Eleanor Roosevelt: In Her Words

ON WOMEN, POLITICS, LEADERSHIP, AND LESSONS FROM LIFE

Nancy Woloch

BLACK DOG
& LEVENTHAL
PUBLISHERS
NEW YORK

Black Dog & Leventhal Publishers
Hachette Book Group
1290 Avenue of the Americas
New York, NY 10104

www.hachettebookgroup.com

www.blackdogandleventhal.com

First Edition: September 2017

Black Dog & Leventhal Publishers is an imprint of Hachette Books, a division of Hachette Book Group. The Black Dog & Leventhal Publishers name and logo are trademarks of Hachette Book Group, Inc.

The publisher is not responsible for websites (or their content) that are not owned by the publisher.

The Hachette Speakers Bureau provides a wide range of authors for speaking events. To find out more, go to www.HachetteSpeakersBureau.com or call (866) 376-6591.

Additional copyright/credits information is on page 329.

Print book interior design by Liz Driesbach.

Library of Congress Cataloging-in-Publication Data

Names: Roosevelt, Eleanor, 1884-1962. | Woloch, Nancy, 1940- editor.
Title: Eleanor Roosevelt : in her words : on women, politics, leadership, and lessons from life / edited by Nancy Woloch.
Description: New York : Black Dog & Leventhal, 2017.
Identifiers: LCCN 2017016588| ISBN 9780316552912 (hardback) | ISBN 9781478976981 (audio download) | ISBN 9780316552943 (ebook)
Subjects: LCSH: Roosevelt, Eleanor, 1884-1962--Quotations. | Presidents' spouses--United States--Quotations. | United States--Politics and government--1933-1945--Quotations, maxims, etc. | BISAC: BIOGRAPHY & AUTOBIOGRAPHY / Women. | HISTORY / United States / 20th Century. | SOCIAL SCIENCE / Feminism & Feminist Theory.
Classification: LCC E807.1.R48 A25 2017 | DDC 973.917092--dc23
LC record available at https://lccn.loc.gov/2017016588

ISBNs: 978-0-316-55291-2 (hardcover), 978-0-316-55294-3 (ebook)

Printed in the United States of America

LSC-C

Printing 3, 2020

Contents

Introduction v

1. Becoming ER 1

2. On Women, Work, and Politics 41

3. Humanizing the New Deal 81

4. This Is No Ordinary Time: World War II 123

5. Civil Rights and Democracy 165

6. The UN and Human Rights 211

7. Postwar Politics 245

8. Lessons from Life 287

Notes 317

Bibliography 327

Photo Credits 329

Index 331

Introduction

ER with her father, Elliott Roosevelt, and her two younger brothers in 1892.

"We had it in the Red Room," Eleanor Roosevelt told her friend Lorena Hickok after the first White House press conference for women reporters on March 6, 1933. "Thirty-five came and of course there weren't enough chairs to go around so some had to sit on the floor."[1] Open only to women, the weekly press conference saved the jobs of women journalists and ensured their access to news; it also provided the new first lady with invaluable publicity and a national audience. Held two days after Franklin Delano Roosevelt's inauguration as president, the press conference marked a turning point in Eleanor Roosevelt's political ascent. What lay ahead: world acclaim as a defender of democratic values, civil rights, human rights, and international peace. ER (as she signed her letters to FDR) had a second career underway as well, as a prolific author, journalist, lecturer, broadcaster, and public personality. *Eleanor Roosevelt: In Her Words* explores the convergence.

ER's patrician roots shaped her childhood; so did misfortune. Born in 1884, ER entered a world of social privilege and emotional neglect. Her rejective mother, Anna Livingston Hall, remote and cold, preferred her younger brothers. Anna died when ER was eight. ER's adored father, Elliott Roosevelt, whom she praised in print for the rest of her life, was the unstable younger brother of Theodore Roosevelt. Sometimes solicitous but often unreliable, Elliott died of alcoholism and depression in 1894. Orphaned at ten, ER was brought up by her maternal grandmother, Mary Livingston Ludlow Hall, a responsible but stern figure, worn out by her own unruly offspring. ER remembered herself as a solemn child, with

A school photo in New York City in 1898.

ER's Allenswood class of 1900, with ER in the top row, third from right. Admired by her classmates and indulged by Mlle Souvestre, ER looked back on her Allenswood years as among her happiest. "I think those three years did much to form my character," she wrote, "and give me confidence to go through some of the trials that awaited me."

an urge to be "useful." But social privilege provided advantage: an education. At fifteen, ER began three years at Allenswood, a girls' school on the edge of London. Marie Souvestre, the enlightened educator who ran the school, made ER a favorite, fostered her curiosity, took her around Europe, and vastly boosted her self-esteem. Ostensibly a finishing school, Allenswood became a starting point for ER. "Whatever I have become since had its seeds in those three years of contact with a liberal mind and strong personality," she wrote.[2]

Mlle Souvestre stirred in her protégée an affinity for social reform. When Eleanor Roosevelt returned to New York in 1902 for her debut into society, she taught at a settlement house and joined a leading reform group, the National Consumers' League, which sought improved conditions for women workers in stores and factories. In 1905, ER married her distant cousin, Franklin Delano Roosevelt. Then a law student, FDR began his political career in the New York State Senate. Between 1906 and 1916 ER had six children, five surviving, and coped with her formidable mother-in-law, Sara Roosevelt, who ruled the household and managed the children's upbringing. Once again, as in her unhappy childhood, ER confronted the iron-willed disapproval of an older female authority. By this time she may have been quietly cultivating an iron will herself.

In 1918, when FDR served as assistant secretary of the Navy in Washington, ER discovered his adulterous affair with Lucy Mercer, her social secretary. To accept divorce, as ER proposed, would have terminated FDR's political career. Instead, the couple persevered, the marriage became a political partnership, and FDR ran for vice president in 1920. In 1921, an attack of polio posed another threat to FDR's future. To keep his prospects in play, ER followed

ER's report card at Allenswood, January to April 1900. "Excellent, she is the most amiable girl I have ever met," Mlle Souvestre commented on the bottom, "eager to learn and highly interested in all her work."

A photo of ER taken at the time of her debut in New York City in 1902.

the counsel of FDR's astute political adviser, journalist Louis M. Howe, who had joined the household after the 1920 campaign. The goal: to keep FDR's name alive. Capitalizing on family position and in accord with Howe's directions, ER began to establish an independent career. She joined the Women's Division of the State Democratic Committee and a roster of women's voluntary organizations, such as the League of Women Voters. By the fall of 1928, when FDR ran for governor of New York, ER had made extensive contacts in the women's movement and in state politics. She had coedited the *Women's Democratic News,* run a state voter registration campaign, and, again with Louis Howe's help, launched her own four-decade career as a journalist. When FDR was governor, ER taught three days a week at the Todhunter School for girls in New York City. By the time FDR ran for president in 1932, ER had established her lifelong pattern of boundless activity and awesome pace. Impelled to be "useful," she had developed leadership skill; no prospective first lady had ever compiled such daunting credentials.[3]

Just as FDR had met the incomparable Louis Howe in the 1920 campaign, in the 1932 campaign ER met her own journalist-

ER and FDR in Hyde Park in 1906, a year after their marriage.

adviser, Lorena Hickok, who covered ER for the Associated Press. Hickok would propose several of ER's leading innovations, including the White House press conferences—there would be 348 in twelve years—and a newspaper column on her daily activities that became "My Day." These ideas were invaluable. A romance between the two women flourished for several years but faded in 1935 as ER backed off, though a long friendship continued. By then Hickok had resigned her job with the AP to do investigative work for a New Deal agency; her career was in decline. ER's career, in contrast, skyrocketed.[4]

In the New Deal years, ER reached national prominence. As the president's surrogate, she traveled continually around the country and reported to FDR. As a political operative, the first lady helped run the 1936 presidential campaign; she served as a link between the president and party leaders James Farley and Molly Dewson at Democratic headquarters. As guardian of the disadvantaged, she built a bridge between Depression victims and the administration. ER often voiced political positions to the left of those of FDR. A champion of civil rights, she forged contacts with National Association for the Advancement of Colored People (NAACP) leader Walter White, educator and National Youth Administration (NYA) official Mary McLeod Bethune, and other activists, as well as with pacifist groups of the 1930s and with the American Youth Congress. Her liberalism gratified her own followers without embroiling the president, who relied politically on conservative Democrats, especially Southerners. ER also befriended labor leaders, promoted a minimum wage, defended the federal homestead program, testified before congressional committees on migrant workers and on discrimination in the armed forces, and became entrenched in the administration of relief programs, notably the NYA and the Works Progress Administration (WPA).

Some of the Depression-era causes that ER endorsed enjoyed only token success, like resident camps for women workers, a counterpart to the Civilian Conservation Corps (CCC) camps for men;

other causes drew controversy, like Arthurdale, a planned community for mining families in West Virginia that she championed. Some causes sank entirely, as did her calls for compulsory health insurance, a child labor amendment, and an anti-lynching law. But ER excelled as a political presence. To challenge boundaries was part of her mode of operation; reforms that she supported might flounder or fail, but ER carved out a path for democratic ideals. Another tactic, fine-tuned in the New Deal years: ER enlarged her influence not by defying traditional roles for women but by extending them. Finally, she generated a media blitz, in the press and on the air. Pressure groups competed for her notice, officials listened to her, newswomen pursued her, and voters admired her. "I am sure, Eleanor dear, that millions of people voted with you in their minds also," ER's friend Rose Schneiderman wrote after FDR's reelection in 1936.[5]

World War II challenged ER in new ways, first, briefly, in 1941–1942, as an administrator at the Office of Civilian Defense, where she sought to promote a wartime New Deal, and thereafter, without title, as an advocate for civil rights and civil liberties. Her concern in wartime extended to blacks, youth, soldiers, and labor; to women defense workers in need of services; to refugees from fascism and to interned Japanese Americans. More than ever, ER stood out as a defender of democracy. The United States, she argued, had to show the superiority of democracy to totalitarianism; racial and economic injustice at home impeded this goal. To fight fascism, according to ER, called for *more* democracy at home. [6]

The postwar era brought further challenge. After FDR's death, ER expanded her scope and won yet greater acclaim. An appointment by President Truman as a US delegate to the United Nations gave ER a place in international affairs (1946–1953); a leadership role in shaping the Universal Declaration of Human Rights (1948); and a reputation as "first lady of the world." Coping with Soviet critiques of the United States in the UN only bolstered ER's commitment to democracy. In postwar politics she became a major voice in the progressive wing of the Democratic Party, a leader of the anticommunist left, and a beacon of liberalism.[7]

But ER had more than one professional life. Entwined with her achievement in politics and diplomacy was a complementary, overlapping career as journalist, lecturer, broadcaster, and public personality. ER wrote continually. Her body of writing—and speaking—was sprawling and prodigious. She reached a mass audience through magazine articles, newspaper columns, and radio talks. Book followed book, and speech followed speech. For almost four decades, ER both generated news and wrote about it. Just as progressivism and the early twentieth-century women's movement shaped ER's preparation for New Deal politics, her career as a writer, speaker, and broadcaster reflected the drive of the "new woman" of the 1920s for "economic independence." Like the publishers, editors, sponsors, and agents with whom she dealt, ER embraced the marketplace.[8]

ER's ventures in journalism began in the 1920s, first with short pieces for the publications of women's organizations and for the *Women's Democratic News*. Louis Howe, a treasury of advice, began to place ER's articles in the popular press. After 1928, when FDR became governor, her rate of productivity accelerated. Most of her work appeared in women's magazines. ER had no hesitation in offering guides to marriage, or to child rearing or running a home, activities that occupied less and less of her own time. Her many articles—such as "Ten Rules for Success in Marriage" or "Today's Girl and Tomorrow's Job"—kept the family name in the spotlight. But she shifted to politics with ease. Her advice to women who sought political roles, "Women Must Learn to Play the Game as Men Do," based on her own experience and published in *Redbook* in 1928, remains a handbook on leadership. Demand for material by ER soared when her White House tenure began. In 1933, she signed an arrangement with the *Woman's Home*

Companion for a monthly essay on topics proposed by readers. In 1935, when *WHC* backed out, ER began a far more successful column, "My Day," where she shared her schedule and activities. Readers in the thousands appreciated her direct, forthright style and her first-person accounts of White House events. Within three years, the six-day-a-week column, syndicated in sixty-two daily newspapers, reached four million readers; over time ER introduced political commentary. With its original blend of the personal and political, "My Day" anticipated the blog; it was also a distinctive publicity tool. "My Day" served the president, ER claimed, by market-testing ideas: "My column could sometimes serve as a trial balloon," for which FDR could disclaim responsibility.[9]

Radio, the newest media outlet of the 1930s, also beckoned. ER began radio talks in 1932–33 and started again in 1934 with a dozen broadcasts sponsored by Pond's Cold Cream. From 1934 to 1941, she worked with sponsors of such products as shoes, mattresses, typewriters, and soap. ("Accept no substitute when you ask for SweetHeart Soap," declared the host/announcer, Ben Grauer, "and

My Day

By ELEANOR ROOSEVELT

HYDE PARK — A few nights ago I read a pamphlet by Harold Taylor, president of Sarah Lawrence college, entitled, "Philosophy as Process." It is, I gather, a reprint of the speech he delivered at Teachers' college last winter. One passage seems to me a very wise one to bring to the attention of any teachers.

It reads: "There are as many roads to the attainment of wisdom as there are people who undertake to walk them. There are as many solid truths as there are people who can search them out and stand on them firmly.

"My Day" column from July 14, 1949.

the microphone is yours again, Mrs. Eleanor Roosevelt.") The Simmons Mattress Company sponsored ER's first important civil rights speech in 1934, an address to a conference on black education, as well her radio talk on "When Will a Woman Become President of the US?" (Not yet, said ER.) The Pan-American Coffee Bureau, a group of Latin American businesses, sponsored a series of NBC broadcasts, "Over Our Coffee Cups," in 1941–1942; the series carried ER's Pearl Harbor address in 1941 and other wartime talks. Meanwhile, public speaking stints multiplied. ER gave 1,400 speeches as first lady, most without fee; these include her pivotal address to the 1940 Democratic Party convention. She also registered in 1935 with a leading lecture agency, the W. Colston Leigh Lecture Bureau, and completed two lecture tours a year, "a few weeks in the spring and fall," until war interrupted in 1941. ER used the speaking trips to inspect New Deal projects, meet "a good cross section of people," and report to FDR. She signed up again with the lecture agency from 1945 to 1962. Even in the late 1950s, ER was on the road for one or two weeks a month.[10]

As her biographers reveal, ER was a competitive professional. She appreciated the income from her writing, speaking, and radio appearances, and relished giving most of it to favored causes, as in the 1930s, when she donated funds to Arthurdale through the American Friends Service Committee. Generally, magazine editors suggested topics. ER wrote her own material, without ghostwriters. Her devoted secretary and traveling companion, Malvina (Tommy) Thompson, typed her articles and columns, though sometimes, when in transit alone, ER worked at a typewriter, too. She edited typed drafts in pen. After Louis Howe's death in 1936, ER turned to literary agents. Her main agent was former journalist George T. Bye, whose client list included many celebrities and who placed her work at magazines such as *Ladies' Home Journal, Look,* and *Collier's*. By the mid-1930s, ER commanded high fees. In the late 1930s, she earned more than $73,000 a year from publication, from lecturing, and especially from radio; the 2017 equivalent would be about $1,240,000. The independent income provided "more money for things I wanted than my husband could afford to give me," ER claimed; she also enjoyed earning as much as or more than FDR.[11]

In the 1940s, ER tried out an engaging interactive form of magazine journalism, her "If You Ask Me" column, first, from 1941 to 1949, in the *Ladies' Home Journal* and then, after 1949, in *McCall's*. Readers submitted questions, editors chose among them, and ER responded. The lively interchanges ranged from inquiries about wartime issues, such as policies for soldiers' leave, to questions about the Roosevelt family (Why did the Roosevelt children attend private school? Was there ever a member of the Roosevelt family killed in combat?) Some questions were startling, if not incredible. ER at first wondered if magazine personnel invented them ("I accused the editorial staff of making them up.") Several readers of the early 1940s challenged ER's civil rights stance. "I don't mean to be rude but do you have colored blood in your family?" a reader asked. Another reader accused ER of "commercialization of the White House" by her earnings in "writing, lecturing, broadcasting." "I personally do not think that earning a small or large amount is commercializing the White House," ER responded. "The point in making money is to earn it honorably and . . . to use your work and what you make out of it for the benefit of the community as a whole as well as for yourself."[12]

More than two dozen books extend ER's legacy in print. *It's Up to the Women* (1933) the first book published by a current first lady, replays topics from ER's articles in women's magazines of the 1920s. To a critic in the *Saturday Review*, "the book may be helpful to the middle class woman who needs to be told that two and two are four." In its defense, the book urged women's involvement in civic life and paid work for married women, a cause that absorbed ER in the 1930s; the book's appearance underscored ER's status as a national public figure. In 1937, her agent, George T. Bye, sold serial rights to *This is My Story,* the first volume of her autobiography, to the *Ladies' Home Journal* for $75,000, a publishing coup. Two subsequent volumes carried the story forward. *This I Remember* (1949), serialized by *McCall's,* covered ER's life through the New Deal. *On My Own* (1958), on the postwar years, was serialized in the *Saturday Evening Post. The Moral Basis of Democracy* (1940), published as war arose in Europe, presents the pursuit of democracy as a spiritual quest. *You Learn by Living* (1960) urged readers to learn through experience, a process for which ER offered examples from her own life. In *Tomorrow is Now* (1963), published posthumously, ER shared her view of the eras of change through which she had lived; she concluded with the civil rights movement, just then entering a new phase with freedom rides of the early 1960s.[13]

Contradictions or inconsistencies pervade ER's life and works. Sincere humility and self-effacement vied with a need for recognition and acclaim. Empathetic and compassionate, ER could be rivalrous, combative, angry, or hostile, and even, on occasion, eviscerate an opponent. Her success in writing, lecturing, and broadcasting fostered a sense of independence from FDR but at the same time relied on her connection to FDR. That her acceptance of equal rights for women was gradual sometimes perplexes modern readers. From the start of her career in public life, ER supported protective laws for women workers, as did the "social feminist" wing of the women's movement with which she was affiliated. An equal rights amendment, first proposed in 1923 by the National Woman's Party (NWP), would invalidate such laws. Moreover, ER disliked the leaders of the NWP, whom social feminists saw as arrogant, elitist, and antilabor (not without reason). ER's commitment to the labor movement was fervent. After Congress passed the Fair Labor Standards Act of 1938, which made the defense of protective laws for women alone less pressing, her resistance to the cause of equal rights began to fade; by the 1940s, she had largely withdrawn from the argument. Still, her old antipathy to an ERA and to its proponents persisted. Her pro–equal rights statements of the postwar era, accordingly, were measured. ER's gifts to the women's movement include her discerning articles on women in politics, from 1928 onward; the way she grasped leadership roles in the White House years and after; the campaign for human rights; and her final stint as chair of President Kennedy's Commission on the Status of Women in 1961–1962.[14]

What themes recur in ER's vast legacy of writing and speech? Three compete for attention. To start with the personal, much of ER's writing, in her columns and articles as well as in her autobiographies, explores facets of her life story. She deals extensively with her childhood memories and early experiences. She often mentions her notable family, its various members, and her famous uncle, Theodore Roosevelt; she revisits Mlle Souvestre, the early years of her marriage, and her controlling mother-in-law. She reflects on her relationship with FDR, and, in the postwar era, reweaves it by speaking *for* FDR. ER reveals yet other facets of herself in "My Day" with her daunting schedules. Candid (to a point), disarming, attuned to detail, and alert to emotion, ER found many ways to share personal narrative.

A related theme, didactic and inspirational, involves learning from experience. "There is no experience from which you can't learn something," ER wrote in 1960. "The learning process must go on as long as we live." Life demanded continual adjustment to new situations, ER posited, and "the process of readjustment never stops." She illustrated the process of readjustment through her own example; each stage of life, from childhood to widowhood, brought with it an imperative to adapt to change of circumstance. At the same time, ER stated, it was important for the individual to transcend circumstance, because "nothing ever happens to us except what happens in our minds." Happiness, like unhappiness, exists "independent of circumstance." ER urged her readers, variously, to defy fear, preserve curiosity, seek challenge, surpass obstacles, connect to others, and distill meaning from experience. Advice from ER reflected a value system.[15]

A third theme is political. To defend democratic ideals, ER often invoked the concept of "interdependence." Democracy rested not just on economic security or on equal opportunity, though these were imperative, but on a cooperative community and a sense of responsibility for one another. "We must learn to work together, all of us, regardless of race or creed or color," as ER told a conference in 1934. "We go ahead together or we go down together." ER's "theory of a Democratic way of life" involved interconnection, mutuality, and service. "[O]ur own success, to be real, must contribute to the success of others," she wrote in 1940. "That means an obligation to the coal-miners and sharecroppers, the migratory workers, the tenement-house dwellers and farmers who cannot make a living." In the 1940s and especially in the postwar years, when ER led the UN commission that drafted the Declaration of Human Rights, her vision of interdependence took global shape. The advance of human rights depended on a shared respect for the rights of others. Nations, like persons, had to nurture a cooperative community and a sense of mutual obligation.[16]

The chapters in *Eleanor Roosevelt: In Her Words* offer excerpts from ER's articles, columns, books, press conferences, lectures, speeches, radio talks, and, occasionally, letters. The selections track ER's concerns from the start of her writing and political careers in the 1920s, when she focused mainly on women and wrote for women's publications; through the White House years, when she won a national audience; to the postwar era, when she achieved worldwide acclaim. Much is omitted; many more selections could be added. ER's legacy in print is full of surprises. On some occasions, to be sure, she wrote (or spoke) to fill the space or meet a deadline. But elsewhere she is exceptional—terse, agile, fast-paced, and powerful. Her concern with democracy is contagious; her political perceptions reach out to new generations. In April of 1945, just before V-E day, looking back on fascist barbarism, ER hurled a warning at her contemporaries and at those who would follow. "There is nothing, given certain kinds of leadership, which could prevent our falling a prey to this same kind of insanity," ER wrote. "If we do not see that equal opportunity, equal justice, and equal treatment are meted out to every citizen, the very basis on which this country can hope to survive with liberty and justice for all will be wiped away."[17]

NOTES

——————

1. Lorena Hickok, *Reluctant First Lady* (New York: Dodd, Mead & Co., 1962), 108–110.

2. "Seven People Who Shaped My Life," *Look* 15 (June 19, 1951), 54–56, 58; Hugh Davis Graham, "The Paradox of Eleanor Roosevelt: Alcoholism's Child," *VQR Online* 62, no. 2 (Spring 1987), 1–15. For ER's early life, see Blanche Wiesen Cook, *Eleanor Roosevelt: Volume 1, 1884–1933* (New York: Penguin, 1992) and Joseph P. Lash, *Eleanor and Franklin* (W. W. Norton, 1971).

3. Joan Hoff-Wilson and Marjorie Lightman, eds., *Without Precedent: The Life and Career of Eleanor Roosevelt* (Bloomington: Indiana University Press, 1984), Part 1 (essays by William Chafe, Elisabeth Israels Perry, and Susan Ware).

4. Susan Quinn, *Eleanor and Hick: The Love Affair That Shaped a First Lady* (New York: Penguin Press, 2016); see also Rodger Streitmatter, ed., *Empty without You: The Intimate Letters of Eleanor Roosevelt and Lorena Hickok* (New York: The Free Press, 1998).

5. Susan Ware, *Beyond Suffrage: Women and the New Deal* (Cambridge: Harvard University Press, 1982), 10. For the New Deal years, see Blanche Wiesen Cook, *Eleanor Roosevelt: Volume 2, 1933–1938* (New York: Viking, 1999).

6. Matthew Dallek, *Defenseless Under the Night: The Roosevelt Years and the Origins of Homeland Security* (New York: Oxford University Press, 2016), 259. For ER in wartime, see also Blanche Wiesen Cook, *Eleanor Roosevelt: Volume 3, 1939–1962* (New York: Viking, 1996), and Doris Kearns Goodwin, *No Ordinary Time, Franklin and Eleanor Roosevelt: The Home Front in World War II* (New York: Simon and Schuster, 1994).

7. E. J. Kahn, "Profiles: The Years Alone–1," *New Yorker* 24 (June 12, 1948), 30–40; Allida M. Black, *Casting Her Own Shadow: Eleanor Roosevelt and the Shaping of Postwar Liberalism* (New York: Columbia University Press, 1996); Mary Ann Glendon, *The World Made Anew: Eleanor Roosevelt and the Universal Declaration of Human Rights* (New York: Random House, 2001).

8. Maurine H. Beasley, *Eleanor Roosevelt and the Media: A Public Quest for Self-Fulfillment* (Urbana and Chicago: University of Illinois Press, 1987).

9. ER, *Autobiography* (New York: Harper, 1961), 193, 197–198; Maurine H. Beasley and Henry Beasley, "Eleanor Roosevelt as Entrepreneur," *White House Studies* 4, no. 4 (October 2004), 522.

10. ER, *Autobiography,* 131, 189, 191, 291. Beasley and Beasley, "Eleanor Roosevelt as Entrepreneur," 524, 525, 527; Stephen Drury Smith, *The First Lady of Radio* (New York: The New Press, 2014), 2–3, 42–50, 189–197.

11. ER, *Autobiography,* 131; Beasley and Beasley, "Eleanor Roosevelt as Entrepreneur," 518; Beasley, *Eleanor Roosevelt and the Media,* 78.

12. ER, *Autobiography*, 198; "If You Ask Me," *Ladies' Home Journal* (September 1941, November 1941, and June 1942); Beasley and Beasley, "Eleanor Roosevelt as Entrepreneur," 518.

13. Beasley and Beasley, "Eleanor Roosevelt as Entrepreneur," 526.

14. ER, "My Day," May 14, 1945; May 25, 1951; and June 7, 1951; Beasley and Beasley, "Eleanor Roosevelt," 522. For the labor movement, see Brigid O'Farrell, *She Was One of Us: Eleanor Roosevelt and the American Worker* (Ithaca and London, Cornell University Press, 2010).

15. ER, *You Learn By Living: Eleven Keys for a More Fulfilling Life* (New York: Harper & Row, 1960) 5–6, 78, 82, 83.

16. "Address of Mrs. Franklin D. Roosevelt," National Conference on Fundamental Problems in the Education of Negroes, May 11, 1934; ER, *The Moral Basis of Democracy* (New York: Howell, Soskin, & Co., 1940) 14, 77; Glendon, *A World Made A New,* 239; Cook, *Eleanor Roosevelt: Volume 3, 1939–1962,* 307.

17. "My Day," April 30, 1945.

CHAPTER 1

Becoming ER

FDR, flanked by his mother, Sara Roosevelt, and ER in 1920, as he
finished his term as assistant secretary of the Navy under Woodrow Wilson.
In the next decade, ER would veer away from her domestic role
and find a place in public life.

Eleanor Roosevelt's apprenticeship in public life began after World
War I and continued through FDR's terms as New York's governor from 1929 to 1933. "The war was my emancipation and my
education," ER told Lorena Hickok in a 1932 interview. More likely,
biographers suggest, her discovery in 1918 of FDR's affair with Lucy
Mercer, followed by FDR's polio attack of 1921 and subsequent
paralysis, steered her into a decade of transition. In the 1920s ER
entered the vibrant world of women's organizations, with which
she had been briefly involved before her marriage. Her new commitments included Democratic women's groups that arose after

women won the vote in 1920. At the same time, she began to write articles for political journals and popular magazines. As volunteer or journalist, ER identified herself as "Mrs. Franklin D. Roosevelt." Both types of activity served to keep FDR's name in public view. Ironically, the need to be useful to FDR provided the rationale that enabled ER to achieve an independent life.

At the century's start, before her marriage, ER had joined the National Consumers' League and had volunteered at the College Settlement in New York City. After World War I, in Washington, DC, as FDR completed his term as assistant secretary of the navy, ER served as a translator at an international congress of women workers and joined the women's peace movement. Her pace of activity escalated in New York in the 1920s. ER had not joined the woman suffrage crusade but was soon deeply involved in women's politics. In 1920 she enrolled in the League of Women Voters (LWV), where she led the legislative committee and rose to vice chair of the New York State league. In 1922 she joined the Women's Trade Union League, where she first met labor leader Rose Schneiderman, a lifelong friend; in 1923 she joined the Women's City Club of New York and the Women's Division of the New York Democratic Party. In 1924, at the request of the Democratic National Committee (DNC), ER chaired the DNC platform committee on women's issues. She organized a successful get-out-the-vote campaign in 1928, when FDR won election as governor of New York. Throughout the decade FDR's adviser Louis M. Howe, an expert in political publicity, provided ER with first-rate guidance in public affairs. As Howe famously told her, "Have something you want to say, say it, and sit down." By the end of the 1920s ER held a significant role in political life.

When FDR became New York's governor in 1929, ER withdrew from state politics. By then she had developed overlapping circles of allies. At the LWV, she met lawyer Elizabeth Read and Read's companion, Esther Lape, who joined ER to coedit the LWV newspaper. In New York politics, she met her future New Deal colleagues Molly Dewson, colleague at the Women's City Club and organizer of women voters, and Frances Perkins, who served as FDR's state labor commissioner. At the state women's division, ER joined forces with Caroline O'Day, Nancy Cook, and Marion Dickerman, with whom she edited the *Women's Democratic News*. With Cook and Dickerman, ER ran Val-Kill industries, a furniture factory on the Hyde Park estate, and bought the Todhunter School for girls in New York City, where ER taught history and other subjects from 1927 to 1933 and cultivated her favorite role, that of educator. Her commitments of the 1920s shaped bonds of friendship as well as enduring professional interests.

Since her days in Washington, ER had fielded interviews with women reporters, which continued through her Albany years and thereafter. She also sought a career as a journalist herself. Again guided by Louis M. Howe, who served as her literary agent, ER submitted articles to many publications, from the journals of women's organizations to mass-market venues such as *Parents* magazine and the *Pictorial Review*. ER experimented in her articles with different voices. Depending on the assignment, she might be a partisan Democrat or a political analyst; or she might be an expert housewife, an authority on child rearing and schooling, or a guide to success in marriage. Notably, ER began to recount—or reimagine—the story of her life; by 1930 she had shaped her own "legend," or backstory, on which she drew to discuss other subjects. She also began to explore aspects of her current experience, as in an embattled essay on the role of the political wife. Finally, she started to analyze facets of women's role in society—in education, the workforce, and politics. Overall, in the decade after World War I, ER seized the chance to reinvent herself, to shape a public persona, and to find a convincing voice as journalist. FDR's terms as governor, especially, provided a rehearsal for the White House years. When ER finally became first lady in 1933, she did so well prepared. "With such ease does she live a half dozen lives that it would seem she never tires," declared the exuberant *Women's Democratic News*. "Possibly no woman in the United States is better equipped to become mistress of the White House."

ER with Nancy Cook, Caroline O'Day, and Marion Dickerman in 1929 at New York headquarters of the State Democratic Committee; the four women edited the *Women's Democratic News*. "My friends," wrote ER in the 1930s, "are responsible for much that I have become."

AMBITION

———

Some people consider ambition a sin but it seems to me to be a great good for it leads one to do & be things which without it one could never have been. Look at Caesar. It was because he was ambitious that they killed him but would he ever have been as great a man had he not had ambition? Would his name ever have come down to us if he had not had enough ambition to conquer the world? Would painters ever paint wonderful portraits or writers ever write books if they did not have ambition?

Of course it is easier to have no ambition & just keep on the same way every day & never try to do grand or great things, for it is only those who have ambition & who try & who meet with difficulties, they alone feel the disappointments that come when one does not succeed in what one has meant to do. . . . But those who have ambition try again, & try till they at last succeed. It is only those who ever succeed in doing anything great.

Ambition makes us selfish and careless of pushing others back & treading on them to gain our wish it is true, but we will only be able to push back the smaller souls for the great ones we cannot tread on. . . .

Is it best never to be known and to leave the world a blank as if one had never come? It must have been meant it seems to me that we should leave some mark upon the world and not just live [&] pass away. For what good can that do to ourselves or others? It is better to be ambitious & do something than to be unambitious and do nothing.

Ambition is essential for any kind of success. . . .

School essay, c. 1898

I BECAME A MUCH MORE
ARDENT CITIZEN AND FEMINIST

That spring of 1919, on the side of my official duties, I had my first personal contact with the cause of woman suffrage. Back in the Albany days [when FDR served in the New York State Senate], you will remember, my husband had been for woman suffrage. Through the years, courageous women carried on a constant fight for ratification of woman's suffrage by the different states. It looked as though their fight was nearing a successful end and, therefore, the opposition rallied its forces.

Coming down on the train one day to Washington from New York, I happened to meet Alice Wadsworth [daughter of Secretary

At the suggestion of FDR's political adviser Louis M. Howe, ER accompanied FDR on his campaign train when he ran for vice president in 1920. Here, ER with Lucy Cox, wife of the Democratic presidential nominee James M. Cox.

of State John Hay], wife of Senator James Wadsworth [of New York], who, with her husband, had always been much opposed to woman suffrage. We lunched together and she spent the time trying to persuade me to come out against the ratification. I was very noncommittal, for I considered any stand at that time was quite outside my field of work. I think she had hopes that she might make a convert of me. Fortunately, before she succeeded, the [woman suffrage] amendment was ratified, and soon after I undertook work which proved to me the value of a vote. I became a much more ardent citizen and feminist than anyone about me in the intermediate years would have dreamed possible.

This Is My Story, 1937

WHY I AM A DEMOCRAT

Why am I a Democrat? One hears it very often said that fundamentally there is no difference between the two major parties, and that the issues, aside from the old question of a high or a low tariff, are practically non-existent. For those of us who do not wish to take the trouble of going any deeper this is a very satisfactory way out, as it permits our voting for the man we like best, with little regard to the principles of the party to which he belongs. . . . Therefore, to be helpful to the political life of the country, it seems to me one must decide for oneself which of the two parties presents the greater opportunity for the mass of the people, to become articulate, to express their desires and aspirations and choose their leaders . . . [T]o my mind the Democratic party is the one at present working to this end. . . .

On the whole the Democratic party seems to have been more concerned with the welfare and interests of the people at large, and less with the growth of big business interests. Now we all realize that a country, to prosper, must have its big businesses; these must have fair opportunity and bring in fair returns to attract the interest and hold the ambition of able men, but we must not lose sight of the fact that the ultimate result should never be the welfare and achievement of a few men, but the bettering of the whole country. . . . This, it seems to me . . . has been more visibly the trend of the Democratic party and of the people who compose it, than of the Republican party and the Republicans. . . .

My last reason for being a Democrat is open to much difference of opinion. All women will, I think, agree that they wish to take all possible steps for the prevention of war; the division comes on the methods, and I can only say that my feeling is that the Democratic party has made more constructive efforts toward this end than has the Republican party, and is today more conscious of our world responsibility and more anxious to see sane steps taken toward international cooperation.

Junior League Bulletin, 1923

I am a Democrat—Because it seems to me that the Democratic party is the only party whose fundamental principles promise progressive growth in a sane way. It is the only party which on the whole meets the question of deepest interest to women in a way to help the majority that need help and not only a favored few. This is where it differs from the Republican party. In its policy on international affairs it meets more hopefully and constructively than the Lafollette group [Progressives] the greatest interest to all women—the steps which we shall take to end war.

Women's Democratic Campaign Manual, 1924

HOW TO INTEREST
WOMEN IN VOTING

———

The most difficult problem before women leaders today is "How are we to interest the women of the state in voting and get them to change from their uninterested and apathetic attitude to an attitude of intelligent and active interest in their Government?" . . . Of course, no one woman has a right to say what the mass of women want to accomplish with their vote, but I can at least say what I hope the Democratic women wish to achieve.

First: Honest, clean administration in party organizations, coupled with a real desire to have the people understand fundamental issues. . . .

Second: We want to see a real use of the primaries so that they will express the will of the people. . . .

Third: We desire to see a greater interest taken by our Government in what is best for the mass of the people, as opposed to groups among the people. This does not mean that I am unmindful of the necessity that business must prosper and that capital should have its just reward, but the balance must be kept proportionate among the various interests of our people. . . .

Fourth: From this interest in the mass of our own people, we wish to see a growth in the real interest taken in the welfare of the world as a whole. Without this real interest we will not enter any League or Association of nations, we will take no steps to prevent war, we will remain selfish individualists, each scrambling for our own little place in the sun. Like the old story, "For myself and my wife, my son John and his wife, us four and no more," forgetting that the great cloud over others may easily spread and cover our little patch as well.

Women's Democratic Campaign Manual, 1924

ER met members of the National Women's Trade Union League (NWTUL) when she served in 1919 as a translator (French) at the First International Congress of Working Women in Washington, DC, above. Joining the New York branch of the NWTUL in 1922, ER remained a loyal member thereafter.

WHAT I WANT MOST OUT OF LIFE

I suppose if I were asked what is the best thing one can expect out of life, I would say—the privilege of being useful. For when all is said and done I think that no one can expect more out of life than to be of some real use to the world and to other people. Most persons want to be happy in life, but to me being happy is entirely a matter of individual character. If one has the temperament for it, one will be happy without, apparently, any reason for happiness, even with every reason against serenity, whereas I think one can be unhappy and have, apparently, everything in the world. . . .

But I started to speak of usefulness, and it is, I think, along this line that woman's main objects lie. She wants to be happy and she can only be happy by being useful, which resolves itself into a proposition that calls for an opportunity for service—this and nothing more. I have particularly in mind the woman who has passed forty and whose life is revolving in a well-ordered groove. She is removed from the necessity of any material consideration, and now, with her children grown and married, she finds herself fairly alone and with far more leisure than ever before. What, then, is she to do?

Nothing remains but for her to find something that will engage her energies, just as her homemaking and childrearing engaged them during the earlier years of her married life.

It is probably safe to say that there are more things in the world for women to do today than there ever were before. For this reason alone any woman of intelligence can find an outlet for her surplus energy. I confess it is rather difficult for me to understand the feeling of being idle, useless, drifting, as so many have confessed being, for I have never found myself without anything to do. . . .

For my own part I happened to have been born into a politically minded family. The late Theodore Roosevelt was my uncle. My husband went into the state senate shortly after we were married and, till 1920, he continued to be active in politics. It was natural, therefore, that I should be deeply interested in the machinery of government, even though women could not be of much practical use in the early days. They could at least, however, be good listeners, I learned, which is a full-time job in itself. I might add, especially in the city of Washington.

Washington is a city where paying calls has been transformed from a pleasure into a science. You have to call on everyone who holds a position higher than your husband's. It is all cut and dried. Every official has a "day." On every day but one you leave your home at three and do not see it again until dinner time. On that day you station yourself at your own tea-table, throw the doors wide open, and devote the afternoon to greeting the many people who must take advantage of the invitation. . . .

When we left Washington, I was thankful beyond words to have lost that job—the job of paying calls. . . . After our return to New York in 1920, I found myself free from social duties and because of the nine years spent in Albany and Washington I became interested in New York State politics and was fortunate to be able to work first with the New York State League of Women Voters and then under Mrs. Daniel O'Day in the Women's Division of the Democratic State Committee.

Many women find it hard to understand just what there is to do between elections, but the necessity of constant work to maintain a skeleton organization keeps us at our desks every day. It provides the individual with a definite interest and a responsibility. We must have a nucleus of women everywhere who are trained, who understand both the practical side of politics and what the objects are they are working to attain, who can take their places at the proper times, distribute literature and explain the issues to voters. In the summer we go into every county in the state and review, in a way, and reinforce, this standing army.

Right here it might be well to say that this nucleus should be greater, politics should be interesting to every woman voter, if for no other reason than one of self-interest, and I believe that it is rapidly becoming so. But there is still a long way to go. . . .

My object in politics at present is to create an interest in citizenship. I want my children to grow up interested and constructive citizens, and I think if women become intelligently interested in public affairs it will do much to bring about an enlightened citizenship which is particularly necessary in a democracy. . . .

I only have two little boys at home now and both go off to school. I don't find it difficult to plan my day with reference to them and yet with due regard for the things I want to do. One of my boys comes home to lunch, and I usually manage to be there. After I have gone down to the kitchen in the morning and written out the menus and done the ordering I am through for the day, as is the case with most women who do not have to do their own household tasks. Then I come down to the Democratic State Committee office, where I am at my desk for several hours every day. Then there are the Industries [at Val-Kill]—as we call our plan for making reproductions of furniture—some charitable boards and some club committees, in all of which I am interested. . . .

I think women look upon their homes as the first objects of their lives. I see no change in their attitude at present, and no hint of a change for the future. Home comes first. But—in second and third and last place there is room for countless other concerns. This, women understand now, and the present tendency is to avoid purely selfish interests and do something which is of some use to somebody in the world, other than one's self. And so if anyone were to ask me what I want out of life I would say—the opportunity to be useful, for in no other way, I am convinced, can true happiness be obtained.

Success, 1927

FDR's mother, Sara Roosevelt, bought adjoining townhouses at 47–49 East 65th Street in 1908 for herself and for FDR and his family. ER spent some time in number 49 in the 1920s, when she became active in New York State politics. Here, she hosts an election celebration in 1924 at a gathering of the Democratic Party's Women's Division. ER sits opposite political adviser Louis M. Howe, front right.

ER's article on "What I Want Most Out of Life" appeared in *Success* magazine in May 1927. The article included this photo taken at Campobello Island, New Brunswick, in 1920. ER is with Elliott, FDR Jr., John, Anna, and "Chief."

HOW TO VOTE
FOR PRESIDENT IN 1928

I am for Governor [Alfred E.] Smith, because of his astonishing knowledge of government, his power of clear, straight thinking, his intolerance of trickery and chicanery, his courage and unswerving honesty, but above all because he has a human heart and does not consider that success in the life of the individual or nation can be measured by a bank balance or treasury credit. . . .

He is of the people and understands them and respects them, but also realizes that they must be led.

He is a leader because his whole political life shows that he has a wonderful power of convincing people regardless of their usual political affiliations that he is right; a power due, I think, to the fact that he believes himself to be right with all his heart and soul, and never goes ahead until he is himself convinced. It is fortunate that a man of this rare ability has also the keen power of analysis and clear thinking which make his conclusions in the great majority of instances the right answers to the problems of the hour. Compared to these qualities his personal attitude on Prohibition is of minor importance, especially in view of the fact that, in my opinion, this is not a question between parties, but within the parties, between individuals who wish their party to be either completely wet or completely dry. So far no group has won out in either party, and as a President, with all his influence, cannot vote on any law, this question remains one to be settled in Congressional Districts, regardless of whether the President wishes the Volstead Act [the law enforcing Prohibition] modified or not. When we elect enough Congressmen who are convinced that their constituents want the Volstead Law or any other law strictly enforced, we will have it done and not before.

As to the religious question, Governor Smith has made his own answer and the country seems as a whole to approve. If a few captious souls still fear the influence of Rome, it is because they must find something to fear and this is nearest at hand.

North American Review, 1927

SHALL ARISTOCRATS RULE?

The outstanding issue today is much as it was in Jefferson's day—trust in the people or fear of the people. . . .

The Democrats today trust in the people, the plain, ordinary, everyday citizen, neither superlatively rich nor disastrously poor, not one of the "best minds" but the average mind. The Socialists believe in making the Government the people's master; the Republicans believe that the moneyed "aristocracy," the few great financial minds, should rule the Government; the Democrats believe that the whole people should govern. They have no quarrel with big business; they know we need business, big and little, for prosperity, but they do not believe the Government should be in control of any business group. The old dictum, "Equal rights for all, special privileges for none," still is the old democratic principle accepted by all. The country has been since 1920 under Republican rule, and our particular difficulties of the moment have developed logically from the Republican theories of government.

The Republicans fear their own people; therefore they distrust other people, and, instead of trying to eradicate an evil when it appears, they cover it up. . . .

ER with her friends, Marion Dickerman, center, and Nancy Cook, right, at Campobello in July 1926.

Therefore, it looks to me as if the fundamental issue between Republicans and Democrats must be fought out again: Is the Government to be in the hands of the aristocrats, some of whom may have been corrupt but who will, on the whole, give as they say an "able" administration with great material prosperity for a few perhaps and a fair amount of it for many, or shall it be in the hands of the people who may make more mistakes but who will be free, responsible citizens again?

Current History, 1928

THE MODERN WIFE'S DIFFICULT JOB

[Interviewer:] What is the master key to success in the modern wife's job?

Of the three fundamentals of her task—being a partner, being a mother, and being a homemaker—what is the most vital to success in married life?

A generation ago we should probably have answered, "Being a mother, of course," with the housekeeping next, and the partnership last. But now, according to Mrs. Franklin D. Roosevelt, wife of New York's Governor, if we are up to date we realize that the most important part of a wife's job is to be a good companion—that everything else depends upon the success of the wife and the husband in their personal relation....

Mrs. Roosevelt believes that modern conditions compel the wise wife to change her ways or adopt new ones.... Remarking that the most successful marriage she has ever known was the most complete in its partnership, she continues:

"Partnership! Companionship! And fitness for it! It is the major requirement for modern marriage.

"I am not saying that the wives of today can hope to be better companions than were some wives of the past. The great change is that, far more generally we recognize the importance of such companionship. Today, I think, there are far more wives who are good companions than there used to be.

"How well we realize today that it is essential for a woman to develop her own interests—in music, literature, club life, church, community activities, and hobbies, for instance—so as not to lose the possibility of being a stimulating personality! . . .

"More than ever before a wife must be able to take an intelligent interest in her husband's interests. Notice that I say in her husband's 'interests,' not merely in his 'job.' Her interest must not cease with his job. Women have found it a terrible thing to be just a heavy partner, sharing business and home cares only, and not a light partner, sharing in the diversion of pleasure hours.

"The modern way means that she must fit herself, and keep herself fit to share not only responsibilities and burdens but intellectual pursuits, recreation, diversion, and pleasures of all kinds.

"On the other hand, each should, I think, have the opportunity for some experiences and interests that are not entirely shared by the other. As one sociologist put it, 'Each must have a separate foothold, personal activities which are entered upon alone, and which are not immediately rehashed in lieu of other conversation. These detached and personal activities maintain that sense of "illusiveness" characteristic of courtship days. So that their companionship may not pall, there must always be some distinct territory in the life of each that has never thoroughly been explored by the other.'"

[Interviewer:] Mrs. Roosevelt, we are told, goes from Albany to New York to teach in a girls' school three days of each week, because she loves to teach. That is her "separate foothold" at present.

When the interviewer asked her to name "the particularly modern aspects of the mother phase of the wife's job," she replied:

"How much more we know today about the care and rearing of children than women formerly knew!

"The difference between the methods of today and those of yesteryear consist mainly in this: We do not have the old-fashioned idea of making a child do a thing simply because he is told to do it. From his earliest days we teach him the reason back of what is asked of him. As much as possible, we let him learn by experience. Nevertheless, we still tell him what to do and require his obedience.

"If he does not quite understand the reason for what is asked of him, he must, nevertheless, obey, if for no other reason than that he has learned that mother is trustworthy. In the future, of course, he may demand an explanation, and this the wise mother will do her best to give. . . .

"The essential thing for a mother to realize is that smothering should and can be avoided. The great safeguard lies in this. As her children grow older, and do not require physical care, a mother may take pains to develop new interests of her own in church, community, or welfare activities, say. She must not let herself be completely dependent for her interests in life on the lives that her children live."

[Interviewer:] The homemaker's part of the wife's job has changed utterly since the days when most of the necessities of life were produced in the home, says Mrs. Roosevelt; now most homes have the necessities, and the wife has to "plan on what are the next greatest values for the family after the necessities are taken care of—in itself an important and momentous new task." She continues:

"Think of the things a woman must know today! So much more reliable information is available as to what are the proper things

In 1924 ER joined her friends Nancy Cook and Marion Dickerman to found
Val-Kill Industries, a small factory on the Hyde Park estate that made
reproductions of early-American furniture. In 1936, when the factory closed,
ER turned one of the Val-Kill houses into a cottage for herself. Here,
with a Val-Kill craftsman circa 1929.

to eat, and how they should be cooked. If it is a home where she
does most of her own work, she has the problem of systematizing
that work, and of using as many labor-saving devices as she can
afford. She must learn to do it in the easiest and quickest possible
way so that all goes as smoothly as possible and so that it may not
seem a burden to her. . . .

*[Interviewer:] To succeed as a wife in this age requires a tremen-
dous fund of energy, the Governor's wife has discovered, and it is
important "to budget not only expenditures, but time and energy."
In order to do this, she says, one must learn to choose the things that
are most important, and eliminate the rest:*

"Many women, floored by the rapidity of movement in the world
today, have said to me: 'I cannot keep up with my children! Motor-
cars carry them so fast! Now they want to fly! There are so many
things I should, but cannot do. I cannot read or hear or see enough
to keep up to date.' To these women I say: 'The first thing to do is

sit down and become immovable. Get possession of yourself! Let the world go by altogether until you have decided for yourself just exactly what you want.'"

The Literary Digest, 1930

VAL-KILL SHOP
HYDE PARK, N. Y.
WHOLESALE PRICES

Feb. 1, 1929

(Write for prices if you wish special furniture, sizes or woods)

No.		WOOD	PRICE
1—Cambra Table		Walnut	$115.00
24¼ " x 70 "		Mahogany	115.00
29½ " high		Oak	110.00
2—Sofa Table with drawers		Walnut	125.00
22 " x 73 "		Mahogany	125.00
29½ " high		Oak	120.00
3—Double Gate Leg Table		Walnut —	*160.00*
(Dining Table 4' 6")		Maple	
		Mahogany	
		Oak	
		Pine	
4—Oblong Table (to seat 4 or 6)		Walnut —	*165.00*
		Maple	
		Mahogany —	*160.00*
		Oak	
		Pine	
5—Pine Tavern Table with Drawers		Walnut	125.00
27 " x 53 "		Maple	115.00
29 " high		Oak	120.00
		Pine	110.00
6—Large Table, 2 leaves		Maple	95.00
36 " x 69 "		Oak	98.00
29½ " high		Pine	87.00
7—Oblong Trestle Table,		Walnut	98.00
Narrow—2 leaves		Maple	90.00
35 " x 55 "		Mahogany	98.00
29½ " high		Oak	95.00
		Pine	88.00
8—Gate Leg Table—spool		Walnut	94.00
36 " round		Maple	88.00
28 " high		Mahogany	94.00
		Cherry	90.00
		Oak	90.00

[1]

A Val-Kill price list from 1929.

EDUCATION
AND CITIZENSHIP

———

As girls went in those days, I suppose my own education was fairly typical, and I confess with some shame that at the age of twenty, when asked by an Englishwoman how our government functioned, I was as completely floored as if she had asked me to describe the political events on the moon! I had heard the men in the family mention political happenings, but it was not a subject of general or frequent conversation in our presence.

Women did not vote and were not expected to be interested. Besides there was something dark and sinister about politics, and it was more respectable not to know politicians or political methods too well. Business might necessitate some dealings with these rather inferior and nefarious beings, but the general attitude of the righteous was like that of a high-minded and upright citizen of New York City who once remarked to me that a certain political organization was undoubtedly corrupt, but he preferred (though belonging to an opposite political party) to keep the wicked organization in power as "you paid for what you wanted and were sure to get it, whereas reform administrations were not so reliable in this ability to 'deliver the goods'!"

I do not think I am unfair in saying that in most secondary schools, at least, the teachers of American history in those days laid more emphasis on the battle of Bunker Hill than they did on the obligations of citizenship. . . .

Gradually a change has come about. More young men and more young women (since the latter have had the vote) are doing political work. And even if they do not hold political office they have felt the need to understand their own government. In our schools are now given courses in civics, government, economics, current events. But there still remains a vast amount to be done before we accomplish our first objective—informed and intelligent citizens, and secondly, bring about the realization that we are all responsible for the trend of thought and the action of our times.

How shall we arrive at these objectives? We think of course of history as a first means of information. Not the history which is a mere recital of facts, dates, wars, and kings, but a study of the life and growth of other nations, in which we follow the general moral, intellectual, and economic development through the ages. . . .

It is not, however, only in courses bearing directly on history and government that citizenship can be taught. The child taking Latin and mathematics is learning invaluable lessons in citizenship. The power of concentration and accuracy which these studies develop will later mean a man or woman able to understand and analyze a difficult situation. . . .

The practical side of good citizenship is developed most success-fully in school because in miniature one is living in a society, and the conditions and problems of the larger society are more easily reproduced and met and solved. To accomplish this, however, pre-supposes a high grade of teaching, a teacher who not only teaches a subject but is always conscious of the relation of the subject to the larger purpose of learning to live.

Learning to be a good citizen is learning to live to the maximum of one's abilities and opportunities, and every subject should be taught every child with this in view. The teacher's personality and character are of the greatest importance. I have known many er-udite and scholarly men and women who were dismal failures as teachers. I have known some less learned teachers who had the gift of inspiring youth and sending them on to heights where perhaps they themselves were unable to follow. . . .

When I was fifteen I came in contact with a really remarkable teacher [Marie Souvestre], a strong and vital personality. All my life I have been grateful for her influence. She has been dead for many years, but to this day her presence lives with me. . . . She had great charity for mistakes, for real limitations in knowledge or experience, but if you tried to "get by" with inadequate research and preparation, you felt her scorn because she believed in you and felt you could do better and you had fallen down.

I think few of us worked under her without acquiring a conception of intellectual integrity and obligation at all times to do our best. I still remember evenings when she read to us and by her comments opened up avenues of thought. If ever in small ways I may do any good work in the world the credit will not be mine, but in part at least it will belong to the most inspiring teacher I ever knew. . . .

The school alone cannot teach citizenship, however, any more than it can really educate a child. It can do much in directing thought and formulating standards, in creating habits of responsibility and courage and devotion. In the last analysis our home surroundings are the determining factor in development. . . .

Eleanor Roosevelt ran a triumphant voter recruitment drive in New York state in 1928, when FDR won election as governor. Here, ER and FDR join Democratic campaign workers in Albany.

As the great majority of our children are being educated in public schools, it is all-important that the standards of citizenship should be of the best. Whether we send our children to private school or public school we should take a constant interest in all educational institutions and remember that on the public school largely depends the success or failure of our great experiment in government, "by the people, for the people."

Pictorial Review, 1930

BUILDING CHARACTER

D o not feel sorry when you cannot fulfill every wish your child expresses. Children coming from a home where there is just money enough to give them healthful surroundings but where they are obliged to struggle to a certain extent to obtain opportunities for progress have an advantage over children who have always dropped into their laps the greatest opportunities for development, with no effort on their own part. It is impossible artificially to create a situation which will give the incentive of struggle, which has an advantage in creating firmness and steadiness of character. There is one thing, however, which we can all do, namely, we can make it possible for our children to appreciate what work is. A child's zest in life will not be lessened and his strange character-building process will go on much better when he is envisaging new fields of endeavor. Nothing is more pathetic than a bored child; and one becomes bored when there is nothing new that is of interest. So open up all the avenues of rich experience to your children and encourage them to follow them for themselves.

The Parents Magazine, 1931

TEN RULES
FOR SUCCESS IN MARRIAGE

———

Marriage is not only a responsibility, but an opportunity, a never-ending source of growth and education. In this school one never graduates. It takes time, trouble, patience to make a marriage go. You must *grow* along with it. It is a relationship that must always be looked after. . . .

In many respects marriage will always remain a gamble. If we could take the gamble out of it, it would be far less interesting. On no phase of the question dare one be hard and fast. However, as I think over the marriages I have known and the experiences that have been confided to me, I am tempted to say that there are ten rules, not hard and fast, but safe and sane, the observance of which makes for success in marriage.

1. Have a plan, some central idea, as definite a pattern for your life as possible, and a clearly understood object for the joint project.

2. Remember that sooner or later money is apt to be a cause of friction. Keeping a budget is a practical way of eliminating the irritations and dissatisfactions that come to married people over the outlay of money.

3. Apportion your time and energy, allowing each his share for the joint homemaking duties, as well as for individual responsibilities.

4. Let neither husband nor wife strive to be the dominating person in the household. A victory for either in this respect means failure for the partnership.

5. Expect to disagree. Two people may hold entirely different views on many subjects and yet respect and care for each other just the same.

6. Be honest. Each must be honest with himself and with the other, not trying to think and be things he is not.

7. Be loyal. Keep your differences to yourselves. The less said about your married troubles, except between yourselves, the better. The feeling that many young married people have, that they can complain to their parents when things do not go just right, is bad for them, and brings more serious trouble later on.

8. Talk things over. When hurt do not keep it to yourself, brooding over it. Meet every situation in the open. Troubles that seem momentous quickly vanish when frankly dealt with.

9. Avoid trivial criticisms. Grumbling and complaints use up the vital forces of man or woman.

10. Keep alive the spirit of courtship, the thoughtfulness which existed before marriage. Look for traits in the other that can be admired and praised. You can accomplish much by stimulating self-confidence in your partner. For one who reacts to encouragement with, "But I'm afraid I can't," there are ten who feel, "I'm really quite a fellow after all! I mustn't let her (or him) down in what she (or he) expects of me!"

As a result of my experience and observation there are two things which I would counsel fathers and mothers and all "in-laws" to bear in mind. First, I would say, "Offer as little advice to the newly

ER, as first lady of New York State from 1929 to 1933, greets visitors in Albany.

married as possible, preferably none. Once the young people have begun their life together, their elders can be of great service simply by standing by, ready to help if called upon in real crises. Volunteering advice is not the privilege of the older generation; it is a serious infringement of the rights of the younger."

Second, "I have known many promising marriages to be wrecked because the young people began their life together in the home of their parents or had parents come to live with them. Even though father and mother are lonely, it is better for the young people to start out alone. It is exceedingly difficult for several generations to live under the same roof. Only the most exceptional people can work it out successfully."

Perhaps I have more definite views as to the function of the engagement than many seem to. As I see it, it should be nothing less than a period of almost daily contact. Do not misunderstand me! I am not advocating trial marriage! I mean that, short of trial marriage itself, the engaged couple should have almost constant association with the object of discovering whether they can really stand the jars and jolts and routine of life together and whether they have similar conceptions of what they want to make of their lives.

Pictorial Review, 1931

TODAY'S GIRL
AND TOMORROW'S JOB

Three days a week I teach at a private school [the Todhunter School for girls] which takes girls up to the point of college entrance. I have a family of my own, a daughter and four sons. I have also taken a fairly active part in politics. I present these facts for the reason that they have a special bearing on the subject of youth and its place in the community. My observations, in some respects, cover a greater variety of experiences than usually falls to the lot of the average person. I am especially interested in the girl of today because she fits into my job as a teacher, a mother, a civic worker. I have occasion to see her as a child, a growing girl, and a young woman. Judging from my experience with her I am bold enough to say that she is meeting life exactly as she has been prepared to meet it.

To fit the girl of today for her experience of tomorrow is a large order, in many respects a larger order than our parents and grandparents had to fill for us. The world grows increasingly larger in the number of things there are to do and to think about, but increasingly smaller in respect to distance. A young person today is caught in a flux of changing vibrating life and what to choose, what to discard, what to concentrate upon, become increasingly difficult to decide. Without help or direction of some sort she is lost. Yet fundamentally the problem of parents today is no different from the problem of parents of all time. The purpose of education and child-training has not changed. First and foremost is the building of character. Second in importance is stimulation of curiosity about the world we all live in.

In my own life some of the things I look back upon with the greatest happiness are the hours I spent with my father at an early age. He died when I was very young but the memories of his sympathy and understanding patience in dealing with the growing mind of a child I shall never forget. His brother was Theodore Roosevelt; their father, my grandfather, was the type of man who felt keenly his duty toward the community and this duty involved giving time and thought to his children. You can also put it the other way around. He felt that his duty toward his family and children included a duty toward the community. My father passed on this atmosphere to me, young as I was, and it never quite left me; for later I found myself receptive to certain ideas because they recalled stories and emotions of my childhood.

My grandmother, under whose care I came directly from the time I was seven, was an extremely lovable but an extremely old-fashioned woman. Her idea of education was equipping a girl with the things that would make her agreeable in a drawing room. She had a responsibility toward the community but for her that responsibility could be expressed only in charitable activities, never in civic or community affairs. I learned and followed all the rules and taboos laid down by her; I neither rebelled nor revolted. My life, in other words, was not unusual in its preparation for maturity other than in the vitally important fact that together with the background of an old-fashioned upbringing, there was the inspiration of a man, my father, who had felt it important to acquaint a child with a world in which all the people were living.

The next great influence on my life was a remarkable woman, Mademoiselle Souvestre, the daughter of the French writer, Emil Souvestre. Under her care I lived for three years in Europe. She was the head of the school I attended and she took me traveling with her during many vacations. To her I owe more than I can ever repay for she gave me an intellectual curiosity and a standard of living which have never left me.

For a long time I did nothing constructive with this curiosity which had been aroused in me. At eighteen, together with a friend of mine, I took a class in a settlement on Rivington Street. Shortly afterward I married and the next ten years were spent in having children and caring for them. It was not until the war came that I began taking a really active interest in things beyond the immediate boundaries of the home. But those years of apparent inactivity in the social or community sense were not lost years. The interest, the curiosity, fostered and nurtured in childhood were there waiting for the proper moment of expression.

I have gone into these personal details not because I think of my life as exceptional but because I know that the things which have brought me the greatest happiness and satisfaction never fail to lead me back to the influences of my childhood, the things that so many children of today are missing. Over and over again it is impressed upon my mind that this is the place where parents make their greatest mistake. If it were possible I should like the adult generation of today, which decries youth's irresponsibility, to hear its children tell them the things that home life means to them. Parents might then be able to get some notion of the inevitable connection between cause and effect, might get some idea why the lives of their children are spent within a narrow vitiating circle of pleasure that either does not know or refuses to recognize its relationships to mankind in general and its obligation to do something in a world beyond the one bounded by social pleasures. . . .

The purpose of education is not the accumulation of facts. Certain fundamentals must of course be absorbed. . . . But that alone is not education. No human being can learn all the facts and information that have been piled up over the years but every human being who has within his reach the advantages of an education can forge the tools which will make his life . . . a fuller and richer one. Apart from character, the greatest thing that education can give is curiosity about the changing life about us.

In my work with the girls in school I have two current events classes. One of them consists of older girls, some of whom are graduates of the school; the second is made up of girls of about sixteen. The older class this year elected to study the government of the City of New York. It seemed to me a good way to do this was to see the various departments of the city in action. We visited City Hall and sat in on some of the meetings, we visited schools, the department of labor, police headquarters. I also took my class last year down to the children's court and the things they heard there shocked them into a realization of what the streets of New York and poverty and poor heredity and no chance at the start of life can do to young human beings.

With the younger class of current events students, I start with a background of the explanation of government and the reading of the daily newspapers. It is important that they know the relationship between state and city government, the difference between state and federal government. Very few, I find, can at the start tell me what departments there are in national government and what in the state.

Awakening curiosity in minds that prefer to slumber is no small task. . . .

We cannot know life unless we live it. If the function of a school is to prepare young people for life, then let them see it, feel it, know it, during their formative years. Often when I speak of the work of my classes in civics and current events, I am told that a very

HISTORY *[handwritten: dark ages from fall of Rome to Renaissance 15th & 16th cent. The conquest of the Greeks by the Turks brought ... What were the results of the Crusades? How did a middle class arise in Europe ...]*

Coolumbus 1492 *[handwritten notes]*

1498 Vasco da Gama *[handwritten notes]* East. Marco Polo - *[handwritten]*

Norse Vikings - 10th Century *[handwritten: Humanists ... printing ... what century was ...]*

[handwritten: ... Paper introduced & by whom? What was ...]

Haiti - 1st permanent settlement *[handwritten: National State? Portugal?]*

The Pope's Decree

Amerigo Vespucci - 1501

How we got out name - Waldsumuller)

1513 Balboa from Haiti - Isthmus of *[Panama]*   "Mar del Sur" -Pacific-

1519 Ferdinand Magellan - Portuguese 1519 - 22 *[Pacific]*

What made the discovery that the world is a sphere a certainty.

Sixteenth Century - Three reasons for exploration, missionary zeal, gold,
            Fountain Perpetual Youth.

1521 - Spaniards. Conquest of Mexico. Hernando Cortez. Aztecs. Mexico
            City, Montezuma
10 yrs. later - Francis Pizarro - Peru. Inca. Riches were hindrance. Why?
            Ponce de Leon, Florida
            Cabeza de Vaca, across Texas to Gulf of California
            Hernando de Soto, Georgia to Arkansas
            Coronado , Pacific Coast of Mexico to Kansas
1565 - St. Augustine, first permanent settlement in U.S. *[handwritten]*
            (Verrazana, sent by French King, Francis I (1515 - 1547)
1524 - North Carolina to Nova Scotia *[handwritten: He was Italian but sent by the King]*
1534 Jacques Cartier, Gulf St. Lawrence
1535 *[handwritten]* village ... Royal (...)

1498 - John Cabot (Italian) King Henry VII of England
       Henry VIII 1509 - 1549 Foundation Eng. Navy,

1577 - Francis Drake "Sea Dog" *[handwritten]*
1588 - "The Armada" What poem is written about this?
1583 - Sir Humphrey Gilbert   *[handwritten]*
1585 - 1587 Walter Raleigh - Virginia
1743 - Discovered Rockies
1805 - Pacific coast marked

For Monday read to p. 45. + *[handwritten: prepare charts.]*

In 1927 ER and her friends Nancy Cook and Marion Dickerman bought the Todhunter School, a private primary and secondary school for girls on New York City's Upper East Side. Dickerman, who became principal, had taught at the school for five years. ER, vice principal, taught history, literature, and current events; she continued with her work at the school during FDR's two terms as New York governor. As ER told a reporter in 1932, "I like it better than anything else." Above, one of ER's lesson plans for her history class at the Todhunter school.

small percentage of the girls in them will take an active interest in politics and that therefore such studies are wasted on them. That sort of criticism leaves me speechless. Are people ignorant enough to believe that the girl who marries has no place in the life of her community, that as a wife, as a mother, as a member of society, she can do nothing, influence nothing or nobody in making her community a better place for herself and family to live in, a finer place for her children and other people's children to grow up in?

Woman's Home Companion, 1932

ER leads a group of Todhunter students on a trip to George Washington's home at Mount Vernon in May of 1932, the final year that she would teach at the school.

THE POLITICAL WIFE

———

It is imperative that a wife should not interfere with her husband while he is in office. She must fulfill her obligations, perform her duties, and then, *though she may keep her own convictions—she must keep them to herself.*

Decidedly she should not attempt to meddle with her husband's plans, his procedure, or his principles. Nothing is worse, more futile when a man is strong, or politically more ruinous if he is weak. The first duty of the wife of an officeholder is to help him in her own domain, never to control him.

There is no place for conflict where a husband's political career is concerned. The wife's opinions must be subordinated.

It has been my experience that if my husband and I differed upon any important matter, we would talk it out. Then, as with any other person, if we still differed, he would go his way and I mine. We could only have such independence when he was neither holding office nor was candidate for office. When he is actively engaged in public or party business, and I disagree with the stand he takes, I do not discuss it with him or in any way attempt to place my reaction to his action before him.

A wife, I have always held, has a right to her own opinion, but she should never *nag* her husband. She has a right to state her opinion, but she should not go on, in the privacy of their home, emphasizing their differences, nor need she make them public. . . .

Family differences are always the subject of great public interest. Many other members of the Roosevelt family are Republicans. Yet unless my husband is running for office they do not make a point of discussing their differences. Families are families in spite of political opinions. If, however, my husband's interests clashed with theirs politically, I should support my husband to the best of my ability. . . .

There are few avenues of life where men and women agree on everything. In politics they differ along very definite lines.

Men tend to look at things from a legalistic point of view; women from a practical one.

Women will ask, "What result will this bring?"

Men will question, rather, "How can this be done?" . . .

Women generally are more interested in reforms than in tax laws. Consequently, if a bill dealing with maternal and infant welfare is before the legislature a wife is quite likely to consider it the most important measure before the body. Her husband might disagree, insisting that income-tax revision should take priority. Here there is no adjustment of opinion. Each must keep his own. The approach is fundamentally different.

My own experience has been that of many women of my generation, namely, an approach to social and economic problems via the route of a personal interest in the miseries of humanity. Women have thought more in the trend of homes, and of charity to alleviate hardship in homes, in illness, and growing children. When participation in politics was thrust upon them they seized upon the side of life they knew. Only lately have they become accustomed to other sides of the government and recognized their relations to the things in which they are interested. They are just beginning to realize that questions of tariff, of organization, of running town and state, keeping down civic expenses, are nothing but group housekeeping, and that foreign relations are nothing but relations between neighbors. . . .

Since 1920 the intrafamily divergence of political opinion has occasionally taken a virulent form, demanding drastic measures. The dangerous phase of this disturbance comes when both members of the marriage have embarked upon political careers. When they belong to the same party and subscribe to the same policies, it is possible. When they differ, it is a catastrophe.

IT IS IMPOSSIBLE FOR HUSBAND AND WIFE BOTH TO HAVE POLITICAL CAREERS. It requires all the energy and united effort of an entire household to support one.

Liberty, 1932

ER, Anna, FDR, and Curtis Dall, Anna's husband, enter the inaugural ball for FDR's second term as New York's governor, January 1, 1931.

The Roosevelt family in the fall of 1931, within a year of FDR's
nomination for president in the summer of 1932.

WE WOMEN HAVE
GREAT OPPORTUNITY
FOR USEFULNESS

This column will I hope be a method of keeping in touch with many of my New York State friends who will always be my friends even though I may be temporarily leaving them. . . .

As I am still in this state and haven't yet moved to Washington, my words to you this month must be on something in which I personally am deeply interested and in which I also hope you will take an interest.

We all of us are concerned about the unemployment relief work and should try to help in every way possible any new schemes which this state's unemployment relief administration has undertaken, particularly where they have a vision for the future good embodied in their plans. . . .

Many of us have learned that real rest is not always found in doing nothing, but is often found in changing one occupation to another, and that is something which people who work hard should learn. If you work with your hands all day, some other type of work is a relief. If you work with your brain all day, some work with your hands is a relief. . . .

It seems to me that we women have great opportunities for usefulness at present and if we do not take them up, I fear that there may be some rather serious results to the future generation.

Women's Democratic News, 1933

CHAPTER 2

On Women, Work, and Politics

Eleanor Roosevelt greets enthused supporters after addressing
a Democratic Party rally in New York City in October 1932,
just as the presidential campaign neared an end.

"At the President's press conferences, all the world's a stage, at
Mrs. Roosevelt's, all the world's a school," wrote Associated Press
reporter Bess Furman in the 1930s. "Give Mrs. Roosevelt a room-
ful of newspaperwomen, and she conducts classes on scores of
subjects, always seeing beyond her immediate hearers to 'the

women of the country.'" Started at the suggestion of reporter Lorena Hickok, the weekly press conferences were a masterpiece of public relations. ER shared her schedules, interests, and pet projects; she introduced women officeholders, promoted New Deal programs, and provided a forum for women's issues. With the prodding of reporters, other subjects soon arose; the realm of women's issues served ER as a springboard to public policy in general. Still, the focus on questions of interest to "the women of the country" prevailed. Topics discussed at the press conferences resonated in other forums—in ER's radio speeches and her "My Day" column, both begun in 1936; in her outpouring of magazine articles, now picked up by major publications; and in her 1933 book, *It's Up to the Women.* The varied venues enabled ER to share her ideas about women's roles in the workforce and in politics, as well as to shape her image, expand her following, and secure a foothold in national public life.

Women's place in the workforce was a contested issue in Depression-era America. "Quite a number of people feel that if you took women out of all jobs, there would be plenty of jobs for men," ER told a press conference in 1938, "and that would solve the unemployment problem." To compound the issue of anti-women bias, white-collar workers (often women) held onto jobs more easily than did blue-collar workers (mainly men). Working wives were a crux of conflict. The women's movement denounced a clause in the Economy Act of 1933 that forced wives of federal employees to resign federal posts. ER steadily defended working wives who supported families when men lost jobs, as well as those who sought employment as a preference, "because something in them craves the particular kind of work which they are doing." Like her wing of the women's movement, ER also defended protective laws for women in industry; accordingly, she opposed the National Woman's Party and its call since 1923 for an equal rights amendment. Women-only laws, wrote ER, were the best solution at hand. Her long affiliation with the National Women's Trade Union League and her friendship with Rose Schneiderman bolstered her support for women-only protective laws; so did her central position among like-minded women who were New Deal officeholders, such as Frances Perkins at the labor department and Mary Anderson at the Women's Bureau. Conflict over the potential impact of an equal rights amendment endured for decades.

ER's main field of expertise was electoral politics. Her focus on women in politics drew on her experience in Albany as well as in Washington. In 1928, in a major article in *Red Book,* ER argued for women's roles as what she called political "bosses," women leaders who could mobilize a female constituency and who could "talk the language of men." ER denied seeking power for herself; she resisted the suggestion of Louis M. Howe to consider a run for political office. Her directives to others stressed skill development: diligence, diplomacy, efficiency, and interchange with constituents; the aspiring woman leader had to become "active among the mass of women voters . . . mixing with women and getting their point of view." In short, ER urged readers to follow the path to leadership she had pursued herself in New York State. She continued her focus on political activism by issuing advice to women engaged in political campaigns; by repeatedly tackling the question of whether a woman could be president; and by persistent analyses of the impact—or lack of impact—of the women's vote. In 1940 ER published a stunning trio of articles in *Good Housekeeping,* "Women in Politics," starting with a survey of women's unprecedented contributions to New Deal political life. In the final article, ER analyzed the tensions in feminist politics between women's roles as individuals and as a group. The paradox that she described in 1940 would remain relevant in the women's movement for decades to come.

WOMEN MUST LEARN TO PLAY THE GAME AS MEN DO

———

Women have been voting for ten years. But have they achieved actual political equality with men? No. They go through the gesture of going to the polls; their votes are solicited by politicians; and they possess the external aspect of equal rights. But it is mostly a gesture without real power. With some outstanding exceptions, women who have gone into politics are refused serious consideration by the men leaders. Generally they are treated most courteously, to be sure, but what they want, what they have to say, is regarded as of little weight. In fact, they have no actual influence or say at all in the consequential councils of their parties.

In small things they are listened to, but when it comes to asking for important things, they generally find they are up against a blank wall. That is true of local committees, state committees, and the national organizations of both political parties.

From all over the United States, women of both camps have come to me, and their experiences are practically the same. When meetings are to be held at which momentous matters are to be decided, the women members often are not asked. When they are notified of formal meetings where important matters are to be ratified, they generally find all these things have been planned and prepared, without consultation with them, in secret confabs of the men beforehand. If they have objections to proposed policies or candidates, they are adroitly overruled. They are not allowed to run for office to any appreciable extent and if they propose candidates of their own sex, reasons are usually found for their elimination which, while diplomatic and polite, are just pretexts nevertheless. . . .

Politically, as a sex, women are generally "frozen out" from any intrinsic share of influence in their parties. . . .

Beneath the veneer of courtesy and outward show of consideration universally accorded women, there is a widespread male hostility—age-old, perhaps—against sharing with them any actual control.

How many excuses haven't I heard for not giving nominations to women! "Oh, she wouldn't like the kind of work she'd have to do!" Or, "You know she wouldn't like the people she'd have to associate with—that's not a job for a nice, refined woman." Or, more usually, "You see, there is so little patronage nowadays. We must give every appointment the most careful consideration. We've got to consider the good of the party." "The good of the party" eliminates women! . . .

Personally, I do not believe in a Woman's Party. A woman's ticket could not possibly succeed. And to crystallize the issues on the basis of sex-opposition would only antagonize men, congeal their age-old prejudices, and widen the chasm of existing differences.

How, then, can we bring the men leaders to concede participation in party affairs, adequate representation and real political equality?

Our means is to elect, accept and back women political bosses.

To organize as women, but within the parties, in districts, counties and states just as men organize. And to pick efficient leaders—say two or three in each State—whom we will support and by whose decisions we will abide. With the power of unified women voters behind them, such women bosses would be in a position to talk in terms of "business" with the men leaders; their voices would be heard, because their authority and the elective power they could command would have to be recognized. . . .

Perhaps the word "boss" may shock sensitive ears. To many it will conjure all that is unhealthy and corrupt in our political machinery. Yet when I speak of women bosses, I mean bosses actually in the sense that men are bosses. The term *boss* does not necessarily infer what it once did. Politics have been purged of many of the corruptions prevalent a quarter of a century ago. . . . As things are today, the boss is a leader, often an enlightened, high-minded leader, who retains little of the qualities imputed by the old use of this obnoxious word, but who still exercises authority over his district. I therefore use the word, as it is the word men understand.

If women believe they have a right and duty in political life today, they must learn to talk the language of men. They must not only master the phraseology, but also understand the machinery which men have built up through years of practical experience. Against the men bosses there must be women bosses who can talk as equals, with the backing of a coherent organization of women voters behind them. . . .

The trouble with many women is that they won't work. They won't take up their jobs as men do and put in seven or eight real working hours a day. They lack knowledge, and at that many won't take the pains to study history, economics, political methods or get out among human beings. If they take a volunteer political job, it is a thing of constant interruptions, with no sense of application, concentration, business efficiency or order. One of the reasons why men leaders so often do not consider as important what a woman says is that they do not feel sure she has been active among the mass of women voters and has learned what they want. In fact, many women do make the mistake of "talking out of a blue sky" instead of going about, mixing with women, and getting their point of view from close personal contact and practical experience. When a man leader says his following want certain things, the men higher up realize that he knows what he is talking about, and that he has gone through his district. . . .

Women are different. Many of them have no professional careers. If they go into politics it is usually because of some interest which they realize is dependent on government action. I know women who are interested in education, in health conditions, in the improvement of rural life, in social problems in housing, and all active in politics because they have come to realize by that way they may further their particular cause. Politics is less of a game to them because they haven't had the same training for games as men, and their first contact with great groups of people is an exciting and disturbing experience, not to be taken lightly. . . .

Remember, women have voted just ten years. They have held responsible positions in big business enterprises only since the war, to any great extent. . . . Can you blame them if the adjustment to modern conditions is somewhat difficult?

Certain women profess to be horrified at the thought of women bosses bartering and dickering in the hard game of politics with men. But many more women realize that we are living in a material world, and that politics cannot be played from the clouds.

To sum up, women must learn to play the game as men do. If they go into politics, they must stick to their jobs, respect the time and work of others, master a knowledge of history and human nature, learn diplomacy, subordinate their likes and dislikes of the moment and choose leaders to act for them and to whom they will be loyal. They can keep their ideals; but they must face facts and deal with them practically.

Red Book Magazine, 1928

WHAT TEN MILLION WOMEN WANT

What do ten million women want in public life? That question could be answered in ten million different ways. For every woman, like every man, has some aspirations or desires exclusively her own. We women are callow fledglings as compared with the wise old birds who manipulate the political machinery, and we still hesitate to believe that a woman can fill certain positions in public life as competently and adequately as a man. For instance, it is certain that women do not want a woman for President. Nor would they have the slightest confidence in her ability to fulfill the functions of that office. Every woman who fails in a public position confirms this, but every woman who succeeds creates confidence.

Judge Florence Allen on the Supreme Court Bench in Ohio, and Frances Perkins as Labor Commissioner in New York, have done much to make women feel that a really fine woman, well trained in her work, can give as good an account of her stewardship as any man, and eventually women, and perhaps even men, may come to feel that sex should not enter into the question of fitness for office. When it comes to the matter of having a woman as a member of the President's Cabinet, there are I think, many women who feel that the time has come to recognize the fact that women have practically just as many votes as men and deserve at least a certain amount of recognition.

Take the Department of Labor, for instance. Why should not the Secretary of Labor be a woman, and would not a woman's point of view be valuable in the President's Council? There are many other places to which women may aspire, and the time will come when there will be new departments, some of which will undoubtedly need women at their heads. When we come to finances we realize that after all, all government, whether it is that of village, city, state or nation, is simply glorified housekeeping. Little by little we are getting budget systems into our public housekeeping and budgets are something all women understand. . . .

Do women want to take part in framing our laws? I think the answer to that is decidedly yes. There are more and more women elected to legislative bodies every year. This session of Congress has six

Congresswomen on its roll, three Democrats and three Republicans.
. . . Welfare legislation touches very closely the home life of every
woman, and therefore demands her interest and careful criticism.
. . . Because these laws are interpreted and enforced by our courts,
I think women feel they are entitled to places on the bench.

Women judges are no longer a novelty, and in some classes of courts,
particularly those dealing with juvenile defenders, the women have
proven themselves decidedly superior to the men. I do not think
women would approve of having women heads of police departments. I do think they feel policewomen and matrons a necessity
for the proper care of girl and women offenders. As for a national
police commissioner, male or female, I think women are decidedly
opposed to it. . . .

Women, to whom, after all, the education of the child is largely
entrusted by the men, understand far better than the average man
the need of education and improvement in teaching. Too often,
the father's actual knowledge of how his child is being educated is
gleaned from a hasty scanning of the report card once a month,
but the mother knows all the virtues of the successful teacher and
the faults of the poor one. . . .

There is much research that a department of education might be
doing. What actual education possibilities does each state offer? Are
all children furnished with standard textbooks? Are libraries accessible for all children? Do we need, for a great majority of children,
more specialized and vocational training? . . .

Then we come to the [final] point, which, after all, while it is entirely
in the hands of the national government, still comes back to the home
of every individual woman. She may wake up someday to find that
her nation is at war and her boys and even her girls in one war or
another, are drafted into a service from which they may not return. . . .

The only danger that women will not get what they want lies in the fact that there are still a goodly number who do not know how to use their influence and to make known their ideas. . . .

If ten million women really want security, real representation, honesty, wise and just legislation, happier and more comfortable conditions of living, and a future with the horrors of war removed from the horizon, then these ten million women must bestir themselves. They can be active factors in the life of their communities and shape the future, or they can drift along and hide behind the men. Today is a challenge to women. Tomorrow will see how they answer the challenge.

The Home Magazine, 1932

Molly (Mary W.) Dewson (left), shown here with Labor Secretary Frances Perkins, was head of the Women's Division of the Democratic National Committee. Sometimes called "More Women Dewson," to fit her initials, Dewson urged the appointment of women to federal positions, including those of Judge Florence Allen and Frances Perkins.

A PLACE FOR WOMEN
IN POLITICS

That there is a place for women in politics I am absolutely convinced. But politics is a comparatively new field for women and for their own good as well as for the women who will come after them, to say nothing of the community at large, they should keep out of office until they are confident they can hold it with ability and personal integrity. And when I say personal integrity I mean more than dollars-and-cents honesty. I mean the consistent loyalty to an intelligent idea of service which does not allow itself to be swayed by what older people in office might call politic or expedient.

Paradoxically the world expects a better job from a woman in office than from a man and although it seems unfair, and is unfair, I am glad that it is so. In a manner of speaking it is a safeguard for women. It will put into office and keep in office only those who are preeminently fitted for the job and that, as I see it is the only reason they should have it. Perhaps this sounds discouraging to many women. It shouldn't. I want to see women taking an interest in politics, taking active part in campaigns, organizing their strength for proper legislation and proper legislators. But I cannot say too often that taking an interest in politics is not synonymous with holding political office. It is more important for a million women to know whom to vote for than it is for one to hold office. It is a matter, again, of intelligent public opinion, of breadth of interest, of training and education.

Woman's Home Companion, 1932

Eleanor Roosevelt with reporters at her first White House press conference, held only for women members of the press, March 6, 1933. "You are the interpreters to the women of the country," ER told the reporters.

ER'S FIRST WHITE HOUSE PRESS CONFERENCE

TOPIC: MRS. ROOSEVELT'S UNOFFICIAL
STATEMENT AS HER REASONS FOR HOLDING
PRESS CONFERENCES

Mrs. Roosevelt: "The reason that I am glad to see you all is that I think in the first place it is much more convenient for you to come at the same time and in the second place it saves me time. I imagine there will be times when various ones will ask for special interviews and I will try to grant them.

"It will save my time enormously if I see you all together once a week and do not have to see three now and three later and so on. I feel that your position as I look upon it is to try to tell the women throughout the country what you think they should know. That, after all, is a newspaper woman's job, to make her impressions go to leading the women in the country to form a general attitude of mind and thought. Your job is an important one and if you want to see me once a week I feel I should be willing to see you, and anything that I can do through you toward this end I am willing to do.

"The idea largely is to make an understanding between the White House and the general public. You are the interpreters to the women of the country as to what goes on politically in the legislative national life, and also what the social and personal life is at the White House."

Press Conference of March 6, 1933

ER with four fellow journalists on a trip to Puerto Rico in March 1934. Left to right: Emma Bugbee of the New York *Herald Tribune*; Dorothy Ducas of the New York *Evening Post* and later the *Herald Tribune*; Ruby Black, White House correspondent for the United Press; and Bess Furman from the Washington Bureau of the Associated Press.

ON THE NATIONAL WOMAN'S PARTY, WOMEN WORKERS, AND THE ERA

TOPIC: NATIONAL WOMAN'S PARTY AND THE EQUAL RIGHTS AMENDMENT

Mrs. Roosevelt: "I think the National Woman's Party ignores the fact that there is a fundamental difference between men and women. I don't mean by that women can't make as great a contribution, nor if they do the same work they should not be paid the same wages. The mere fact that women basically are responsible for the future physical condition of the race means for many restrictions. It is a physical difference, not a mental.

"In my mail the most violent protestation against employment of married women comes from women themselves.

"There is from my point of view a value in work. It is un-American to say anybody should not work. It is class legislation of the very worst kind to say that any particular class of people can't work.

"Women do need a certain amount of protection. I'm not sure I'd think so if women were well enough developed to run their own unions. But they [unions] are run by men and the women can't defend themselves and are exploited. They work for a very limited high type group of women who are able to defend themselves. The rest work at anything until they marry. They don't see far enough ahead either to be unionized or to prepare themselves for better jobs.

"I'm in perfect sympathy with many things the National Woman's Party stands for."

Press Conference of July 6, 1933

Officers of the National Woman's Party meet in the 1920s to plan the dedication of the NWP's new Washington, DC, headquarters; the party's leader, Alice Paul, is at the far left. In 1923 the NWP proposed to Congress the first version of an equal rights amendment. ER's branch of the women's movement opposed the prospect of an ERA because it would vitiate state protective laws for women workers, such as maximum hours laws, minimum wage laws, and night work laws.

WOMEN AND WORKING CONDITIONS

Great efforts have been made to make working women realize the necessity for union organizations but very little result in the way of actual organizations can be seen. Now and then you will find women are organized in some trade, but it is very apt to be a trade where they are allowed to enter the same union with the men and where the men's union had already been established.

One would think that enough women of intelligence would have recognized this problem and educated the great body of working women. This, however, does not seem to be the case and women in industry continue, largely because of their own lack of initiative, to receive lower wages than men and to pull down the wage scale of the men as well as their own.

In occupations where the higher type of women with a better education are employed, they are more nearly getting to an equality and I think before many years in the professions and the more skilled trades and more executive jobs, we shall see very little difference in the earning capacity of women as compared with men. Women should receive equal pay for equal work and they should also work the same hours and insist on the same good working conditions and the same rights of representation that the men have. If they accept longer hours and unsanitary working conditions, they may injure the cause of labor. This may mean, however, if they are not allowed to join the men's unions, the forming of a union of their own, but I hope it will not be as difficult in the future as it has been in the past to awaken them to the necessity of organization. I think women have a right to demand equality as far as possible but I think they should still have the protection of special legislation regarding certain special conditions of their work and until we actually have equal pay and are assured of a living wage for both men's and women's work, I believe in minimum wage boards and regulating by law the number of hours women may work. They should also be allowed a certain number of days off before and after the birth of a child. This legislation is primarily necessary because as yet women are not as well organized or as able to negotiate for themselves with the employers, but it is also necessary in the interests of the state, which must concern itself with the health of the women because the future of the race depends upon their ability to produce healthy children. The new codes [NRA codes of 1933] aim to accomplish many of these things, but the codes must be enforced and public opinion must insist on this.

It's Up to the Women, 1933

WOMEN IN PUBLIC LIFE

———

The basis of all useful political activity is an interest in human beings and social conditions, and a knowledge of human nature.

This is not something which can be acquired overnight and that is why I suggest that young people—particularly young women—come to their political activities from the bottom rather than from the top. If they come from the bottom, there will undoubtedly be times when they will feel that political life is sordid, that human beings are disappointing, that their aspirations and desires are frequently rather low, and it is just as well to realize all this, for no useful work is accomplished until facts are faced and accepted. If you are going to be discouraged by finding that people do not always measure up to what you expected of them and by finding out that everybody does not always believe in the old adage that "honesty is the best policy," the sooner you get over that discouragement the better. It is well to remember the old fable of the tortoise and the hare. Pegging along day by day is a dull way of changing the world . . . but probably it is the plodders who in the long run accomplish the most.

When a woman has mastered the details of party organization and has gained a certain amount of knowledge of her fellow human beings, then she may be ready to accept either an appointive or an elective office. She will be far more effective because of this service in her party organizations.

Every few days somebody writes and asks me whether I think we will some day have a woman President of the United States and I am afraid that I look upon this question with a certain amusement, for it is really unimportant of what sex a President may be. We certainly will not have a woman President until some woman worthy of being President appears on the horizon. In the meantime, men both worthy and un-worthy will probably fill that office. In the course of human events it may come to pass that we shall consider an individual's qualifications and the sex will pass unnoticed, but that is some years away and in the interim, I do not advise any woman to try to be President, or in fact to hold any important office until she has gained experience in minor offices first and feels herself capable of filling easily whatever office she is striving for. During the next few years, every woman in public office will be watched more carefully than a man holding a similar position, and she will be acting as a pioneer preparing the way for many other women who will follow in her footsteps.

It's Up to the Women, 1933

ER TO LORENA HICKOK: TWO LETTERS

Journalist Lorena Hickok covered Eleanor Roosevelt for the AP during the 1932 campaign and proposed to ER the idea of the all-women White House press conferences. Resigning from the AP in June 1933, Hickok next worked as chief investigator for the Federal Emergency Relief Administration. Above, ER and Hickok on a trip to Puerto Rico in March 1934; the two friends explored an impoverished section of San Juan with local officials.

[May 23, 1934]

The White House
Washington

Hick Dearest, I know how you felt today, you couldn't let go for fear of losing control & being with me was hard & I imagine I made it worse by sending you to say goodbye to Tommy [Malvina Thompson] but she spoke of it at breakfast & I was so afraid she'd come & stay & spoil our little time together. Darling I love you dearly & I am sorry for letting my foolish temp[e]rament make you unhappy & sorry that your temp[e]rament does bad things to you too but we'll have years of happy times so bad times will be forgotten. July is a long way off but when it comes we'll be together.

Perhaps this will reach you tomorrow night so sleep sweetly & and a world of love dear one,

E.R.

With Lorena Hickok at a concert, 1935.

[May 13, 1935]

The White House
Washington

Dear one,

Your wire came this morning to my joy & I found 3 letters here which was also a joy, Wed. Thurs. and Friday & the last has made me think & try to formulate what I believe about happiness. I think it is this way, to most of us happiness comes thro' the love we give & the return love we feel comes to us from those we love: There does not have to be a balance however, we may love more or less some since there is no measure of love. Over the years the type of love felt on either side may change but if the fundamental love is there, I believe the relationship adjusts to something deep and satisfying to both people. For instance, I know you often have a feeling for me which for one reason or another I may not return in kind but I feel I love you just the same & so often we satisfy each other that I feel there is a fundamental basis on which our relationship stands. I love other people in the same way or differently but each one has their place & one cannot compare them. I do know for myself that if I know someone I love is unhappy I can't be happy and I would be happier to see or to know they were happy even if it meant giving up my own relationship to them in whole or in part. I'd probably hope to get it back enriched someday but if not, well, I know no one I love I wouldn't rather see happy & I hope they wouldn't worry about my hurt because it would be so much less than watching them hurt. I don't think I'd run away either, unless they wanted me to! I'm not worried tho' for this means that I am a person of little depth & really don't know what suffering such as you go thro' is really like.

Well, I must go to bed. I love you dearly & miss you much dear person. Sleep sweetly,

E.R.

Lorena Hickok Papers, 1934–1935

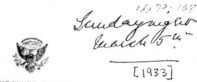

THE WHITE HOUSE
WASHINGTON

Sunday night
March 5th
[1933]

Hick my dearest — I cannot go to bed to-night without a word to you. I felt a little as though a part of me was leaving to-night, you have grown so much to be a part of my life that it is empty without you even though I'm busy every minute.

These are strange days & very odd to me but I'll remember the days & try to plan pleasant things & count the days between our times together!

Eleanor Roosevelt's letter to Lorena Hickok of March 5, 1933, one day after FDR's inauguration and on the eve of ER's first White House press conference. By mid-1935, ER had started to retreat from the intense relationship.

WHEN WILL A WOMAN BECOME PRESIDENT?

———

Announcer: Mrs. Roosevelt promised us that she would give her opinion of the question "When will a woman become president of the United States?"

ER: "I do not think that it would be impossible to find a woman who could be president, but I hope that it doesn't happen in the near future. There are exceptional women just as there are exceptional men, and it takes an exceptional man to be a successful and useful president. Though women are doing more and more, and are proving every year that they are capable of assuming responsibilities which were considered to be out of their province in the past, I do not think that we have yet reached the point where the majority of our people would feel satisfied to follow the leadership and trust the judgment of a woman as president. And no woman could, therefore, succeed as president any more than could any man who did not have the trust and confidence of the majority of the nation, for this is a democracy and governed by majority rule.

"People say no woman could stand the physical strain, but that I think is nonsense and answered over and over again by women through the length and breadth of the land. No man works harder in the fields than the farmer's wife, in her home and on the farm. Women have carried the same jobs in factories, even in mines, up to a few years ago. And besides their industrial jobs [women] have almost always carried on the work of the home. Sometimes badly, to be sure, but that work has always been before them when the other work was done. . . .[T]hey have as much endurance and ability to bear strain as the male of the species.

"Women have not as yet had, however, as many years of background in public life. Or as many years of experience in learning how to give and take in the world of affairs. And I personally would be sorry to see any woman take any position of responsibility which she was not well equipped to undertake and where she could not command the following which she would need for success. Someday a woman may be president, but I hope it will not be while we still speak of 'a woman's vote.' I hope it will only become a reality when she is elected as an individual because of her capacity and [because of] the trust which the majority of the people have in her integrity and ability as a person.

"It is not a new thing for women to wield political power. They have done it through men in the past and women have been independent rulers in their own right. Witness Catherine of Russia and Queen Elizabeth of England. In fact, birth seems to have created more confidence in some countries of the past than does ability today! The future lies before us, however. And women have a big contribution to make. So let us hope that when a woman does assume any important office, it will be because the services she can render are apparent to all."

Radio Broadcast of September 3, 1934

ADVICE TO WOMEN
IN POLITICS

———

You cannot take anything personally.

You cannot bear grudges.

You must finish the day's work when the day's work is done.

You cannot get discouraged too easily.

You have to take defeat over and over again and pick up and go on.

Be sure of your facts.

Argue the other side with a friend until you have found the answer to every point which might be brought up against you.

Women who are willing to be leaders must stand out and be shot at. More and more they are going to do it, and more and more they should do it.

Democratic Digest, 1936

SHOULD WIVES WORK?

———

Hyde Park, Friday— . . . I received the other day an appeal from an organization which had as its purpose the removal from all employment of any married women whose husbands earned enough to support them. Who is to say when a man earns enough to support his family? Who is to know, except the individuals themselves what they need for daily living or what their responsibilities are, often hidden from the public eye? There are few families indeed who do not have some members outside their own immediate family who need assistance, Added to this, who is to say whether a woman

Boston women picket against the employment of married women in public service jobs in the 1930s. Their argument: working wives deprived male "breadwinners" and their families of income. ER and her New Deal allies, in contrast, defended the working wife.

needs to work for the good of her own soul outside her home? Many women can find all the work they need and all the joy they need and all the interest they need in life in their own homes and in the volunteer community activities of their environment. Because of this I have received many critical letters from women complaining that other women were taking paid jobs who did not need them; that they were working for luxuries and not for necessities, that men were kept out of jobs who had families to support by these selfish and luxury-loving creatures. I have investigated a good many cases and find that, on the whole, the love of work is not so great; those who are gainfully employed are usually working because of some real need. There are a few, however, who work because something in them craves the particular kind of work which they are doing, or an inner urge drives them to a job. They are not entirely satisfied with work in the home. This does not mean that they are not good mothers and good housekeepers, but they need some other stimulus in life. Frequently they provide work for other people and if they suddenly ceased their activities, many other people might lose their jobs. As a rule these women belong to the creative type.

It seems to me that the tradition of respect for work is so ingrained in this country that it is not surprising that some fathers have handed it down to their daughters as well as their sons. I wonder if we are not going to feel more respect in the coming years for the women who work and give work to others, than for the women who sit at home with many idle hours on their hands.

"My Day," July 24, 1937

FOR SOME PEOPLE, WORK IS ALMOST A NECESSITY

TOPIC: MARRIED WOMEN IN THE LABOR FORCE

Mrs. Roosevelt: "For some people, work is almost a necessity to development. . . . [Y]ou certainly can't deny that human being the right of development permanently.

"I have always cited the fact that work was necessary to the development of the country and dignified the individual and was of value to the community, and that any young man who could live on his income without working and who did not work has always had the feeling that he was a slacker.

"Why should we feel that in an age when someone's work is not needed in the home, she should, out of necessity, be made a slacker, is something I have never been able to understand. . . ."

Mrs. Weed [A member of the National Woman's Party]: "I expected you to say that there might be, in times of stress, a reason for women to work without salary."

Mrs. Roosevelt: "Not for women to give up their work. I think you have to realize that there are always individual situations. . . ."

Mrs. Weed: "Do you think there is a greater moral obligation on women to give up their work, when they have other means of support, than there is on men in the same circumstances, married or single?"

Mrs. Roosevelt: "I think if the single woman has to support herself, the question does not arise if she is under more moral obligation than a man.

"So I think it boils down to a married woman, and then comes the question whether the man or woman should be the main support in a family. My own instinct is a feeling that most women, if it comes to a decision, have more ability to find employment for themselves than most men have. But that doesn't always hold true. . . ."

May [May Craig, correspondent for Maine newspapers]: "What is a woman's duty? Her first duty is to stay home and take care of her family, and the other is to take a job in the economic situation where jobs are scarce."

Mrs. Roosevelt: "Who is going to be the person to decide whether it is a woman's duty to stay at home and take care of her family?

"Second, who should say that where the skills of the woman were such that she could do that particular job better than anybody else, better than she could do any other, probably it would be economically sound as well as spiritually a good thing? On the other hand, there may be a great many people for whom it would neither be spiritually or economically the best thing for their children for that individual."

Press Conference of June 16, 1938

WORKING WOMEN
IN THE DEPRESSION

TOPIC: A REPORT ABOUT WOMEN
IN THE LABOR FORCE

Mrs. Roosevelt: ". . . Quite a number of people feel that if you took women out of all jobs, there would be plenty of jobs for men and that would solve the unemployment problem.

"I think the men would have a feeling that a lot of people support, in general . . . that these statistics are entirely true. But like so many statistics they only tell half the story. They don't say that, very likely, the reason there has been a disproportionate increase of women who earn their living, very likely, is that, in many cases, men have lost their jobs, and women have had to go back and take jobs; because perhaps it is possible for them to get a job, where the man couldn't get one. And in many cases the man's income may have been so much reduced that it was necessary for the woman, if she could get a job, to go out and get it in order to keep a standard of living to be anywhere near what it had been before.

"Therefore, I don't feel that these statistics . . . really give us any very great information that is worthwhile.

"I think that the Women's Bureau should take those same figures and try to break them down, to find out why they were as they were. We might find out that there is a disproportionate increase and might find out the reason why. We might find the reason is a desire for a higher standard [of living]. We might find that there was not as much advantage in the home. We might find a great many reasons.

"I am much more interested in knowing the reasons why things are than in just knowing, in a blank way, that a certain thing exists, without having any idea why."

Press Conference of October 10, 1938

ER with her devoted secretary and personal assistant, Malvina "Tommy" Thompson, center, and her White House social secretary, Edith Helm. Thompson, who first met ER in 1917, traveled everywhere with the first lady; typed her speeches, articles, and correspondence; took notes at conferences; and provided years of loyal company and support.

PLENTY OF
CAPABLE WOMEN

———

TOPIC: NATIONAL LEAGUE OF WOMEN VOTERS'
REPORT [ON FALLING NUMBERS OF WOMEN SERVING
IN STATE LEGISLATURES AND CONGRESS]

Mrs. Roosevelt: ". . . I think the reason why there are so many men in our state legislatures and Congress is not so much that women would be unwilling to run but the fact that women as a whole do not back women's running and do not back them for positions and are not really trying to get them to represent the women's point of view.

"I think just as soon as you have found a genuine demand among women for the representation of their point of view, you would find plenty of women capable and willing to run; and until there is genuine demand, you don't find women who are willing to go out and do that.

"I think we will probably have something jolting us into waking up some day. We waste our energy so many times. I think there are plenty of capable women."

Press Conference of December 27, 1938

WORKING WIVES

———

New York, Thursday—A number of people have written me in opposition to my stand that married women should be allowed the privilege of working. They plead with me to consider how cruel it is that these married women, with husbands well able to support them, should be taking jobs away from young people.

They insist that most of these married women are simply doubling good incomes and acquiring luxuries for themselves. They think that they are taking the bread out of the mouths of single women who are helping to support members of their families.

It sounds a bit hysterical, so let us consider the question calmly. Basically, is it wise to begin to lay down laws and regulations about any particular group? If we begin to say that married women cannot work, why shouldn't we say next that men with an income of more than a certain sum shall not work, or that young people whose parents are able to support them have no right to look for jobs? It seems to me that it is the basic right of any human being to work.

Many women, after marriage, find plenty of work in the home. They have no time, no inclination or no ability for any other kind of work. The records show that very few married women work from choice, that they are working only because a husband is ill or has deserted them, or there are special expenses caused by illness or educational requirements in the home. There may even be fathers, mothers, sisters or brothers to be supported. It seems to me that it is far more important for us to think about creating more jobs than it is for us to worry about how we are going to keep any groups from seeking work.

"My Day," June 16, 1939

WOMEN IN POLITICS

Where are we going as women? Do we know where we are going? Do we know where we want to go?

I have a suggestion to make that will probably seem to you entirely paradoxical. Yet at the present juncture of civilization, it seems to me the only way for women to grow.

Women must become more conscious of themselves as women and of their ability to function as a group. At the same time they must try to wipe from men's consciousness the need to consider them as a group or as women in their everyday activities, especially as workers in industry or the professions.

Let us consider first what women can do united in a cause.

It is perfectly obvious that women are not all alike. They do not think alike, nor do they feel alike on many subjects. Therefore you can no more unite all women on a great variety of subjects than you can unite all men.

If I am right, as I have stated in a former article, women have caused a basic change in the attitude of government toward human beings, then there are certain fundamental things that mean more to the great majority of women than to the majority of men. These things are undoubtedly tied up with women's biological functions. The women bear the children, and love them even before they come into the world. Some of you will say that the maternal instinct is not universal in women, and that now and then you will find a man whose paternal instinct is very strong—even stronger than his wife's maternal instinct. These are the exceptions which prove the rule, however. . . . [A] man can nearly always be more objective about his children than a woman can be.

This ability to be objective about children is one thing women have to fight to acquire; never, no matter what a child may do or how old he may be, is a woman quite divorced from the baby who once lay so helpless in her arms. This is the first fundamental truth for us to recognize, and we find it in greater or less degree in woman who have never had a child. From it springs that concern about the home, the shelter for the children. And here is the great point of unity for the majority of women.

It is easy to make women realize that a force which threatens any home may threaten theirs. . . .

I have heard people say that the United States is a matriarchy—that the women rule. That is true only in the nonessentials. . . .

This country is no matriarchy, nor are we in any danger of being governed by women. I repeat here what I have often said in answer to the question: "Can a woman be president of the United States?" At present the answer is emphatically "No." It will be a long time before a woman will have any chance of nomination or election. As things stand today, even if an emotional wave swept a woman into office, her election would be valueless, as she could never hold her following long enough to put over her program. It is hard enough for a man to do that, with all the traditional schooling that men have had; for a woman it would be impossible because of the age-old prejudice. In government, in business, and in the professions there may be a day when women will be looked upon as persons. We are, however, far from that day as yet. . . .

There may be a woman's crusade against war, which will spread to other countries. I have a feeling that the women of the United States may lead this crusade, because the events of the last few months have left us the one great nation at peace in the world. . . .

The consideration of future possibilities for peace seem to me of paramount importance; but other things of worth enter into our present considerations. Great changes in our civilization have to be considered, and the women are going to weigh the effect of these changes in the home. I believe women can be educated to think about all homes and not so much about their own individual homes. If certain changes have to be made in industry, in our economic life, and in our relationship to one another, the women will probably be more ready to make them if they can see that the changes have a bearing on home life as a whole. That is the only thing that will ever make women come together as a political force. . . .

Now let us consider women in the other phases of activity where they wish to be persons and wipe out the sex consideration.

Opposition to women who work is usually based on the theory that men have to support families. This, of course, is only saying something that sounds good, for we know that almost all working women are supporting someone besides themselves. And women themselves are partly to blame for the fact that equal pay for equal work has not become an actuality. They have accepted lower pay very often and taken advantage of it occasionally, too, as an excuse for not doing their share of their particular job.

If women want equal consideration they must prepare themselves to adjust to other people and make no appeals on the ground of sex. Whether women take part in the business world or in the political world, this is equally true.

A woman who cannot engage in an occupation and hold it because of her own ability had much better get out of that particular occupation and do something else, where her ability will count. Otherwise, she is hanging by her eyebrows, trying to exploit one person after another, and in the end she is going to be unsuccessful and drag down with her other women who are trying to do honest work.

In the business and professional world women have made great advances. In many fields there is opportunity for them to work with men on an equal footing. To be sure, sometimes prejudice on the score of sex will be unfair and a woman will have to prove her ability and do better work than a man to gain the same recognition. . . .

In the political field they haven't gone so far. This field has long been exclusively the prerogative of men; but women are on the march. I do not think it would be profitable or desirable to form them into a separate women's political unit. Too many questions arise in government which are not fundamentals that stir women as women. Women will belong to political parties; they will work in them and leave them in much the way that men have done. It will take some great cause that touches their particular interests to unite them as women politically, and they will not remain united once their cause is either won or lost.

I do not look therefore, for a sudden awakening on their part to a desire for greater participation in the government of the nation, unless circumstances arise that arouse all the citizens of our democracy to a feeling of their responsibility for the preservation of this form of government. Otherwise I think it will be a gradual evolution.

There is a tendency for women not to support other women when they are either elected or appointed to office. There is no reason, of course, why we should expect any woman to have the support of all women just because of her sex; but neither should women be prejudiced against women as such. We must learn to judge other women's work just as we would judge men's work. . . . A woman may fail; but women must begin to impress it upon everyone that a woman's failure to do a job cannot be attributed to her sex, but is due to certain incapacities that might as easily be found in a man. . . .

There is one place, however, where sex must be a cleavage in daily activity. Women run their homes as women. They live their social lives as women, and they have a right to call upon men's chivalry, and to use their wiles as women to make men do the things that make life's contacts pleasanter in these two spheres. Sex is a weapon and one that women have a right to use, because this is a part of life in which men and women live as men and women and complement but do not compete with each other. They are both needed in the world of business and politics to bring their different points of view and different methods of doing things to the service of civilization as individuals, with no consideration of sex involved; but in the home and in social life they must emphasize the difference between the sexes because it adds to the flavor of life together.

Good Housekeeping, 1940

TO FIGHT THE AMENDMENT: ER TO ROSE SCHNEIDERMAN

February 11, 1944

Dear Rose:

I will try to see Elizabeth Christman [an officer of the National Women's Trade Union League] very soon. To tell you the truth, I do not think it matters even if both political parties endorse the Equal Rights Amendment. It will take a long time to get it through. However, I feel we must do a lot more than just be opposed to an amendment. I believe we should initiate through the Labor Department a complete survey of the laws that discriminate against women and the laws that are protective; that we should then go to work in every state in the Union to get rid of the discriminatory ones and to strengthen the protective ones; and if the time has come when some of them are obsolete, we should get rid of them even though they were once needed as protective.

If we do not do this, we are not in a good position to fight the amendment. I am sending a copy of this letter to Frances [Frances Perkins], because I think the work should be started as soon as possible. Women are more highly organized, they are becoming more active as citizens, and better able to protect themselves, and they should, in all but certain very specific cases which are justified by their physical and functional differences, have the same rights as men.

Affectionately,
[Eleanor Roosevelt]
Miss Rose Schneiderman
Department of Labor
50 Centre Street, NYC

ER Papers, 1944

ER with her mother-in-law, Sara Delano Roosevelt, at a school dedication ceremony in Hyde Park in 1940. Sara would die in 1941; her dominance had shaped the early years of ER's marriage. "It is dreadful to live so close to someone for 36 years & feel no deep affection or sense of loss," ER wrote to her friend and future biographer, Joseph P. Lash.

ON THE ERA

Hyde Park, Sunday—. . . . I have been getting a good many letters of late about the Equal Rights Amendment, which has been reported out favorably to the House by the House Judiciary Committee. Some of the women who write me seem to think that if this amendment is passed there will be no further possibility of discrimination against women. They feel that the time has come to declare that women shall be treated in all things on an equal basis with men. I hardly think it is necessary to declare this, since as a theory it is fairly well accepted today by both men and women. But in practice it is not accepted, and I doubt very much whether it ever will be.

Other women of my acquaintance are writing me in great anxiety, for they are afraid that the dangers of the amendment are not being properly considered. The majority of these women are employed in the industrial field. Their fear is that labor standards guarded in the past by legislation will be wrecked, and that the amendment will curtail and impair for all time the powers of both state and federal government to enact any legislation that may be necessary and desirable to protect the health and safety of women in industry.

I do not know which group is right, but I feel that if we work to remove from our statute books those laws which discriminate against women today, we might accomplish more and do it in a shorter time than will be possible through the passage of this amendment.

"My Day," May 14, 1945

I DO NOT SUPPORT
THE EQUAL RIGHTS AMENDMENT

———

[LETTER TO NORA STANTON BARNEY]

November 25, 1946

Dear Miss Barney:

I am sorry you have been misinformed on my attitude for equality for women. I do not oppose it and I have never opposed it in the United States.

The confusion arises because I do not support the Equal Rights Amendment. I believe we still need the existing protective laws for women in industry. I know full well of the various state laws which are discriminatory to women. I believe we should work to have such laws repealed in the states. It takes two thirds of the states to ratify an amendment and that means a lot of work.

Some day women in industry will not need protective legislation and then they can work with the women in professions for an Equal Rights Amendment. This has nothing to do with the political rights which were under discussion. We have those.

Very sincerely yours,
[ER]

ER Papers, 1946

CHAPTER 3

Humanizing the New Deal

ER with residents of a federal camp for unemployed women in 1933.

"The century-old White House wore a startled air today as its new mistress took over," Associated Press reporter Bess Furman announced on March 3, 1933. Two days later, with her first White House press conference, Eleanor Roosevelt affirmed her role as a trendsetter. Her functions multiplied. As presidential deputy, ER traveled continually; as respondent to hard times, she defended the disadvantaged, disfranchised, and unemployed. As an outspoken liberal, she veered to the left of FDR, especially in her contact with civil rights activists, pacifists, and the National Youth Congress. Her liberalism spared the president some critiques from the left; it also boosted her own constituency and helped bring black Americans into the New Deal voting coalition. Embedded in a network of women officeholders—in the labor department, the Works Progress Administration, and other agencies—ER used her influence to intercede for her associates with FDR. She promoted the causes she endorsed at White House meetings and press conferences, and in radio talks, articles, and columns; journalists and photographers trailed after her. To her following, ER embodied the process that United Press White House correspondent Ruby Black called "humanizing the New Deal."

Concern for those facing hardship filled ER's correspondence and her publications. Thousands wrote to her about their struggles with job loss, homelessness, and downward mobility. In *It's Up to the Women* (1933), she offered menus for austerity to housewives on reduced budgets. Developed by the White House housekeeper, the menus, famously, included recipes like those for watery vegetable stew and boiled prunes. ER reminded magazine readers that "the unemployed are not a strange race" and pressed the administration to include unemployed women in federal jobs programs. Relief efforts constituted much of her portfolio. A main concern was Arthurdale, a pioneer resettlement community in West Virginia. In 1933, ER's friend Lorena Hickok reported to Harry Hopkins, head of emergency relief, about the dire condition of jobless miners and tenant farmers in the area. Alert to the plight of the unemployed, ER leaped into the effort to shape Arthurdale. Under the wing of the Department of the Interior, the subsistence homestead program sought to provide housing, jobs, education, and recreation. ER contributed time, energy, funds, initiative, and influence; her involvement brought publicity. Arthurdale never fulfilled its ambitious goals, but it represented ER's commitment to humanitarian relief. The people of Arthurdale had been "restored to usefulness and given confidence in themselves," she wrote. "The human values were most rewarding even if the financial returns to the government were unsatisfactory."

ER also focused on the growing labor movement; union membership rose in the 1930s and soared in wartime. Long concerned with labor issues—she had been involved with the National Women's Trade Union League since the 1920s—ER saw unions as essential in a democratic state. New Deal legislation—the Wagner Labor Relations Act of 1935 and the Fair Labor Standards Act of 1938—helped ensure basic labor rights, including the right to join a union and engage in collective bargaining, and laid a foundation for a "New Deal for workers." But ER was yet more fervent; she sought alliance with union leaders, supported striking workers, and refused to cross picket lines. In 1936 she joined the American Newspaper Guild, a union of journalists, and remained a member for life. As she told a group of striking electrical workers, "the ideals of the labor movement are high ideals." To ER the future of labor involved the future of democracy. By the end of the 1930s, as Americans watched war make inroads in Europe, ER became increasingly absorbed in democratic ideals and their preservation in yet another era of emergency.

THE FEELING THAT WE ARE RESPONSIBLE FOR EACH OTHER

[O]ne part of the country or group of countrymen cannot prosper while the others go downhill and . . . one country cannot go on gaily when the rest of the world is suffering. . . . [T]hey must survive together. . . . In our complicated modern civilization, we are so separated from each other, that we forget our interdependence. If we can get back to the feeling that we are responsible for each other, these years of Depression would have been worthwhile.

Democratic News, 1932

THE BRIGHT SIDE
OF THE DEPRESSION

For four years now we have been going over and over again the ills that have befallen us. We know that the Depression has brought us an added burden of debt as a nation. We know that as individuals it has meant to many people loss of jobs, loss perhaps of their home or their farm. To young people sometimes it has meant the inability to educate themselves in a way which they desired, possibly a sense of hopelessness in their inability to find either a way to earn a living or to feel themselves necessary in their homes and in their communities.

To many old people it has meant despair as their savings were wiped out, or their incomes so reduced that they saw themselves a burden upon their children already overburdened with their own difficulties.

All of this tale of woe we are familiar with, and I think the time has come for us to look back over the past seven years and see if we cannot find some bright side to this picture. . . .

[W]e have added to our debt, obliged to do so because of the war on the Depression, but in doing so we have lent and given primarily money to our own people so that the money has remained in America to be spent for American goods.

In addition while we have had to help many of our citizens, they have [gone] on relief work, or on CWA [Civil Works Administration], or PWA [Public Works Administration], or under the NYA [National Youth Administration], and in the CCC [Civilian Conservation Corps] camps, things which we can point to in every community in this country as improvements for the future which we owe to the Depression.

I can think, for instance, of a park near one of our middle western cities which will bring pleasure and recreation to many people for many years. I can think of swimming pools and community houses, improved aviation fields in communities both small and great; soil erosion and reforestation work which can be looked upon as bright spots in our Depression gloom.

Now for the personal things we have gained. It seems to me that as individuals we have more character because we faced the Depression, met our problems and solved them, because we were obliged to try new things, to use our ingenuity, to take our courage in our hands and take advantage of anything which the government offered. None of the government plans would have succeeded if the people had not made them succeed. In the last analysis we were responsible for our own solution. We were pioneering again for our homes and our country just as surely as our great-grandfathers did. . . .

Out of the Depression has come to both young and old, I think, a greater ability to meet life and conquer it. With it has perhaps come the realization that man must have faith in the future, faith in himself, faith in some kind of divine Providence which is willing to help those who help themselves.

Draft of article, 1933

DEPRESSION MENUS

———

I am putting together here a sample week's menus and recipes prepared for the Temporary Emergency Relief Administration by the New York State College of Home Economics of Cornell University. These recipes will serve a family of six. Many of these meals we have used ourselves at the White House. They have been worked out under the direction of experts on home economics and will serve as a sample for balanced, inexpensive home rations. . . .

TUESDAY

Breakfast

Oatmeal-milk-sugar,
Whole Wheat Toast-Butter,
Milk for Children, Coffee for Adults.

Dinner

Hot Stuffed Eggs-Tomato Sauce,
Mashed Potatoes,
Whole Wheat Bread-Butter,
Prune Pudding,
Milk for Children.

Supper

Apple and Cabbage Salad,
Peanut Butter Sandwiches,
Cocoa for All.

For the 2- or 3-year-old child the tender leaves of cabbage may be chopped and put in a sandwich.

HOT STUFFED EGGS: 5 eggs, hard cooked; ½ teaspoon minced onion, I teaspoon vinegar or tomato juice, ¼ teaspoon salt, pinch of pepper.

Cut the eggs in half lengthwise, removing the yolks. Mash the yolks thoroughly, mix with other ingredients. Stuff the egg whites. Put in a dish, cover with tomato sauce, reheat in a slow oven and serve. A white sauce may be used instead of tomato sauce. . . .

PRUNE PUDDING: ¼ pound prunes, 1½ cups cold water, ½ cup sugar, 2 cups prune water, 1 inch stick cinnamon or ¼ teaspoon powdered cinnamon, 4 tablespoons flour, 4 tablespoons cold water.

Soak the prunes overnight in the 1½ cups cold water. Cook in the same water until they are tender. Drain, but save the liquid. Remove the seeds and cut prunes into bits. Add sugar, cinnamon and hot prune juice. If juice does not measure 2 cups, add enough water to make up the measure. Bring to the boiling point and simmer for 10 minutes. To the flour add the 4 tablespoons cold water and mix to a smooth paste. Add this slowly to the prune mixture, stirring carefully, and cook for 10 minutes over a slow fire or over boiling water. Remove stick cinnamon (if used) and pour into bowl or a mold. Serve cold. . . .

WEDNESDAY

Breakfast

Tomato Juice for Children,
Oatmeal-Milk, Bread-Butter,
Milk for Children, Coffee for Adults.

Dinner

Vegetable Stew, Whole Wheat Bread-Butter,
Caramel Blanc Mange,
Milk for Children.

Supper

Scalloped Potatoes with Milk,
Carrot Relish,
Whole Wheat Bread-Butter,
Tea for Adults, Milk for Children.

VEGETABLE STEW: 1½ cups dried lima, navy, kidney beans or lentils, 2 quarts cold water, ½ cup rice, 2 cups tomatoes, 1 onion, 4 tablespoons drippings.

Wash and soak the beans overnight in water. Drain and add fresh water to cover well. Boil for three hours. Brown sliced onion in frying pan, with drippings; add this to the cooked beans, together with tomatoes, washed rice, and seasonings. Simmer for one-half hour.

It's Up to the Women, 1933

FAIR WORKING CONDITIONS

No matter how fair employers wish to be, there are always some who will take advantage of times such as these to lower unnecessarily the standards of labor, thereby subjecting him to unfair competition. It is necessary to stress the regulation by law of these unhealthy conditions in industry. It is quite obvious that one cannot depend upon the worker in such times as these to take care of things in the usual way. Many women, particularly, are not unionized and even unions have temporarily lowered their standards in order to keep their people at work. If you face starvation, it is better to accept almost anything than to feel that you and your children are going to be evicted from the last and the cheapest rooms which you may have been able to find and that there will be no food.

Cut after cut has been accepted by workers in their wages, they have shared their work by accepting fewer days a week in order that others might be kept on a few days also, until many of them have fallen far below what I would consider the normal and proper standard for healthful living. If the future of our country is to be safe and the next generation is to grow up into healthy and good citizens, it is absolutely necessary to protect the health of our workers now and at all times.

It has been found, for instance, in Germany, in spite of the Depression and the difficulty in making wages cover good food, that sickness and mortality rates have been surprisingly low amongst the workers, probably because of the fact that they have not been obliged to work an unhealthy number of hours.

Limiting the number of working hours by law has a twofold result. It spreads the employment, thereby giving more people work, and it protects the health of the workers. Instead of keeping a few people working a great many hours and even asking them to share their work with others by working fewer days, it limits all work to a reasonable number of hours and makes it necessary to employ the number of people required to cover the work.

Refusing to allow people to be paid less than a living wage preserves to us our own market. There is absolutely no use in producing anything if you gradually reduce the number of people able to buy even the cheapest products. The only way to preserve our markets is to pay an adequate wage.

It seems to me that all fair-minded people will realize that it is self-preservation to treat the industrial worker with consideration and fairness at the present time and to uphold the fair employer in his efforts to treat his employees well by preventing unfair competition.

Scribner's Magazine, 1933

On May 21, 1935, a *New York Times* headline announced that
"First Lady Tours Coal Mine in Ohio." The photo captures ER, in miner's cap,
at the entrance to Willow Grove Mine Number 10, a model mine in Bellaire,
Ohio; company managers and union officials showed her around.

ON STARTING ARTHURDALE

For many years past I have taken an interest in certain mining communities because as far back as 1915 a gentleman who was in a position to know, told me that there had been several investigations and reports on the general conditions of the coal mining industry but that nothing was ever done about it; the reports were simply pigeonholed and conditions were growing constantly more unsatisfactory.

This is one of the basic industries of our country and perhaps serves as the best example to prove what I think we are all of us going to realize, namely, that no business can be fundamentally sound where the human beings connected with it who actually are the basis of whatever that business may produce do not receive in return for their labor, at least a minimum of security and happiness in life. They must have enough to eat, warmth, adequate clothing, decent shelter and an opportunity for education.

No business can prosper where the workers do not at least receive this in return for their labor. For some time past it has been widely known that a great many of the workers in the coal mining industry fall far short of these minimum standards. So partly because I was interested in seeing something of these conditions for myself and partly because I was interested in seeing how relief was being administered in an area where I had heard it had been intelligently and adequately done from the beginning, I wanted a chance to talk to the people themselves and spend a day without their really knowing anything beyond the fact that a casual visitor had come to see them. This I accomplished. . . .

I do not believe if most of us knew the conditions under which some of our brothers and sisters were living that we would rest complacently. . . . [C]hange may have to be slow and I pray that it may come about through our own volition and in a peaceful manner. But of one thing we may be very sure, that is that if we do not bring it about because we recognize the justice of what should be done, then we can be expecting that history will repeat itself in this country as it has in many other countries, for it is misery that drives people to the point where they are willing to overthrow anything simply because life is not worth living any longer.

Women's Democratic News, 1933

DEFENDING ARTHURDALE

TOPIC: REPLY TO CHARGE BY DR. WILLIAM A. WIRT,
CRITIC OF THE NEW DEAL, THAT THE ARTHURDALE PROJECT
IN REEDSVILLE, WEST VIRGINIA, WAS "COMMUNISTIC."

Mrs. Roosevelt: ". . . I do not understand exactly how he considers it communistic to give people a chance to earn their own livings and buy their own houses. It is a fact that the government will provide the initial capital but if any private enterprise wishes to do it, and I hope that many private enterprises will do it, the government is simply attempting to point the way for what may be done by many industries throughout the country in the future. Never in this country to my knowledge has it been considered communistic for an opportunity to be given to people to earn their own livings

ER arrives in Arthurdale in 1933, surrounded by reporters, photographers, officials, and townspeople. The "social experiment in community life" that ER envisioned far exceeded its projected costs. According to Secretary of the Interior Harold Ickes, whose department ran the subsistence homestead program, "We are spending money down there like drunken sailors."

and buy their own houses. What the government is doing in its homestead projects is a drop in the bucket in a big country like this and its value, while it may be helpful to a few people, really lies in the suggestions which it is making to the industry of the country that by decentralizing and moving out of large cities, it may make it possible for great numbers of people to have more in their lives than they would otherwise have."

Press Conference of April 11, 1934

Guest of honor at the senior prom of the class of 1938 at the Arthurdale school, ER celebrates with an unidentified partner. Journalists and photographers who trailed the first lady to Arthurdale and covered her participation in community events noted what *New York Times* reporter Bess Furman called "a marathon of devotion." ER's goals for Arthurdale included, for instance, public health services, community cooperatives, a handicraft business, a progressive system, and cultural programs to preserve the Appalachian heritage. She also urged integrated housing, which Arthurdale residents rejected.

THE HOMESTEAD PROGRAM

———

I am going to tell you a little about that much discussed, and at times vilified, project near Reedsville, West Virginia. . . .

They say that Scott's Run, West Virginia . . . is the heart of the most concentrated bituminous coal fields in the world. Many of the people working there come from farms and mountains in the days of fabulously high wages when the miners knew what it was to wear silk shirts. . . .

Then came the crash and in its wake years of misery. Men were out of work one and two and more years, working only occasionally. The Quakers came at last to lend a helping hand. Finally, the government set men to work again, repairing roads, clearing water ways, improving sanitation. . . .

I went to West Virginia, and by dint of careful planning, succeeded in spending time in various mining camps without being recognized. To the families whom I visited, I was simply a friend brought in by the social workers who visited them in any case, at regular intervals. I had heard that relief work had been intelligently handled from the beginning in Fairmont and Morgantown, but I wanted to talk to the people themselves and see their homes and their children. This I accomplished.

The people I saw had begun to realize that hundreds of these men would never work again in the mines and that they had to face the problem of devising what they should do in the future and many of the women did not want to see their husbands and children continue in mining.

The government[,] realizing their need, started the first experiment in subsistence homesteading in Arthurdale, near Reedsville, West Virginia. This land was chosen by an agricultural expert and considered to be good average farming land for that region. There was a large, old house, the Arthur Mansion, on the ground, with a few outbuildings. Amongst other things there was an old log cabin well over a hundred years old and on a hillside, an old graveyard where were buried some of the early pioneers.

In the Interior Department this new division of subsistence homesteads had just been set up, some young architects were put to work on possible plans and went to live in the Arthur Mansion. They had nothing to guide them, they had to make surveys of the land, and decisions as to how it should be divided, where roads should go and over and above all, hovered the thought of the families living nearby in dire poverty, illness, and distress. In the haste of those first few weeks, it was decided that fifty portable houses of a type which had withstood the rigours of the climate of Labrador, might be used to expedite the moving in of those families. The families were not hard to find, for lists of applicants were already available, of those who wished to return to farming. . . .

These unemployed men were taken on and put to work at building cellars for the houses which were to arrive and be put up as quickly as possible. But difficulties soon appeared as they do in every project of this kind. Land had to be drained which they had not expected to have to drain, and draining is fairly costly. The winter of this hill country also made work extremely slow and meant heavy losses in time and money. The houses, when they came, were not entirely suitable to the needs of the families who were to live in them. Changes were difficult and yet vital. . . .

The administrative personnel in the Interior Department in Washington, as well as in the field, had not shaken down as yet, nor become a well-rounded organization. This first experiment, like all experiments, was proving far more costly than had originally been planned. In spite of it all, however, these houses were built and they had cellars and barns and at last fifty families moved in. . . .

The number of families eventually to be housed was raised from one hundred to about two hundred. The property adjoins the railroad and is easily accessible. . . . The first factory, which will employ fifty people, is now being built near the railroad line. . . .

Even more important than what each individual is able to do for himself, is the idea of what, as a community, they can accomplish for each other. . . . The idea of community activity for the good of all rather than the interest of the individual, has grown largely through the influence of the school.

The school is purely an experiment, an experiment in which the state and county boards of education are taking a great interest. There are two hundred and forty-six pupils, all children of the homesteaders, and it is run by Miss Elsie Clapp, who has degrees from Vassar, Barnard, and Columbia, but more important than her degrees is her understanding that school life and the entire subsistence homestead experiment has value only if it succeeds in giving the people of the community a more abundant opportunity

One of several noted photographers who followed ER to Arthurdale, Marion Post Wollcott depicted mining families in Scott's Run in the 1930s. Wollcott worked for the Farm Security Administration.

to live better and more fruitful and more satisfying lives. This school is supported in part by the county and in part by the interest and generosity of outsiders who see an opportunity to develop through experiment a new method of education. . . .

Arthurdale is a social experiment in community life which centers around its school. It has cost the government money, more money perhaps than it should have cost, but I wonder how many inventions and experiments developed by industry and science do not cost those industries money before the actual returns come in. . . . That is the way I look at the Arthurdale experiment.

I doubt if anyone can go there, with an open mind, and spend a day or better still a day and a night, and attend a community dance where the community orchestra provides the music, and not come away with the feeling that if we could multiply such communities and make them successful, even on a basis far below the millennium we wish for an ultimate goal, we would still have a degree of contentment and well-being which has never in the past been the lot of many people in our land.

Draft of article, 1935

WHETHER THE DEPRESSION IS HALF OVER

TOPIC: WHETHER THE DEPRESSION IS ENDING.

Mrs. Roosevelt: "In the first place, I would hardly be in a position to know whether the Depression is half over or more than half over, or less than half over. I can only judge from what the papers print and any conversations I have had. . . . I happened to hear, while at Cornell at a meeting of economists, that their consensus of opinion was that we would be back by 1936. . . . That I give you for what it is worth. I would have no way of formulating an opinion of my own."

TOPIC: OBJECTIVES OF THE NEXT TWO YEARS
IN PROMOTING ECONOMIC RECOVERY

Mrs. Roosevelt: 1. "I could name more than three or four out-standing things. I think that the things I would like best to see accomplished in the next two years are complete realization of both labor and industry or capital of their responsibility towards each other and the public; of the necessity of their interdependence or the fact that neither prospers without the other. On the part of industrial leaders, I would like to see a willingness to realize that labor must share to a greater extent and receive a fairer return for its part in the world's work, and that capital shall accept the fact of a more limited and reasonable return. On the part of organized labor, I should like to see a greater understanding and recognition of their responsibilities to the people at large and a recognition of the necessity that they look upon problems not only as problems of organized labor, but as problems of the country as a whole.

2. "I hope that we will have a greater realization of our international interdependence and our responsibility toward the rest of the world.

3. "I hope we will realize the problem of youth and make a more determined effort to be helpful to the rising generation.

4. "I hope very much to see a security program really launched on its way which will include old age pensions, a permanent ban on child labor, better unemployment insurance, better health care for the country as a whole, better care for mothers and children generally. I do not expect that program to be static, that is, that within the next two years we will have completely written a security program, but I hope it will be started. Many things will have to be

changed, year by year, in as big an undertaking as this. But I hope we can get it started."

TOPIC: ACCOMPLISHMENTS OF
THE NEW DEAL TO DATE

Mrs. Roosevelt: "The banking bill, the insurance of bank deposits. The beginning that we have made in making it more difficult for the gullible public to be sold things which they should not buy. The TVA [Tennessee Valley Authority] is a decided accomplishment, the whole utility program is a decided step forward. The CCC camps have been an accomplishment. . . .

"I should also say that one of the things which was a great accomplishment was the beginning of a subsistence homestead program. I do not agree with those who think it is a menace. I believe that if properly developed it will be of great assistance in furnishing greater security in connection with industry."

TOPIC: GOVERNMENT
RESPONSIBILITY FOR WELFARE

Mrs. Roosevelt: "The big achievement of the past two years is the great change in the thinking of the country. Imperceptibly we have come to recognize that government has a responsibility to defend the weak. I also think that in spite of criticism, the administration of relief has been a great achievement."

TOPIC: PRESIDENT ROOSEVELT'S
FIRST INAUGURAL ADDRESS

Mrs. Roosevelt: "The President's inaugural address is a most historic event—'the only thing we have to fear is fear' will go down in history, I hope."

Press Conference of February 27, 1935

ER first called a White House conference on November 2, 1933, to discuss "Emergency Needs of Women." A major goal: work projects to which unemployed women might be assigned, a counterpart to CCC camps for men. By 1936, about ninety camps, nicknamed "She, She, She," included about 5,000 women. Here, ER speaks to residents of a pioneer project, Camp Tera (for "Temporary Emergency Relief Administration") in Bear Mountain, New York, in August 1933.

FIRST LADY'S DICTIONARY

[COMPILED FROM ER QUOTES BY
AP REPORTER BESS FURMAN]

AVOCATION—"Something in life which occupies either your mind or your hands, and which will change your trend of thought when you wish to change it."

BUDGET—"A necessary evil no matter how dull you may find it, equally necessary for the woman with $15 a week as for the woman of unlimited means."

CHARITY—"Not only the immediate alleviation of distress, but the up-building of the individual or the family to a point of independence so that charity will be unnecessary. Charity, meaning the giving of material things, should be taken out of our planned society."

CITIZENSHIP—"No more apathy, no more accepting ideas handed to you, no more accepting labels, nor even facts just because they are told to you as facts—instead, an open mind, a real inquiry as to how to use that mind to the best advantage, a real determination that what you have gained you are to give back to your country and its people."

ECONOMY—"Cost curtailment based on a weighing of what will do possible harm and what can be done without harm to future generations. If we get false economy it will be because we did not take the trouble to get the right kind of economy."

FEAR—"A bad thing at all times. It should be eliminated from our lives as much as possible."

GARDENING—"Not just a question of enjoying the flowers or the vegetables; it is something like rearing a child. You have taken so much trouble about it that you cannot help getting a tremendous satisfaction out of it."

HOLIDAYS—"The time when one gets that grand feeling of letting oneself go into whatever one wants to do, thus developing individuality, originality, and personality."

LADY—"In essentials, a lady remains exactly what she always was. The essentials are kindliness of spirit, and the kind of naturalness which is not dependent on birth or circumstances surrounding the person, but is dependent on the inner assurance that if you are doing the right and kind thing it must be the right way to act, therefore you do not worry about what people may think, or whether what you do seems to them right or wrong."

MONEY—"Only a token, but a token which represents real things—somebody's work or the production of some material things for which some human beings have in some way worked. Real work of some kind must attend the honest making of money."

NEIGHBORLINESS—"Not to be interested just in family affairs, but to be interested in everything which touches the neighborhood."

POLITICIAN—"A public servant unselfishly giving his time to carry out the wishes of a majority of the people, and devoting to that task all his education and experience."

SNUB—"The effort of a person who feels superior to make someone else feel inferior. To do this, it is necessary first to find someone who can be made to feel inferior."

SOCIETY—(as was)—"A little group of people, set apart from the rest. Fortunate people who had not only money but through some accident of birth or circumstance were thrown in with those whose word or action carried weight in the community, and who were the people looked to and copied by the rest of their fellowmen."

SOCIETY—(as is)—"Means that human beings need contact with each other, and must have opportunities for knowing each other, and for being mutually helpful. Society today means the big society of all men and women, and each one of us in our own little sphere may have real society if we cultivate making friends and drawing around us congenial people."

TRADITION—"[T]he continuity of comradeship and experience which really binds people, especially families, together."

ER Papers, 1935

THE UNEMPLOYED ARE NOT A STRANGE RACE

Another task for us to undertake and a very important one, is to convince many unthinking people that the unemployed are not a strange race. They are like we would be if we had not had a fortunate chance at life. Some of us regard the unemployed remotely, as if they were thousands of miles away, and had no personal call on anyone's sympathy. It isn't the intention to be cruel and indifferent. It's just that it is very hard for people who do not come face to face with suffering to realize how hard life can be.

I have a feeling that in the next few years in addition to helping themselves, we in this group must take on the task of educating the fortunate people into an understanding of the lives of the unfortunate.

If the fine characters can be developed against such odds as we see about us, we surely can and must solve these problems that make it difficult for the great majority of our people to live decent lives.

We simply cannot sit back and say, "all people cannot live decent lives." We've got to try to make this goal our particular responsibility. I'm not a very wise person but I do know that this cannot be accomplished unless people who have much get to know about people who have little.

We must all see how well worthwhile it is to help those who are struggling heroically, for if once we have this kind of understanding, goodwill and brains and enthusiasm will put over a magnificent job.

Democratic Digest, 1936

ARE YOU FREE
IF YOU CANNOT VOTE?

———

New York, Wednesday— . . . Are you free if you cannot vote, if you cannot be sure that the same justice will be meted out to you as to your neighbor, if you are expected to live on a lower level than your neighbor and to work for lower wages, if you are barred from certain places and from certain opportunities? It seems from my mail that there are people in this country who do not feel as I do about personal freedom, even though they might agree that they are better off than they might be somewhere else.

I think of the little girl who wrote me not long ago: "Why do the other children call me names and laugh at my talk? I just don't live in this country very long yet."

Are you free when you can't earn enough, no matter how hard you work, to feed and clothe and house your children properly? Are you free when your employer can turn you out of a company house and deny you work because you belong to a union?

There are lots and lots of things which make me wonder whether we ever look ourselves straight in the face and really mean what we say when we are busy patting ourselves on the back!

Somewhere someone must be having a quiet laugh, I think, if there is a place where real truth is dealt in!

"My Day," December 8, 1938

DEFINING DEMOCRACY

———

TOPIC: DEFINITION OF DEMOCRACY

Mrs. Roosevelt: "You must have a minimum of economic security in order to have true democracy and for people to love their government and their country.

"You must have an assurance of a certain amount of education which makes it possible for you to understand questions which face your country.

"And your sources of information must be kept free. While you must guard against government controlled sources of information, there are other ways of controlling those sources which you must guard just as carefully, such as banks, advertisers and subscribers.

"People cannot love a government or a country which does not allow them to have anything which makes life worth living."

Press Conference of January 17, 1939

ON THE AMERICAN YOUTH CONGRESS

———

There is a growing wave in this country of fear, and of intolerance which springs from fear. Sometimes it is a religious intolerance, sometimes it is a racial intolerance, but all intolerance grows from the same roots. I can best illustrate fear by telling you that a short time ago someone told me in all seriousness that the American Youth Congress was a Communist organization and that the World Youth Congress was Communist controlled. This person really believed that the young people who were members of these organizations were attempting to overthrow the governments of the countries to which they belonged.

Undoubtedly, in the World Youth Congress there were young Communists, just as there are a group of young Communists and a group of young Socialists in the American Youth Congress, but this does not mean that either of these bodies is Communist controlled. It simply means that they conform to the pattern of society, which at all times has groups thinking over a wide range, from what we call extreme left to extreme right. The general movement of civilization, however, goes on in accordance with the thinking of the majority of the people, and that was exactly what happened in both the American Youth Congress and the World Youth Congress.

ER chats with Joseph P. Lash, a leader of the American Youth Congress, when he was subpoenaed to testify before the House Un-American Activities Committee in November 1939. A hostile witness, Lash refused to cooperate with the committee (to supply names of Communist Party members). ER and Lash, who had met only recently, became lifelong friends. Later a cofounder of Americans for Democratic Action (ADA), an anti-communist pressure group, Joseph P. Lash won a Pulitzer Prize in biography in 1972 for his admired study *Eleanor and Franklin*.

The resolutions finally passed by both bodies were rather sane and calm, perhaps a trifle idealistic and certainly very optimistic. There were amendments offered for discussion, and voted down, which many people might have considered radical; but since there is radical thinking among both young and old, it seems to me wiser to discuss and vote down an idea than to ignore it. By so doing we know in which direction the real trend of youth is growing. If we take the attitude that youth, even youth when it belongs to the Communist party, cannot be met on the basis of equal consideration and a willingness to listen, then we are again beginning to allow our fears of this particular group to overwhelm us and we are losing the opportunity to make our experience available and useful to the next generation.

The Virginia Quarterly Review, 1939

CHILDREN AND COMMUNITY

I have seen many things in different parts of the country, and I have seen children that I think everyone who is listening today would agree with me had very little chance of being valuable citizens in a democracy.

Democracy is being challenged today, and we are the greatest democracy. It remains to be seen if we have the vision and the courage and the self-sacrifice to give our children all over the nation a chance to be real citizens of a democracy.

If we are going to do that, we must first see that they get a chance at health, that they get a chance at an equal opportunity for education. We must see that they get a chance at the kind of education which will help them to meet a changing world. We must see that, as far as possible, these youngsters, when they leave school, get a chance to work and get a chance to be accepted and to feel important as members of their communities.

I think there is nothing that helps one to develop so much as responsibility, and for that reason I think it is well for us to try to bring home to every one of our citizens the fact that our young people must be given an opportunity to feel real responsibility in their communities.

I also feel that it is a pity we do not, some of us, retire from some of our responsibilities and turn them over to younger people in our communities, because we learn by doing and they will learn by doing too.

White House Conference, 1940

ER visits a WPA nursery school for African American youngsters in Des Moines, Iowa, 1936.

INSURING DEMOCRACY

W e are learning that rural slums may be quite as bad as city slums. We are learning that it is not because of the adult members of the family alone that we must do away with these slums. The children born and brought up in them are apt to be conditioned for the future by their earliest environment. What happens to our children is the concern of a whole nation because a democracy requires a standard of citizenship which no other form of government finds necessary. To be a citizen of a democracy a human being must be given a healthy start. He must have adequate food for physical growth and proper surroundings for mental and spiritual development. Under a dictatorship it may be sufficient to learn to read and write and to do certain things by rote, but in a democracy we must learn to reason and to think for ourselves. We must make our decisions on the basis of knowledge and reasoning power. In a democracy we must be able to visualize the life of the whole nation. When we vote for candidates for public office to be our representatives, we must decide on the qualities to be required of the men and women who are to hold public offices. . . .

Poor schools in our communities today mean poor citizens in these communities in a few years—men and women ill-prepared to earn a living, or to participate in government. . . .

One minority group of American children that I feel deserves particular attention are about five million Negroes, Indians, Mexicans and Orientals under sixteen years of age. They have all the handicaps of other children with the addition of a number of special handicaps of their own. Their families are usually in the lowest income groups and the restrictions put upon the opportunities offered them for health, for education, for recreation and later for employment, are very great because of prejudice and lack of understanding or appreciation of their needs and capabilities. This conference should set the example and perhaps start our thinking in a new way—in America good standards apply to all children regardless of race or creed or color.

Child labor has frequently flourished in underprivileged groups. Child labor, of course, is a menace not only to other young people but to all workers. We have been handicapped by the fact that many people have thought that the regulation of child labor would mean interference in the home and prevention of ordinary home training in work habits. This, of course, is not child labor, and there is much child labor in this country which we should make every effort to control. We are concerned about the children before they are born, but we should follow them through every step of their development until the children are firmly on their feet and started in life as citizens of a democracy. . . .

I have often heard people say they would rather have a democracy, even if it had to be inefficient, than regimented efficiency. We love our freedom, but must we of necessity have freedom coupled with stupidity? Is it not possible to face our situation and recognize the inequalities in the economic background of America's children, inequalities in educational opportunities, in health protection, in recreation and leisure-time activities and in opportunities for employment?

I began by telling you how inadequate I felt when bringing up my own children. I feel the mistakes I made serve to give me a little more wisdom and understanding in helping people who are trying today to preserve our democracy. We cannot direct youth altogether but we can give courage to the next generation and stand back of them so that they will feel our protection and goodwill.

Collier's, 1940

THIS IS NO ORDINARY TIME: ADDRESS TO THE DEMOCRATIC CONVENTION

Delegates to the convention, visitors, friends. It is a great pleasure for me to be here and to have an opportunity to say a word to you.

First of all, I think I want to say a word to our National Chairman, James A. Farley.

For many years I have worked under Jim Farley, and I think nobody could appreciate more what he has done for the party, what

Suddenly arranged and unexpected, ER's speech at the Democratic Convention in Chicago on July 18, 1940, conveyed the need to reelect FDR; the nation, ER explained, faced a new emergency. ER's presence, meanwhile, pressed delegates to accept FDR's controversial choice of Henry Wallace as his running mate.

he has given in work and loyalty. And I want to give him here my thanks and devotion.

And now, I think that I should say to you that I cannot possibly bring you a message from the president because he will give you his own message. But, as I am here, I want you to know that no one could not be conscious of the confidence which you have expressed in him.

I know and you know that any man who is in an office of great responsibility today faces a heavier responsibility, perhaps, than any man has ever faced before in this country. Therefore, to be a candidate of either great political party is a very serious and solemn thing.

You cannot treat it as you would treat an ordinary nomination in an ordinary time. We people in the United States have got to realize today that we face a grave and serious situation.

Therefore, this year the candidate who is the president of the United States cannot make a campaign in the usual sense of the word. He must be on his job.

So each and every one of you who give him this responsibility, in giving it to him assume for yourselves a very grave responsibility because you will make the campaign. You will have to rise above considerations which are narrow and partisan.

You must know that this is the time when all good men and women give every bit of service and strength to their country that they have to give. This is the time when it is the United States that we fight for, the domestic policies that we have established as a party that we must believe in, that we must carry forward, and in the world we have a position of great responsibility.

We cannot tell from day to day what may come. This is no ordinary time. No time for weighing anything except what we can do best for the country as a whole, and that responsibility rests on each and every one of us as individuals.

No man who is candidate or who is president can carry this situation alone. This is only carried by a united people who love their country and who will live for it to the fullest of their ability, with the highest ideals, with a determination that their party shall be absolutely devoted to the good of the nation as whole and to doing what this country can to bring the world to a safer and happier condition.

Press Release, 1940

ER gave the 1940 convention speech from a page of notes.

Postmaster General James J. Farley, FDR's campaign manager in 1932 and 1936, left, with ER and FDR in 1938. In the 1936 campaign, ER had served as an intermediary between the White House and Democratic headquarters, run by Farley and Molly Dewson. In 1940, Farley opposed a third term for FDR.

MEMO FOR FDR

MEMO FOR THE PRESIDENT:

I have just heard that no meeting was ever held between colored leaders like Walter White [executive secretary of the NAACP], Mr. Hill [Herbert Hill, NAACP labor director] and Mr. Randolph [A. Philip Randolph, organizer and leader of the Brotherhood of Sleeping Car Porters], with the secretary of War and Navy on the subject of how the colored people can participate in the services.

There is a growing feeling amongst the colored people, and they are creating a feeling among many white people. They feel they should be allowed to participate in any training that is going on, in the aviation, army, navy, and have opportunities for service.

I suggest that a conference be held with the attitude of the gentlemen: these are our difficulties, how do you suggest that we make a beginning to change the situation?

There is no use of going into a conference unless they have the intention of doing something. This is going to be very bad politics, besides being intrinsically wrong, and I think you should ask that a meeting be held and if you cannot be present yourself, you should ask them to give you a report and it might be well to have General Watson [Edwin M. Watson, FDR's military aide and secretary] present.

E.R.

FDRL, 1940

HIGH IDEALS:
ADDRESS TO WORKERS AT THE LEVITON STRIKE

I have always been interested in organizations for labor. I have always felt that it was important that everyone who was a worker join a labor organization. Because the ideals of the organized labor movement are high ideals.

They mean that we are not selfish in our desires, that we stand for the good of the group as a whole, and that is something which we in the United States are learning every day must be the attitude of every citizen.

We must all of us come to look upon our citizenship as a trusteeship, something that we exercise in the interests of the whole people.

Only if we cooperate in the battle to make this country a real democracy where the interests of people are considered, only when each one of us does this will genuine democracy be achieved. . . .

[M]y education in the labor movement has come largely through Rose Schneiderman. I happened to join the Women's Trade Union

League years ago and she has taught me many things I wouldn't have known otherwise.

I worked with Hilda Smith on her programs of workers' education throughout the country. I always ask everybody what they are doing in the work project. I get funny answers. They say that they thought it was a dangerous subject. It doesn't seem that way to me. We must have education and the ability of the people to understand the whole problem.

We should have projects to study the employees' problems and I wish we had employers' educational projects, too. The important thing is to try to learn what conditions are throughout the country

Members of the International Brotherhood of Electrical Workers went on strike at the Leviton Manufacturing Company in Brooklyn, New York, to achieve union recognition and improved working conditions. ER, who visited the picket line, spoke to union members, and offered encouragement, addresses 1,500 striking employees in February 1941.

as a whole. And what the people are really thinking and what they are striving for.

As I look over the last few years, the thing that gives me the most hope for the future is the fact that, on the whole, people are standing together, people are working for the good of a group, not just for themselves. When we learn that, I think we are going to move forward faster and faster.

I wish that those of us who are employers would learn that it is through cooperation that we achieve more, that through stating our problems and asking people to work with us to solve them that we really get somewhere. . . .

We find ourselves at a serious moment in the history of the world. We face problems not only as citizens of the United States; we face them as part of the entire world.

The greatest thing we can get out of the present crisis is to develop the habit of working together and realizing that whatever happens is going to affect us all.

I want to leave you this morning and express my gratitude to you for having stood together to gain those things, materially and spiritually, that will make life for your group richer and more productive.

I hope the day will come when all the people of this country will understand that cooperation will bring us greater happiness, and will bring us in the end a better life for the whole country and enable us to exert a greater influence on the world as a whole.

American Federationist, 1941

TO ME,
ORGANIZATION FOR LABOR
SEEMS NECESSARY

———

Golden Beach, Fla., Wednesday— . . . While I am talking about improvements which I should like to see come about, I should like to state the way I feel about labor organizations. To me, organization for labor seems necessary because it is the only protection that the worker has when he feels that he is not receiving just returns for his labor, or that he is working under conditions which he cannot accept as fair. I also feel that dealing with organized labor should benefit the employer and make for better mutual understanding.

Believing in this principle, however, does not mean I think the decisions made by groups of workmen or their leaders are always correct. I do not expect from them infallibility and superhuman

ER with Rose Schneiderman, leader of the New York Women's Trade Union League, and David Dubinsky, head of the International Ladies Garment Workers Union, at a 1938 White House performance of "Pins and Needles," an ILGWU satirical play.

At Hunter College, New York City, in February 1941 with college president George Shuster and student body president Bella Savitzky, later Bella Abzug. Admitted to the bar in 1947, Abzug served in Congress from 1973 to 1977.

qualities, any more than I do from groups of employers, or from politicians or from government officials.

There have been and are abuses in the labor movement, and I think we should fight them. The people who uncover these abuses and speak fearlessly about them, show courage and perform a civic duty. I think, however, they fail in their full duty when they do not point out that it is only the abuses they attack, not the idea and fundamental right of organization for mutual support.

A union organization fails in its duty when it loses the ideal which lies back of all unionization. This ideal, it seems to me, is an unselfish interest in those who are not as strong as others in their ability to defend themselves, and in a willingness to suffer to obtain for others the rights you may have already achieved for yourself.

I do not believe that every man and woman should be forced to join a union. I do believe the right to explain the principles lying back of labor unions should be safeguarded, that every workman should be free to listen to the plea of organization without fear of hindrance or of evil circumstances, and that he should have the right to join with his fellows in a union if he feels it will help others and, incidentally, himself.

"My Day," March 13, 1941

ON DEMOCRACY

Perhaps the greatest sacrifice of all is the necessity which democracy imposes on every individual to make himself decide in what he believes. If we believe in democracy and that it is based on the possibility of Christ-like way of life, then everybody must force himself to think through his own basic philosophy, his own willingness to live up to it and to help carry it out in everyday living.

The great majority of people accept religious dogmas handed to them by their parents without very much feeling of having a personal obligation to clarify their creed for themselves. But, if from our religion, whatever it may be, we are impelled to work out a way of life which leads to the support of a democratic form of government, then we have a problem we cannot escape: we must know what we believe in, how we intend to live, and what we are doing for our neighbors.

Our neighbors, of course, do not include only the people whom we know; they include, also, all those who live anywhere within the range of our knowledge. That means an obligation to the coalminers and the sharecroppers, the migratory workers, to the tenement-house dwellers and the farmers who cannot make a living. It opens endless vistas of work to acquire knowledge and, when we have acquired it in our own country, there is still the rest of the world to study before we know what our course of action should be.

The Moral Basis of Democracy, 1940

CHAPTER 4

This Is No Ordinary Time: World War II

ER welcomes troops to the White House in 1942.

Eleanor Roosevelt began her White House years as a pacifist; she had long urged disarmament and denounced "the war idea." The rise of fascism, however, eroded her commitment to peace. By September 1938, as war threatened Europe, ER wrote, to open the newspaper induced "a feeling of dread." The White House soon knew that US entry into war lay ahead; as ER declared in 1940, this was "no ordinary time." In September 1941, a few months before Pearl Harbor, ER accepted her first official position in government, a job (unpaid) as assistant director of the new Office of Civilian Defense (OCD), an agency tasked with national security and morale; the director was New York City mayor Fiorello La Guardia. The two clashed over priorities. To La Guardia, the OCD mission focused on military mobilization, such as recruitment of air raid wardens and firefighters. To ER, in contrast, civilian defense involved an expanding system of civil liberty and social services; she resigned in five months. By then, as of December 1941, the United States had entered World War II. With an official role out of reach, ER forged her own campaign to crush fascism abroad, build democracy at home, and seek a wartime New Deal.

ER served the administration in ways both familiar and new. Her wartime travels spanned the globe. She visited US troops in the South Pacific, in Latin America, and in England; at home, she toured defense factories, hospitals, and federal housing projects. She made efforts to save European refugees, especially children; supported the rescue work of Varian Fry; and pressed FDR to take action on refugees, without success. She bombarded administration officials and military leaders with suggestions. As always, she welcomed foreign dignitaries, fielded press conferences, and kept up her schedule of column deadlines, radio talks, and public appearances. Women's roles in the wartime labor market and the armed forces drew her attention. ER proposed women's registration for national service; her suggestions to benefit women workers in the defense industry included child-care programs, community kitchens, and shopping facilities; and she urged women workers to join unions. By 1944 an inescapable question arose: whether new women workers would retain their jobs after the war. ER answered positively but at the same time anticipated a competing postwar priority: to ensure jobs for returning veterans.

ER also pursued her signature concerns: civil rights and civil liberties. In her view, the fight against fascism called for *more* democracy; segregation and bigotry at home were wartime liabilities. Black rights assumed new intensity. ER urged equality in voting rights, economic opportunity, education, and justice (see chapter 5). The plight of Japanese Americans dismayed her. In 1942 military commanders on the West Coast evacuated Japanese Americans to relocation centers in seven western states. To ER, who had opposed the prospect of internment, the evacuation program violated civil liberties. Loyal to the administration, she curbed her opposition in public, though barely. In 1943, when, at FDR's request, ER visited the Gila River internment camp in Arizona, her draft of an article voiced disquiet. To fear fellow Americans, ER argued, injured the nation. To act on such fear challenged every citizen's "right to our basic freedoms" and undercut US capacity to "furnish a pattern for the rest of the world."

More than ever, during World War II, ER addressed "the rest of the world." Her involvement with international affairs expanded; to defend democracy demanded a global perspective. Discussing the role of the United States as victory approached, ER stressed the interdependence of nations, their need to rely on one another, and the postwar imperative to cope with "the world as a whole." After 1945, defying her own expectations, she would shape a role as liberal leader and international defender of human rights.

WHY WARS
MUST CEASE

———

If we do not find another way to settle our disputes and solve the problems of our generation, we will probably find our civilization disappearing also, but that will not happen because we are unable to fight, but because we do not find a substitute for war. There is no further use for war in business, or war between labor and capital, or war between the rich and the poor. The time for unbridled competition, or war, is at an end. We must cooperate for our mutual good.

It is high time to look realistically at this war idea. . . . There never has been a war where private profit has not been made out of the dead bodies of men. The more we see of the munitions business, of the use of chemicals, of the traffic in other goods which are needed to carry on a war, the more we realize that human cupidity is as universal as human heroism. If we are to do away with the war idea, one of the first steps will be to do away with all possibility of private profit.

It does not matter very much which side you fight on in any war. The effects are just the same whether you win or whether you lose. We suffered less here in America in the World War [World War I] than did the people of European countries, but . . . today as a country we are realizing that economic waste in one part of the world will have an impact on other parts of the world. We profited for a time commercially, but as the rest of the world suffers, so eventually do we.

Why Wars Must Cease, 1935

WE WOULD LIKE
TO STAY OUT OF WAR

———

Eastport, Maine, Friday—. . . I understand from a newspaper item which I read that my congressman [Hamilton Fish, representative for New York's 26th district] has received an overwhelming number [of replies from constituents to a questionnaire] stating that the United States should stay out of war. That seems to me fairly natural.

If I thought I had a choice in the matter, I should answer wholeheartedly that I did not wish to enter any war anywhere in the world. But it seems to me that my congressman has oversimplified the question which confronts us at the moment.

We would like to stay out of war. The people of Norway, Holland and all the other countries in Europe, even France and Russia, and Germany itself, would probably have liked to stay out of war. But that wasn't ever put before them as a choice. The war was suddenly upon them. In some cases, their government in the form of a dictator decreed it so. In others, because they woke up one morning and found soldiers of an enemy government marching down their streets.

I can think of a number of questions, Mr. Congressman, which you could have asked your constituents that would have been more enlightening to them and to you. Just as a suggestion, why not ask: "Shall the US allow any enemy nation to obtain possessions which may menace, under modern conditions of warfare, the safety of the US?" Or: "Shall we accept restrictions on our trade or the abrogation of our right to travel in neutral waters throughout the world?"

We have always been a proud and independent people, Mr. Congressman. As a woman, I pray for peace not only now, but in the future. But I think we must look a little beyond next week if we

ER sworn in as assistant director of the Office of Civilian Defense in September 1941, with New York City Mayor Fiorello La Guardia, director, in his Washington office. The first wife of a president to hold an official (though unsalaried) job in federal government, ER drew criticism and feuded with the director. La Guardia urged a militarized home front; ER envisioned a progressive social agenda. Both soon resigned.

expect to ensure an independent USA to our children. There is such a thing, too, as the moral values of a situation, and I do not think we are a nation that has given up considerations for right and wrong as we see it.

"My Day," June 28, 1941

WE KNOW WHAT WE HAVE TO FACE: ON PEARL HARBOR

Good evening, ladies and gentlemen. I am speaking to you tonight at a very serious moment in our history. The cabinet is convening and the leaders in Congress are meeting with the president. The State Department and Army and Navy officials have been with the president all afternoon. In fact, the Japanese ambassador [in reality, a Chinese diplomat] was talking to the president at the very time that Japan's airships were bombing our citizens in Hawaii and the Philippines and sinking one of our transports loaded with lumber on its way to Hawaii.

By tomorrow morning, the members of Congress will have a full report and be ready for action. For months now, the knowledge that something of this kind might happen has been hanging over our heads. And yet it seemed impossible to believe, impossible to drop the everyday things of life and feel that there was only one thing which was important: preparation to meet an enemy, no matter where he struck. That is all over now and there is no more uncertainty. We know what we have to face and we know that we are ready to face it.

I should like to say a word to the women in the country tonight. I have a boy at sea on a destroyer. For all I know he may be on his way to the Pacific. Two of my children are in coast cities on the Pacific. Many of you all over the country have boys in the services who will now be called upon to go into action. You have friends and families in what has suddenly become a danger zone. You cannot escape anxiety. You cannot escape a clutch of fear at your heart. And yet I hope that the certainty of what we have to meet will make you rise above these fears.

We must go about our daily business more determined than ever to do the ordinary things as well as we can. And when we find a way to do anything more in our communities to help others to build morale, to give a feeling of security, we must do it. Whatever is asked of us, I am sure we can accomplish it. We are the free and unconquerable people of the United States of America.

To the young people of the nation, I must speak a word tonight. You are going to have a great opportunity. There will be high moments in which your strength and your ability will be tested. I have faith in you! I feel as though I was standing upon a rock. And that rock is my faith in my fellow citizens.

Now we will go back to the program which we had arranged for tonight. . . .

Radio Broadcast of December 7, 1941

In her scheduled radio program of December 7, 1941, the day of the Japanese attack on Pearl Harbor, ER assured the nation of her confidence in "the free and unconquerable people of the United States." FDR spoke to Congress the next day of the "date that will live in infamy."

THE GREATEST TEST THIS
COUNTRY HAS EVER MET

––––––

Washington, Monday—We are back in Washington [from a trip to the West Coast]. . . . We know that there are German and Italian agents and people representing other sympathetic Axis nationalities who have been very active in this country during the past few years, just as the Communists have been. We know that now, there are Japanese as well as these other agents, who are here to be helpful to their own nation and not to ours. But these people are gradually being rounded up by the FBI and the Secret Service.

We, as citizens, if we hear anything suspicious, will report it to the proper authorities. But the great mass of our people, stemming from these various national ties, must not feel that they have suddenly ceased to be Americans.

This is, perhaps, the greatest test this country has ever met. Perhaps it is the test which is going to show whether the United States can furnish a pattern for the rest of the world for the future. Our citizens come from all the nations of the world. Some of us have said from time to time, that we were the only proof that different nationalities could live together in peace and understanding, each bringing his own contribution, different though it may be, to the final unity which is the United States.

If out of the present chaos, there is ever to come a world where free people live together peacefully, in Europe, Asia or in the Americas, we shall have to furnish the pattern. It is not enough to restore people to an old and outworn pattern. People must be given the chance to see the possibilities of a new world and to work for it.

Perhaps, on us today, lies the obligation to prove that such a vision may be a practical possibility. If we cannot meet the challenge of fairness to our citizens of every nationality, of really believing in the Bill of Rights and making it a reality for all loyal American citizens, regardless of race, creed, or color; if we cannot keep in check anti-Semitism, anti-racial feelings as well as anti-religious feelings, then we shall have removed from the world, the one real hope for the future on which all humanity must now rely.

"My Day," December 16, 1941

STARVATION AND HORROR LIVE WITH THEM DAY BY DAY

New York, Thursday—Yesterday afternoon I joined in a broadcast to the women of Poland on the third anniversary of the loss of their country's freedom. . . . I was glad to be able to say how deeply the women of this country sympathized with the sufferings of the women in Poland.

Starvation and horror live with them day by day. I wonder more and more at the Nazi psychology when I read descriptions of what happens to people in the occupied countries under Nazi control. How can the Nazis hope to create loyal and friendly citizens in a country which they have conquered by cruel treatment? Certainly, if they want goodwill, they go about it in a strange fashion.

I have before me a description of the Ravensbruck Women's Preventive Detention Camp in Poland. One of the items reads: "People are regarded as ill only when they drop. . . . Prisoners have to go barefoot in streets sprinkled with coarse gravel. In consequence prisoners get sore and festered heels, but they have to go on walking barefoot. . . . No food is provided during the examination period, so if they bring none of their own, they go hungry until they are finally assigned to barracks.

. . . One of the punishments consists of transferring to punishment barracks where degenerates are detained. . . . If a Polish woman talks to a Jewess, she is punished with 42 days in a dark cell. . . . There is one month of quarantine on entrance to the camp. . . . There are no books. . . . At the end of the month they are set to work. . . . Kitchen work starts at 4:00 a.m. and includes the carrying of heavy sacks of food from the lorries. . . . They (the women) are used in building houses for German prisoners, carrying bricks, lime and stones."

This is only the description of one camp, and I should not think it would tend to make the conquered people love their conquerors. The Nazi psychology is a strange one, because fear and suffering do not create love and loyalty.

"My Day," September 25, 1942

WHAT WE
ARE FIGHTING FOR

I think most of us will agree that we cannot and do not want to go back to the economy of chance—the inequalities of the '20s. At the end of that period we entered an era of social and economic readjustment. The change in our society came about through the needs and the will of society. Democracy, in its truest sense, began to be fulfilled. We are fighting today to continue this democratic process. Before the war came, all the peoples of the world were striving for the same thing, in one way or another. Only if we recognize the general rising of the peoples of the world can we understand the real reason why we are in the war into which we were precipitated by the Japanese attack. Only if we realize that we in the United States are part of the world struggle of ordinary people for a better way of life can we understand the basic errors in the thinking of the America First people.

A few short months ago the America First people were saying that they would defend their own country, but that there was no menace to this country in the war going on in Europe and Asia. Why would we not stay within our own borders and leave the rest of the world to fight out its difficulties and reap the benefit ourselves of being strong from the material standpoint when others were exhausted? We would make money out of other nations. We would lose nothing, we would only gain materially, and we would be safe. Why stick our necks out? This sounded like an attractive picture to many people, but unfortunately, it wasn't a true one.

One phase of the world revolt from which we could not escape concerns something which people do not like to talk about very much—namely our attitude toward other races of the world. Perhaps one of the things we cannot have any longer is what Kipling called the "White Man's Burden." The other races of the world may be becoming conscious of the fact that they wish to carry their own burdens. The job which the white race may have had to carry alone in the past may become a cooperative job.

One of the major results of this revolution may be a general acceptance of the fact that all people, regardless of race, creed, or color, rate as individual human beings. They have a right to develop, to carry the burdens which they are capable of carrying, and to enjoy such economic, spiritual, and mental growth as they can achieve.

In this connection, a problem which we Americans face now at home is the activity of the Japanese and the Germans in sowing seeds of dissension among the ten percent of our population comprising the Negro race. The Negroes have been loyal Americans ever since they were brought here as slaves. They have worked here and they have fought for our country, and our country fought a bloody war to make them citizens and to insist that we remain a united nation.

They have had equality only in name, however. Therefore, they are fertile grounds for the seeds of dissension. They want a better life, an equality of opportunity, a chance to hold jobs according to their ability, and not to be paid less because their skins are black. They want an equal break with the men and women whose skins happen to be white. . . .

They must have, too, a sense that living in a democracy, they have the same opportunity to express themselves through their government and the same opportunity as other citizens for representation. They aspire to the same things as the yellow and brown races of the world. They want recognition of themselves as human beings, equal to the other human beings of the world.

Of course, they are a part of this revolution—a very active part because they have so much to gain and so little to lose. Their aspirations, like those of other races seeking recognition and rights as human beings, are among the things we are fighting for. This revolution will, I think, establish that the human beings of the world, regardless of race or creed or color, are to be looked upon with respect and treated as equals. We may prefer our white brothers, but we will not look down on yellow, black, or brown people. . . .

Lastly, we are fighting, along with many other people, in other countries, for a method of world cooperation which will not force us to kill each other whenever we face new situations. From time to time we may have other world revolutions, but it is stupid that they should bring about wars in which our populations will increasingly be destroyed. If we destroy human beings fast enough, we destroy civilization. . . . We must set up some machinery, as police force, even an international court, but there must be a way by which nations can work out their differences peacefully. . . .

The American Magazine, 1942

THE RIGHT OF SURVIVAL
OF HUMAN BEINGS

———

Hyde Park, Thursday—I talked a little while yesterday morning with a representative from the group which is trying to formulate plans to save the Jewish people in Europe. Some think of the Jewish people as a race. Others think of them purely as a religious group. But in Europe the hardships and persecution which they have had to endure for the past few years, have tended to bring them together in a group which identifies itself with every similar group, regardless whether the tie is religious or racial.

The Jews are like all the other people of the world. There are able people among them, there are courageous people among them, there are people of extraordinary intellectual ability along many lines. There are people of extraordinary integrity and people of great beauty and great charm.

On the other hand, largely because of environment and economic condition, there are people among them who cringe, who are dishonest, who try to take advantage of their neighbors, who are aggressive and unattractive. In other words, they are a cross section of the human race, just as is every other nationality and every other religious group.

But good or bad, they have suffered in Europe as has no other group. The percentage killed among them in the past few years far exceeds the losses among any of the United Nations in the battles which have been fought throughout the war.

Many of them, for generations, considered Germany, Poland, Roumania and France their country and permanent home. This same thing might happen to any other group, if enough people ganged up against it and decided on persecution. It seems to me that it is part of common sense for the world as a whole to protest in its own interest against wholesale persecution, because none of us by ourselves would be strong enough to stand against a big enough group which decided to treat us in the same way. We may have our individual likes and dislikes, but this is a question which far transcends prejudices or inclinations.

It means the right of survival of human beings and their right to grow and improve. You and I may be hated by our neighbors, but if we know about it we try to change the things within us which brought it about. That is the way civilized people develop. Murder and annihilation are never a satisfactory answer, for the few who escape grow up more bitter against their persecutors and a day of reckoning always comes, which is what the story of Moses in the bulrushes teaches us.

I do not know what we can do to save the Jews in Europe and to find them homes, but I know that we will be the sufferers if we let great wrongs occur without exerting ourselves to correct them.

"My Day," August 13, 1943

TO UNDO A MISTAKE IS ALWAYS HARDER THAN NOT TO CREATE ONE ORIGINALLY: ON INTERNMENT CAMPS

W e are at war with Japan, and yet we have American citizens, born and brought up in this country whose parents are Japanese. This is the essential problem. . . .

In this nation of over 130 million, we have 127,500 Japanese or Japanese Americans. Those who have lived for a long time in the Midwest or in the East and who have had their records checked by the FBI, have been allowed to go on about their business, whatever

Evacuation of Japanese Americans from Los Angeles in September 1942 under US Army war emergency order.

it may be, unmolested. The recent order removing aliens from strategic areas, of course, affects those who were not citizens, just as it affects other citizens, however. . . .

I can well understand the bitterness of people who have lost loved ones at the hands of the Japanese military authorities, and we know that the totalitarian philosophy, whether it is in Nazi Germany or Fascist Italy or in Japan, is one of cruelty and brutality. It is not hard to understand why people living here in hourly anxiety for those they love have difficulty in viewing this problem objectively, but for the honor of our country the rest of us must do so. These understandable feelings are aggravated by the old-time economic fear on the West Coast and the unreasoning racial feeling which certain people, through ignorance, have always had wherever they come in contact with people who are different from themselves. This is one reason why many people believe that we should have directed our original immigration more intelligently. We needed people to develop our country, but we should never have allowed any groups to settle as groups where they created a little German or Japanese or Scandinavian island and did not melt into our general community pattern. Some of the South American countries have learned from our mistakes and are now planning to scatter their needed immigration.

To undo a mistake is always harder than not to create one originally but we seldom have the foresight. Therefore we have no choice but to try to correct our past mistakes and I hope that the recommendations of the staff of the War Relocation Authority, who have come to know individually most of the Japanese Americans at these various camps, will be accepted. Little by little as they are checked, Japanese Americans are being allowed on request to leave the camps and start independent and productive lives again. Whether you are a taxpayer in California or in Maine, it is to your advantage, if you find one or two Japanese American families settled in your neighborhood, to try to regard them as individuals and not to condemn them before they are given a fair chance to prove themselves in the community.

Japanese American children evacuated from Seattle in March 1942 show patriotism as they wave from a train.

ER guided into an internment camp, the Gila River Relocation Center, in Arizona by Dillon S. Myer, director of the War Relocation Authority, on April 23, 1943. She published an article on internment a few months later in *Collier's* magazine.

"A Japanese is always a Japanese" is an easily accepted phrase and it has taken hold quite naturally on the West Coast because of fear, but it leads nowhere and solves nothing. A Japanese American may be no more Japanese than a German American is German, or an Italian American is Italian, or of any other national background. All of these people, including the Japanese Americans, have men who are fighting today for the preservation of the democratic way of life and the ideas around which our nation was built.

We have no common race in this country, but we have an ideal to which all of us are loyal: we cannot progress if we look down upon any group of people amongst us because of race or religion. Every citizen in this country has a right to our basic freedoms, to justice and to equality of opportunity. We retain the right to lead our individual lives as we please, but we can only do so if we grant to others the freedoms we wish for ourselves.

Draft of article, 1943

"IF YOU ASK ME": WARTIME QUESTIONS

Question from a reader: Why wasn't the United States more prepared for war?

Because after the last war we made up our minds that we were never going to have another war. We taught our children at home and on the college campuses that war never settled affairs of state to anyone's satisfaction. We thoroughly convinced our young people of this, and they in turn convinced a great part of the country that we would never again have a period of war. Therefore, as we watched the rest of the world go to war, we simply insisted that staying at peace was something which we decided for ourselves and which had no relationship to the decisions of the rest of the world. Taking this attitude and feeling so secure, we quite naturally sent to Congress people who held the same opinion, and we upheld them in these opinions and would listen to no others.

Would you please tell me if any of your sons in the service is in actual danger?

I have no idea. One son is an ensign on a destroyer which spent the summer going to the Northern Atlantic. He has lately been in other waters, but still far away from this country. Another son is a navigator with a bombing squadron, and up to a few days ago was based in a California camp. He spent the time from last April to September flying over new country in the North. I have no idea where he is at present. A third son is training with his regiment in San Diego, and a fourth is a supply officer at the naval base in San Diego.

What can a young unmarried woman do to help at this time?

If she has no ties which require her to stay at home, she could take training as a nurse. She can work in any of the various Red Cross activities, or she can take up any other kind of work for which her training has fitted her, either on a paid basis or as a volunteer.

What, specifically, can we do now to help bring about a just and lasting peace at the end of this war?

Face the fact that we are going to have to make a worldwide economic adjustment. That we are going to have to be willing to accept much responsibility for the world as a whole. That it is going to mean plenty of work for all of us, inform ourselves on economic and historical questions dealing with the world as a whole. Prepare to be just to all nations and not allow ourselves to seek any personal advantage. . . .

Before you left OCD [Office of Civilian Defense] you were the object of some extremely severe criticism by many sections of the public and press. Do you think that such criticism of a public figure has a place in our accepted freedom of the press?

I think that criticism of any public figure is entirely permissible if it is done constructively, with the object of improving conditions or serving some public purpose, and if the criticism is based on real knowledge of facts and not colored by ulterior motives and a desire to create impressions which have no foundation in fact.

Do you think women, when this war is over, should sit at the peace table with equal voice in solving the problems that must be solved if we are to have a continuing peace?

I think it would be well if we could have some representation of women at the peace table. They certainly will not have an equal voice because they do not have an equal voice in government or in the conduct of the war, and they cannot until they carry equal responsibility in everything.

What do you think of women actually fighting, as they are reported to be doing in Russia?

When the time comes that women are needed in the fighting line, they will be found in the fighting line. They are evidently needed in Russia and they are doing what is necessary for them to do. In the pioneer days of our own country, many a woman fought side by side with her husband, and if the need comes again, women will meet that need.

Negro soldiers guard the railroad bridge in our Maine town. Recently I invited one of the soldiers to dine with us and our whole family (white) is being criticized. Should I have done this?

I see no reason why you should not have invited a Negro soldier to dine with you if you wished to do so. I imagine there are some white people whom you would not like to have in your home, and there might be Negroes whom you would not like to have there either. Just because a person is black, there is no reason why you should not be kind to him if he is a nice person.

After all, we have got to face the fact that we have allies today in India and in China and that our attitude toward the other races of the world must become one of cooperation rather than one of domination, if we are going to lay a basis for a better world in the future. I believe, of course, that the emphasis in our relationship with the Negroes should be to see that they get their full rights as citizens, but the personal equation is one which every person has to decide for himself. We are free to act as our own conscience and our own inclination dictate. We live in a free country where we are not forced to do anything about our personal relationships which we do not feel like doing.

How do you think our boys who have gone to war and risked their lives should treat conscientious objectors after the war?

I should think that the boys who go through the war, and who believe in what they are doing, would have a respect for a conscientious objector who had an equally strong belief that he should not kill other people.

We have put these conscientious objectors to work in this war. They are clamoring for more dangerous work. Some of them are already doing work which requires great courage, but not the taking of another man's life. It would certainly seem a curious thing to me if a boy were not able to understand, having had deep convictions himself, that other people have a right to equally deep convictions and that they should be respected.

Was there ever a member of the Roosevelt family killed on the field of battle in America or any other country?

President Theodore Roosevelt's son, Quentin Roosevelt, was killed during the last World War, being shot down in the air in France. One other member of the Roosevelt family died on a transport on the way home in the last war.

In every war many of the Roosevelt men have served and been wounded, but I do not know enough of the family history to know how many were actually killed previous to the last war. Innumerable people in the collateral branches on all sides of the Roosevelt family have been killed in wars both abroad and in this country.

With what the Germans, Japanese and Italians are trying to do to the democracies of the world—especially our United States—do you really mean you would permit your children to number among their friends any Germans, Japanese, or Italians?

I certainly do. How are we going to live in peace in the world of the future if we cannot be friends with the Germans, Japanese, or Italians? I have friends of all those nationalities, some of them have fled their own countries because they were in disagreement with the policies of the governments of those countries. I imagine there are many people still in those countries who are suffering because they do not agree with what their governments are doing. If we take the attitude that we can never be friends with people of those nationalities, our chance for a peaceful world in the future is slim indeed.

During the First World War, Indians were exempted through their treaty rights. It looks like President Roosevelt doesn't respect our Indian treaty rights because they are being drafted; and yet I thought that is why the United States is in this war—because they are seeking justice. Do you think we should be forced to become citizens against our rights?

During the last World War, Indians were not citizens. According to the Citizenship Act of 1924 and the Nationality Act of 1940, Indians were declared citizens whether or not they were on reservations. As all male citizens of the United States between certain ages are liable for training and service, the Indians could be drafted just the same as any other citizens.

How will our armed forces act toward enemy civilians—like Christians, or like the Germans and the Japs?

I hope that our men will always act as Christians, but war is a grim business, and when it is a question of killing or being killed, instinct seems to make us prefer to remain alive when we can.

Don't you think this country should stop talking about "helping" England and recognize that England kept Germany's weight off us for two years?

Yes I do. We are not helping England. We never have. We realized that we were the next in line for attack if Great Britain fell, and so we helped ourselves.

Is it true that soldiers from the Midwestern states, which are normally Republican, are sent into combat zones before soldiers from Democratic states?

I have never heard anything so idiotic as your question. No soldier is asked what his politics are, and they would be so mixed in the units it would be utterly impossible to separate them. Anyone who believes such a statement as this should go at once to a psychiatrist.

Why are defense workers permitted to strike, while a soldier who deserted his job would be shot?

Because one of the things which we have guarded jealously all through the years of freedom is the right of the individual to strike. A soldier has automatically accepted a different status from that of a civilian.

However, I think during a war it would be better if, voluntarily, workers would give up any and all strikes, but if they are going to do that, then the citizens of the country as a whole must see to it that the workers' rights are safeguarded. By that I mean that the citizens must make it their business to know that the conditions against which a worker is giving up the right to strike are properly investigated and, if found wrong, are corrected. You cannot ask one section of the population to give up the only weapon they have against injustice, unless the people as a whole make it their

Major Lyudmila Pavlichenko, Russian sniper, hero of the Soviet Union, and participant in an International Youth Assembly in Washington, DC, greeted by ER and Supreme Court Justice Robert Jackson in September 1942.

Accompanied by Clementine Churchill, wife of the British prime minister, and Oveta Culp Hobby, director of the Women's Army Auxiliary Corps (WAAC), ER visits an army camp in England in October 1942.

business to see that the rights of that section of the population are really preserved through government channels.

Ladies' Home Journal, 1942–1943

WE KNOW IN THE END
WE WILL WIN: ON D-DAY

It is a great privilege to have this opportunity to speak to the women of this country at this time when they are undergoing such a great strain. I am speaking particularly, of course, to those who have men they love—husbands, sons, brothers, sisters of very

Traveling under the secret service code name "Rover," ER toured areas where troops were stationed in the South Pacific in the summer of 1943, a dangerous voyage. Here, in Bora Bora on August 20, 1943. When visiting troops, ER typically wore a Red Cross uniform, which, beyond its quasi-military flair, cut down on wardrobe and baggage.

dear friends—taking an active part in the European invasion or stationed anywhere in the areas where there may be intensified activity during the next few weeks.

We know in the end we will win, but we do not know what the cost will be. The only thing I can say to you is that every woman, no matter what her church affiliation may be, will be praying daily that the victory will be speedy and that this time the sacrifices, whatever they are, will bring results which will justify in the eyes of those who fight whatever they have gone through.

All that science can do to protect our men will be done and to the care of the wounded will be added all that human devotion will do. We may be sure that all that can be done to alleviate suffering and save human lives will be done. All that we at home can do, however, is to pray and to prepare ourselves to fulfill our obligations to those who fight. They will feel we back them up to attain their objectives if we use our citizenship to attain the ends for which they sacrifice. It is not enough to win the fight—we must win that for which we fight.

In this case it is the triumph of all people who believe that the people of the world are worthy of freedom and that no race has the right to seek domination over any other, so that we may ultimately build a permanent peace.

May we have the courage to do our part for the sake of future generations and may God bring consolation to those who suffer both at home and abroad.

Radio Broadcast of June 6, 1944

Part of the tentative schedule for ER's South Pacific trip in August to September 1943, issued on July 25, 1943.

ER poses in front of a DC-3 on a visit to New Caledonia in 1943.
A French colony in the South Pacific, New Caledonia was the site of wartime
tension between the United States and the Free French. ER made an
unscheduled and incognito stop there to attend a dinner in her honor with
Admiral William Halsey on September 15, 1943. On the left, Major General
Ernest Harmon; on the right Admiral Halsey.

TO WOMEN IN UNIONS

I am glad of this opportunity to congratulate the women of the country for the way in which they have come forward and taken their places in industry, often undertaking jobs which seemed beyond their strength or past skills to perform.

Some of these women will stay on as highly skilled workers, some of them will go back to running their homes and families, all of them will have learned not only something about their jobs, but they will have learned about people, they will be able to work in an organized group, and they will understand the value of the union and the need for leadership in the union, better than ever before.

I hope that they will take places of responsibility in the unions, and I hope that they will realize that the union is not just important for their own interests but that it has an obligation to see that the workers' interest is integrated with the interest of the community. . . .

Above everything else, the men must feel on their return that we have preserved for them a country which is worth the sacrifice which they have made in fighting the war. In addition to that, we must help them when they come back in the even more arduous task of rebuilding the world and of meeting the problems, the solutions of which are vitally important to future generations.

Draft of article, 1944

ER entertained visiting dignitaries from around the world, especially allies of the United States. Here with Clementine Churchill at a radio broadcast in September 1944.

ER with Madame Chiang Kai-shek on the
White House lawn in February 1943.

WOMEN IN THE
POSTWAR WORLD

Just as after the last war, a far greater number of women than ever before found that they could make a place for themselves in the business and professional world, so it seems that in this war there will be a great many women who have made places for themselves in new occupations, occupations very largely that have to do with machinery, and which in the past have been held almost exclusively by men.

It is more than probable that many of the women who are now doing extremely good jobs will nevertheless want to return to their homes at the end of the war. They are doing jobs for patriotic reasons or because they cannot bear to sit with folded hands while their husbands and sons are in danger. In normal times they were fully occupied in their homes and are willing and anxious to return to them.

Many women, however, will have found places in the business world, in the professions, in factories, and in the fields. The breadwinner in many a family may have been taken from them to some faraway battlefields or they may really have found that this added interest in life is something they do not wish to give up.

There is little doubt but that a good proportion of the women now at work will want to continue working when the war is over. That being the case, I think one of the most important things for us to do is to face the fact that no economy of scarcity will reemploy the men in the armed services and keep such women as wish to be at work, at work. I think there is only one way to open up vistas where full employment can be enjoyed throughout the world and that is the vision of world development and the opening up of wider markets for world goods through the increased well-being of the peoples who have in the past existed on a very primitive scale. It is necessary, I think, for men and women alike to study this problem of postwar employment, to convince themselves of what are the steps to be taken, and then to study methods of education by which these steps can actually be made a reality in the near future.

Women have more of a stake in these decisions than ever before, not only because of the interests which have come into their lives, but because it is probable that more women will be the breadwinners and have dependents to support and educate. . . .

[I]t is well to remember that women's interests are not separated from those of the men. What is going to give women a greater responsibility in life will also give men a similar one, and therefore on these problems they must work together if really beneficial results are to be obtained.

Journal of Educational Sociology, 1944

HOW ABOUT WOMEN
AT THE PEACE CONFERENCE?

———

How about women at the peace conference?" is one of the questions frequently asked me these days, and I long to answer with a question: "Where is the peace conference?"

No peace conference seems to be confronting us at the moment. Of course, when and if there is one, I would hope to see women in all the delegations, and I am quite sure they will be represented, not only in the group from the United States, but from many other countries in the world.

The reason I am confident of this is that women have been taking part with the men in fighting this war, and therefore, their interests in any decisions for the future, cannot be ignored.

Men give up their ancient prerogatives of deciding alone without feminine assistance, the great questions of what shall happen in the realm of politics and government rather reluctantly. Nevertheless, gradually they are giving them up. Through the years men have made wars, perhaps it is only fair to suggest that more feminine influence might mean that women would make a peace. Women are, because of their natural functions, the great conservers of the world. They conserve life and men spend it.

But I am not concerned yet about what women will eventually join the gentlemen at a peace conference, or at a gathering of the United Nations to discuss such things as haven't been settled during the war. I am sure there is no nation which will not have its women representatives. . . .

Draft of article, 1944

LETTER TO ROSE SCHNEIDERMAN: ON A FOURTH TERM

August 5, 1944

Dear Rose:

I was so happy to see you the other night and glad to find your letter at Hyde Park when I got home.

Since the president has accepted the nomination, I hope, naturally that he will win and I agree that the next four years will be difficult for the country. I, however, have mixed feelings and personally would much prefer to leave the limelight, but I realize my wishes aren't important.

I shall be delighted, of course, to act as honorary chairman for your benefit and will buy six seats in the second or third row and try to go.

The children have been no hardship and I have had real fun with them.

Affectionately,
[ER]

ER Papers, 1944

Loyal to the cause of labor organization throughout the war, ER addresses the seventh constitutional convention of the Congress of Industrial Organizations (CIO) in 1944.

EXCERPT FROM THE FINAL
WHITE HOUSE PRESS CONFERENCE,
APRIL 12, 1945

———

[The press conference took place in Washington a few hours before FDR's death in Warm Springs, Georgia]

TOPIC: ENGAGEMENTS

Mrs. Roosevelt: "This p.m. I go to the Thrift Shop. Tonight to the American Friends Service Committee dining at the Davis house, the proceeds to go to the Quakers. There will be a report . . . on subsistence homesteads around Birmingham. Tomorrow to the Foreign Policy Association 10:30 to 12. Dean Virginia Gildersleeve [of Barnard College] will come to lunch tomorrow. The Jefferson Day dinner is that evening. A few New York Democrats will be in to tea.

On Monday there will be no press conference—I am going to Forest Glen [rehabilitation post for World War II veterans]. On Tuesday I go to address Bennett College near Hyde Park. Then to Women's Bar Association at Garden City [New York], Wednesday p.m. On Thursday I meet four British and four American trade union women, and at 3:30 to the Crippled Children's Clinic . . . The next conference will be Friday the 20th at 10."

[Note by Furman] She was asked about the United States attitude toward V-E [Victory in Europe] Day.

Mrs. Roosevelt: "It is not up to me to say or know. The question belongs to the State Department or War Department. I hope much on V-E Day we will all have thanksgiving enough to see what to do. American public opinion of some kind will form on Germany and its future. I don't see how we can tell till we know more about what we find in Germany. We can't know what exists outside Nazi Germany and the Nazi government. This evidence should be fully in the hands of State and War Department officials. Although we will be withholding judgment until we have more information we can consider authentic, we are not the only ones to decide what our attitude on Germany should be. We must accustom ourselves to remember we are one of three with the responsibility of waging war.

"And the countries once occupied, once there is a United Nations Organization, have a right to express their opinion.

"We have to get over a habit of ours for many years, to consider only what we will do. What will we do means all the people who have an interest in this question. We will have the United Nations Organization so all the world's opinion will have a clearing place.

"It is very evident that the nations who fought the war will have the first expression of opinion.

"Every nation, ours with others, will have a free expression of the opinion of the people and what we think when we have enough real knowledge to base our opinion on. Until then the State and War Departments will be finding out more."

Question: How soon will the State and War Departments inform us as to what they find in Germany?

Mrs. Roosevelt: "As soon as they can arrive at the truth."

Press Conference of April 12, 1945

FDR and ER with their grandchildren in FDR's White House study
on Inauguration Day, January 20, 1945.

ON FDR'S DEATH

Washington, Monday—When you have lived for a long time in close contact with the loss and grief which today pervades the world, any personal sorrow seems to be lost in the general sadness of humanity. For a long time, all hearts have been heavy for every serviceman sacrificed in the war. There is only one way in which those of us who live can repay the dead who have given their utmost for the cause of liberty and justice. They died in the hope that, through their sacrifice, an enduring peace would be built and a more just world would emerge for humanity.

While my husband was in Albany and for some years after coming to Washington, his chief interest was in seeing that the average human being was given a fairer chance for "life, liberty and the pursuit of happiness." That was what made him always interested in the problems of minority groups and of any group which was at a disadvantage.

As the war clouds gathered and the inevitable involvement of this country became more evident, his objective was always to deal with the problems of the war, political and military, so that eventually an organization might be built to prevent future wars.

· · · · ·

Any man in public life is bound, in the course of years, to create certain enemies. But when he is gone, his main objectives stand out clearly and one may hope that a spirit of unity may arouse the people and their leaders to a complete understanding of his objectives and a determination to achieve those objectives themselves.

Abraham Lincoln was taken from us before he had achieved unity within the nation, and his people failed him. This divided us as a nation for many years.

Woodrow Wilson was also stricken and, in that instance, the peoples of the world failed to carry out his vision.

Perhaps, in his wisdom, the Almighty is trying to show us that a leader may chart the way, may point out the road to lasting peace, but that many leaders and many peoples must do the building. It cannot be the work of one man, nor can the responsibility be laid upon his shoulders, and so, when the time comes for peoples to assume the burden more fully, he is given rest.

God grant that we may have the wisdom and courage to build a peaceful world with justice and opportunity for all peoples the world over.

"My Day," April 17, 1945

ARE WE LEARNING NOTHING?

New York, Sunday. . . . If we do not see that equal opportunity, equal justice, and equal treatment are meted out to every citizen, the very basis on which this country can hope to survive with liberty and justice for all will be wiped away. . . .

Are we learning nothing from the horrible pictures of the concentration camps which have been appearing in our papers day after day? Are our memories so short that we do not recall how in Germany, this unparalleled barbarism started by discrimination directed against the Jewish people? It has ended in brutality and cruelty meted out to all people, even to our own boys who have been taken prisoner. This bestiality could not exist if the Germans had not allowed themselves to believe in a master race which could do anything it wished to all other human beings not of their particular racial strain.

There is nothing, given certain kinds of leadership, which could prevent our falling prey to this same kind of insanity, much as it shocks us now. The idea of superiority of one race over another must not continue within our own country, nor must it grow up in our dealings with the rest of the world who, because of different opportunities and environment, have not progressed as far as other people in what we call civilization. That does not mean, however, that they will forever be inferior in our type of civilization. Given the same kind of opportunities, they may do better than we have done. . . .

We cannot complain that the Germans starved and maltreated our boys if we at home do not take every step—both through our government and as individuals—to see not only that fairness exists in all employment practices, but that throughout our nation all people are equal citizens. Where the theory of a master race is accepted, there is danger to all progress in civilization.

"My Day," April 30, 1945

RADIO BROADCAST
OF MAY 8, 1945: ON V-E DAY

———

ER: I am very happy to have this opportunity to speak to the people of this country on V-E Day. It is a day on which we can be happy that the European war is at an end.

I know my husband would want me to say to you, the soldiers of this country on all the fields of battle, and to the workers at home and the civilians who, side by side, have won through to this day with him, that he is grateful to each and every one of you. I think, also, that he would want to say that we must go on with every power we have until the war is fully won. And that after that, we must give all the backing we can to our own president, to the heads of allied nations, and win through to a permanent peace. That was the main objective for which my husband fought. That is the goal which we must never lose sight of.

It will be difficult. And there will be times when it will be hard to understand other nations and their leaders. But the goal is there. And in one way or another, our leaders and our people must fight through to a permanent peace. That is the only way that we, as a nation, can feel compensation for the sacrifice of thousands of young lives in our own country and in other countries.

Today, I think I want to say again, thank you, from my husband and from myself, as a private citizen. Because it is a wonderful thing to be a private citizen, standing side by side with all other citizens of this great country, knowing that our leaders are worthy and that, we, as citizens, will be worthy of them.

Radio Broadcast of May 8, 1945

ON THE A-BOMB:
THIS DISCOVERY MUST
SPELL THE END OF WAR

New York, Tuesday—The news which came to us yesterday afternoon of the first use of the atomic bomb in the war with Japan may have surprised a good many people, but scientists—both British and American—have been working feverishly to make this discovery before our enemies, the Germans, could make it and thereby possibly win the war.

This discovery may be of great commercial value someday. If wisely used, it may serve the purposes of peace. But for the moment we are chiefly concerned with its destructive power. That power can be multiplied indefinitely, so that not only whole cities but large areas may be destroyed at one fell swoop. If you face this possibility, and realize that, having once discovered a principle, it is very easy to take further steps to magnify its power, you soon face the unpleasant fact that in the next war whole peoples may be destroyed.

· · · · ·

The only safe counterweapon to this new power is the firm decision of mankind that it shall be used for constructive purposes only. This discovery must spell the end of war. We have been paying an ever-increasing price for indulging ourselves in this uncivilized way of settling our difficulties. We can no longer indulge in the slaughter of our young men. The price will be too high and will be paid not just by young men, but by whole populations.

In the past we have given lip service to the desire for peace. Now we must meet the test of really working to achieve something basically new in the world. . . .

This new discovery cannot be ignored. We have only two alternative choices: destruction and death—or construction and life! If we desire our civilization to survive, then we must accept the responsibility of constructive work and of the wise use of a knowledge greater than any ever achieved by man before.

"My Day," August 8, 1945

RADIO BROADCAST OF AUGUST 14, 1945: ON V-J DAY

The day for which all the people of the world have prayed is here at last. There is great thankfulness in our hearts. Peace has not come, however, as the result of the kind of power which we have known in the past, but as the result of a new discovery which, as yet, is not fully understood, nor even developed.

There is a certain awe and fear coupled with our rejoicing today. Because we know that there are new forces in the world, partly understood but not, as yet, completely developed and controlled. This new force is a tremendous challenge to the wisdom of men. . . . We should not think only of its destructive power, for this new discovery may hold within it the germs of the greatest good that man has ever known. But that good can only be achieved through man's wisdom in developing and controlling it. . . .

Before closing, I want to say just one word about my husband. I know that many people have thought of him constantly ever since the war came to an end. I am deeply grateful. He always felt that we could and would fight this war to ultimate victory. And he had complete assurance that with the victory, once won, the people of the United States would turn their full strength and power into making peace a reality and a benefit to mankind.

Radio Broadcast of August 14, 1945

CHAPTER 5

Civil Rights and Democracy

Eleanor Roosevelt presents a civil rights award, the Spingarn Medal, to Marian Anderson on April 9, 1939, at an NAACP Conference in Richmond, Virginia.

In early 1939 Eleanor Roosevelt's enmity to race prejudice caused a storm over black singer Marian Anderson. The Daughters of the American Revolution (DAR), a patriotic organization to which ER belonged, had refused to permit the acclaimed contralto to perform at Constitution Hall, a venue that the DAR owned. ER in response withdrew from the DAR and then referred obliquely to the resignation in her "My Day" column; to remain a member of an organization, ER wrote, implied approval of that organization's action. Even without explicit reference to either the DAR or to Marian Anderson, or to race discrimination, the column channeled outrage toward the DAR and drew widespread press commentary. ER next arranged an alternative recital for Marian Anderson that took place on Easter Sunday, 1939, at the Lincoln Memorial before an audience of 75,000.

A masterful public relations triumph, the Marian Anderson episode came to represent Eleanor Roosevelt's commitment to civil rights, an allegiance that was unexpected, influential, endur-ing, and ever deepening. It began early in the New Deal when ER urged acceptance of black residents at Arthurdale and when Walter White, executive secretary of the NAACP, sought her sup-port, with a barrage of letters, telegrams, and pleas. Serving as an intermediary between the administration and the civil rights community, as well as a buffer, ER endorsed the anti-lynching campaign that White promoted, though a proposed anti-lynch-ing law remained beyond reach. She grasped every chance that arose to address African American groups, to develop contacts among black leaders, to speak out for black tenant farmers and sharecroppers, and to write for the black press. As war arose in Europe, ER's engagement with civil rights increased. Intolerance at home, she argued, imperiled the fight for democracy abroad. In the World War II era, ER defended equal rights: equal economic opportunity and education, equal access to the ballot box, and "justice without prejudice." Facing continual criticism, she used her columns to dispel racist rumors (such as the existence of anti-white "Eleanor Clubs"), to confront hostile insinuations (that she had "black blood"), and to oppose bias of race, religion, or ethnicity; anti-Semitism became another target.

After FDR's death, now free from the constraint of serving ad-ministration policy, ER sought a yet stronger level of engagement with civil rights. In 1945 she joined the NAACP and the Congress of Racial Equality (CORE). She served on the NAACP board of directors and worked with attorney Thurgood Marshall and other black leaders on the NAACP legal affairs committee. She urged President Harry Truman to support fair housing laws, to address the NAACP in 1947, and to integrate the armed forces in 1948. Throughout the postwar decades, from the NAACP push for school integration that culminated in the *Brown v. Board of Education* decision of 1954 through the campaigns for civil rights acts in the 1950s to the start of sit-ins in 1961, ER moved forward with the civil rights movement as its goals expanded and its leverage rose.

Eleanor Roosevelt's commitment to civil rights was always a work in progress; over time she veered away from meliorism toward an endorsement of protest. At the start, her statements urged caution, patience, accommodation, and gradual improvement of race relations. But her very concern for civil rights, without precedent among recent White House occupants, was itself a defiant and extraordinary act. In the 1940s, she assured critics that the civil rights she demanded did not include "social equality"; other civil rights advocates of the day made the same point. In the postwar era, her focus sharpened; civil rights became the crux of her liberal stance. Ignoring detractors, ER seized all opportunities, in her columns and in her public affiliations, to defy critics, press for racial justice, and denounce intolerance. Prejudice, in race or religion, as she had argued in 1939, threatened not just specific victims but everyone: "the real wrong is done to democracy and our nation as a whole."

WE GO AHEAD TOGETHER
OR WE GO DOWN TOGETHER

———

I noticed in the papers this morning the figures given of the cost in certain states per capita for the education of a colored child and of a white child, and I could not help but think as I read that item how stupid we are in some ways, for of course in any democracy the one important thing is to see as far as possible that *every* child receives at least the best education that that child is able to assimilate. . . .

I feel that while we have been fortunate in this country in having many fine men and women interested in the education of the Negro race, we have also been slow, many of us who are of the white race, in realizing how important not only to your race it is, but how important to our race that you should have the best educational advantages. The menace today to a democracy is unthinking action, action which comes from people who are illiterate, who are unable to understand what is happening in the world at large, what is happening in their own country, and who therefore act without really having any knowledge of the meaning of their actions, and that is the thing that we, whatever our race is, should be guarding against today.

There are many people in this country, many white people, who have not had the opportunity for education that they should have, and there are also many Negro people who have not had the opportunity that they should have. Both these conditions should be remedied and the same opportunities should be accorded to every child regardless of race or creed.

Of course I feel this should be done because of our intelligent interest in children, but if we have to put it on a self-interest basis, then it should be done for the preservation of the best that is in the ideals of this country, because you can have no part of your population beaten down and expect the rest of the country not to feel the effects from the big groups that are underprivileged. That is so of our groups of white people and it is so of our underprivileged groups of Negro people. It lowers the standard of living. Wherever the standard of education is low, the standard of living is low, and it is for our own preservation . . . that we are interested today in seeing that education is really universal throughout the country. . . .

I think the day of selfishness is over; the day of really working together has come, and we must learn to work together, all of us, regardless of race or creed or color; we must wipe out, wherever we find it, any feeling that grows up, of intolerance, or belief that one group can go ahead alone. We go ahead together or we go down together, and so may you profit now and for the future by all that you do at this conference.

Speech, 1934

CORRESPONDENCE WITH WALTER WHITE ON THE ANTI-LYNCHING CAMPAIGN

––––––

November 23, 1934

My Dear Mr. White:

I talked with the president yesterday about your letter and he said that he hoped very much to get the Costigan-Wagner bill passed in the coming session. The Marianna lynching [a lynching on October 27, 1934 near Tallahassee, Florida] was a horrible thing.

I wish very much the Department of Justice might come to a different point of view and I think possibly they will.

Very sincerely yours
[Eleanor Roosevelt]

Walter White, executive secretary of the NAACP from 1931 to 1955, campaigned for civil rights with relentless drive. In the 1930s, when White sought administration support for a proposed anti-lynching bill, without success, he corresponded continually with Eleanor Roosevelt; frequently, he urged ER to intercede with the president. Here, White in the late 1930s in front of a painting by Aaron Kameny portraying a victim of lynching. The photo appeared on the cover of *TIME* magazine on January 24, 1938.

January 10, 1935

My Dear Mrs. Roosevelt:

There have come to us a disturbing number [of] expressions of disappointment that the President did not include lynching in his opening address to the Congress, though a great many people had asked him to do so. To all of those who have spoken to me about it, I have urged patience, saying that perhaps the President will send a special message to Congress on lynching or include specific recommendation for passage of the Costigan-Wagner [anti-lynching] bill in his address to the Congress on crime. I wonder if you could advise me if my optimism is well founded. It would help during this very trying period to show that our efforts have not been in vain. . . .

Ever Sincerely,
Walter White
Secretary [NAACP]

[circa March 1935]

My dear Mr. White:

The more I think about going to the [anti-lynching] exhibition, the more troubled I am, so this morning I went in to talk to my husband about it and asked him what they really planned to do about the [anti-lynching] bill because I was afraid that some bright newspaper reporter might write a story which would offend some of the southern members and thereby make it even more difficult to do anything about the bill.

My husband said it was quite all right for me to go, but if some reporter took the occasion to describe some horrible picture, it would cause more Southern opposition. They plan to bring the bill out quietly as soon as possible although two Southern senators have said they would filibuster for two weeks. He thinks, however, they can get it through.

I do not want to do anything which will harm the ultimate objective, even though we might think for the moment that it was helpful and even though you may feel that it would make some of your race feel more kindly toward us. Therefore, I really think that it would be safer if I came without any publicity or did not come at all. Will you telephone me at my New York house at seven o'clock on Friday night? . . . You can then tell me how you feel.

Very sincerely yours,
[Eleanor Roosevelt]

March 16, 1936

My dear Mr. White:

I have spoken to the president about your letter of February 28 concerning the Costigan-Wagner bill. He says, in view of the fact that he is only asking three things of Congress, he does not see how he could specify this particular bill. Of course he is quite willing that it should be pushed by Congress itself, and I feel quite sure he will give it any help he can.

Very sincerely yours,
[Eleanor Roosevelt]

March 19, 1936

My dear Mr. White:

Before I received your letter today I had been in to the president, talking to him about your letter enclosing that of the Attorney General [White had urged Attorney General Homer S. Cummings to punish those responsible for lynching]. I told him that it seemed rather terrible that one could get nothing done and that I did not blame you in the least for feeling that there was no interest in this very serious question. I asked him if there were any possibility of getting even one step taken, and he said the difficulty is that it is unconstitutional apparently for the federal government to step in in the lynching situation. The government has only been allowed to do anything about kidnapping because of its interstate aspect, and even that has not as yet been appealed so they are not sure that it will be declared constitutional.

The president feels that lynching is a question of education in the states, rallying good citizens, and creating public opinion so that the localities themselves will wipe it out. However, if it were done by a Northerner, it will have an antagonistic effect. I will talk to him again about the Van Nuys resolution and will try to talk also to Senator Byrnes and get his point of view. I am deeply troubled about the whole situation as it seems to be a terrible thing to stand by and let it continue and feel that one cannot speak out as to his feeling. I think your next step would be to talk to the more prominent members of the Senate.

Very sincerely yours,
[Eleanor Roosevelt]

ER Papers, 1934–1936

YOU CANNOT EXPECT PEOPLE TO CHANGE OVER NIGHT

We know that many grave injustices are done throughout our land to people who are citizens and who have no equal rights under the law . . . but who are handicapped because of their race. I feel strongly that in order to wipe out these inequalities and injustices, we must all of us work together; but naturally those who suffer the injustices are most sensitive to them. . . .

I would like to urge first of all that you concentrate your effort on obtaining better opportunities for education for the Negro people throughout the country. . . .

I believe, of course, that for our own good in this country, the Negro race in this country must improve its standard of living, and become both economically and ethically of higher caliber. The fact that the colored people, not only in the South, but in the North as well, have been economically at a low level, has meant that they have also been physically and intellectually at a low level. Economic conditions are responsible for poor health in children. And the fact that tuberculosis and pneumonia and many other diseases have taken a heavier toll among our colored groups, can be attributed primarily to economic conditions. It is undoubtedly true that with an improvement in economic condition it will still be necessary not only to improve our educational conditions for children, but to pay special attention to adult education along the line of better living. For you cannot expect people to change overnight, when they have had poor conditions, and adjust themselves to all that we expect of people living as they *should* live today throughout our country.

This holds true of *all* underprivileged people in our country, and in other countries. . . .

I think I am right when I say that it is not just enough to give people who have suffered a better house and better wages. You must give them education and understanding and training before you can expect them to take up their full responsibility. . . .

I have had a number of people tell me that they felt the government in its new efforts and programs was not always fair to the Negro race. And I want to say that though this undoubtedly is so quite often, it is not the intention of those at the top, and as far as possible I hope that we may work together to eliminate any real injustice. . . .

We have long held in this country that ability should be the criterion on which all people are judged. It seems to me that we must come to recognize this criterion in dealing with all human beings. . . .

There is no reason why all of the races in this country should not live together, each of them giving from their particular gift something to the other, and contributing an example to the world of "peace on earth, goodwill toward men."

Opportunity, 1936

ER TO PAULI MURRAY ON HER REJECTION FROM THE UNIVERSITY OF NORTH CAROLINA

Seeking integration in higher education, civil rights activist Pauli Murray, a graduate of Hunter College in New York City, applied to graduate school at the University of North Carolina in 1938. When rejected because of her race, she expressed her grievance in a letter to FDR and started a correspondence with ER, with whom a lifelong friendship ensued. Murray went on to study law at Howard and Berkeley, to challenge inequality of race and sex, and to take a role in the start of the women's movement in the early 1960s.

December 19, 1938

My Dear Miss Murray:

I have read the copy of the letter [to FDR] you sent me and I understand perfectly, but great changes come slowly. I think they are coming, however, and sometimes it is better to fight hard with conciliatory

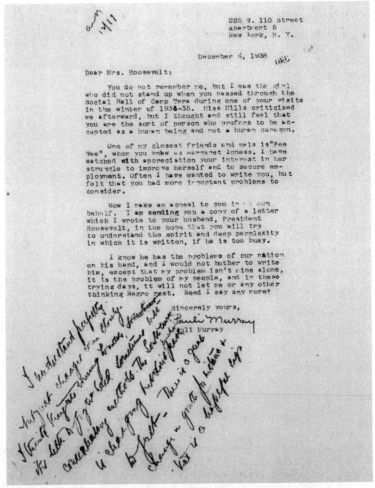

Pauli Murray's letter of December 19, 1938, to Eleanor Roosevelt,
with ER's notes for a response scrawled on the letter.

methods. The South is changing, but don't push too fast. There is a great change in youth, for instance, and that is a hopeful sign.

Very sincerely yours,
[Eleanor Roosevelt]

ER Papers, 1938

RESIGNING FROM THE DAR: A QUESTION WHICH I HAVE HAD TO DEBATE WITH MYSELF

———

Washington, Sunday— . . . I have been debating in my mind for some time a question which I have had to debate with myself once or twice before in my life. Usually I have decided differently from the way in which I am deciding now. The question is, if you belong to an organization and disapprove of an action which is typical of a policy, should you resign or is it better to work for a changed point of view within the organization? In the past, when I was able to work actively in any organization to which I belonged, I have usually stayed in until I had at least made a fight and had been defeated.

Even then, I have, as a rule, accepted my defeat and decided I was wrong or, perhaps, a little too far ahead of the thinking of the majority at that time. I have often found that the thing in which I was interested was done some years later. But, in this case, I belong to an organization in which I can do no active work. They have taken an action which has been widely talked of in the press. To remain as a member implies approval of that action, and therefore I am resigning.

"My Day," February 27, 1939

PRESS CONFERENCE AFTER ER'S RESIGNATION FROM THE DAR

———

TOPIC: RESIGNING FROM DAR
TO PROTEST RACIAL DISCRIMINATION
AGAINST MARIAN ANDERSON

Question: "I have been reading your column ["My Day"] today. Have you resigned from the DAR?"

Mrs. Roosevelt: "Mrs. [Henry M.] Robert [president general of the DAR] better answer that question. I've always had a belief that the organization had a right to give out a resignation."

Question: "Down at the DAR they say that Mrs. Robert is away and no one is opening her mail."

Mrs. Roosevelt: "I can say no more than what I said in my column. One often has to discuss in one's own mind whether one wishes to remain in the organization and make the fight or leave—always before I've remained in and made the fight. But as long as I am in the position I am now and doing little active work, if I decided a certain action was one of which I did not approve I would be constrained to resign."

Question: "Might that action be the refusal to let Marian Anderson sing in Constitution Hall [Washington concert hall owned by DAR]?"

Mrs. Roosevelt: "I'll leave that in limbo, as to what organization I resigned from."

[Note by AP reporter Bess Furman] Followed a long series of questions including the inevitable "Do you deny that you resigned from the DAR?" followed by the inevitable "I neither affirm nor deny". . .]

Question: "Who are you bringing to our [Women's National] Press Club Party?"

Mrs. Roosevelt: "My mother-in-law. I was rather amazed to learn that she is coming down."

Press Conference of February 27, 1939

February 26, 1939.

Henry M.

My dear Mrs. Robert: Jr.

I am afraid that I have never been a very useful member of the Daughters of the American Revolution, so I know it will make very little difference to you whether I resign, or whether I continue to be a member of your organization.

However, I am in complete disagreement with the attitude taken in refusing Constitution Hall to a great artist. You have set an example which seems to me unfortunate, and I feel obliged to send in to you my resignation. You had an opportunity to lead in an enlightened way and it seems to me that your organization has failed.

I realize that many people will not agree with me, but feeling as I do this seems to me the only proper procedure to follow.

Very sincerely yours,

Eleanor Roosevelt's letter of resignation from the Daughters of the American Revolution, sent to DAR president general Mrs. Henry M. (Sarah) Robert, Jr., on February 26, 1939.

Mrs. Henry M. Robert, Jr., president general of the DAR, with Martin Dies of the House Committee Investigating Un-American Activities in December 1938. Mrs. Robert is presenting a six-point program to promote Americanism.

KEEPERS OF DEMOCRACY

For the past few years, nearly all of our organizations and many individuals have said something about the necessity for fighting dangerous and subversive elements in our midst.

If you are in the South someone tells you solemnly that all the members of the Committee for Industrial Organization [Congress of Industrial Organizations] are Communists, or that the Negroes are all Communists. This last statement derives from the fact that, being for the most part unskilled labor, Negroes are more apt to be organized by the Committee for Industrial Organization. In another part of the country someone tells you solemnly that the schools of the country are menaced because they are all under the influence of Jewish teachers and that the Jews, forsooth, are all Communists. And so it goes, until finally you realize that people have reached a point where anything which will save them from Communism is a godsend; and if Fascism or Nazism promises more security than our own democracy we may even turn to them. . . .

Somehow or other I have the feeling that our forefathers . . . would expect us to meet present-day dangers with more courage than we seem to have. It is not only physical courage which we need, the kind of physical courage which in the face of danger can at least control the outward evidences of fear. It is moral courage as well, the courage which can make up its mind whether it thinks something is right or wrong, make a material or personal sacrifice if necessary, and take the consequences which may come.

I shall always remember someone, it may have been Theodore Roosevelt, saying in my hearing when I was young that when you

Marian Anderson onstage at the Lincoln Memorial on April 9, 1939, before an audience of 75,000.

were afraid to do a thing, that was the time to go and do it. Every time we shirk from making up our minds or standing up for a cause in which we believe, we weaken our character and our ability to be fearless. . . .

I do not believe that oppression anywhere or injustice which is tolerated by the people of any country is a healthy influence. I feel that unless we learn to live together as individuals and as groups, and to find ways of settling our difficulties without showing fear of each other and resorting to force, we cannot hope to see our democracy successful. It is an indisputable fact that democracy cannot survive where force and not law is the ultimate court of appeal. Every time we permit force to enter into a situation between employer and employee we have weakened the power of democracy and the confidence which a democratic people must have in their ability to make laws to meet the conditions under which they live. . . .

When we permit religious prejudice to gain headway in our midst, when we allow one group of people to look down upon another, then we may for a short time bring hardship on some particular group of people, but the real hardship and the real wrong is done to democracy and to our nation as a whole. We are then breeding people who cannot live under a democratic form of government but must be controlled by force. We have but to look out into the world to see how easy it is to become stultified, to accept without protest wrongs done to others, and to shift the burden of decision and of responsibility for any action onto some vague thing called a government or some individual called a leader.

It is true today that democracies are in danger because there are forces opposed to their way of thinking abroad in the world; but more than democracies are at stake. When force becomes so necessary that practically all nations decide that they must engage in a race which will make them able to back up what they have to say with arms and will thus oblige the rest of the world to listen to them, then we face an ultimate Armageddon, unless at the same time an effort to find some other solution is never abandoned. . . .

I do still believe that there is within most of us a basic desire to live uprightly and kindly with our neighbors, but I also feel that we are at present in the grip of a wave of fear which threatens to overcome us. I think we need a rude awakening, to make us exert all the strength we have to face facts as they are in our country and in the world, and to make us willing to sacrifice all that we have from the material standpoint in order that freedom and democracy may not perish from this earth.

The Virginia Quarterly Review, 1939

A portrait of Marian Anderson from the late 1930s.

WE HAVE NEVER
BEEN WILLING TO FACE
THIS PROBLEM

———

If we are honest with ourselves today, we will acknowledge that the ideal of democracy has never failed but that we haven't carried it out, and in our lack of faith we have debased the human being who must have a chance to live if democracy is to be successful.

The slave is still with us, but his color is not always black, and I think we will also have to acknowledge that most of our difficulties arise today from the fact that in the rush of material development we have neglected to keep close enough to the Revolutionary idea, guided by religious feeling, which is the basis of democracy. We have undertaken, under our form of government, to carry out the ideal which can exist only if we accept the brotherhood of man as a basic truth in human society. . . .

Our present situation, our present difficulties arise from the fact that in the development of civilization we have neglected to remember that the rights of all people to some property are inviolate. We have allowed a situation to arise where many people are debased by poverty or the accident of race, in our own country, and therefore have no stake in democracy, while others appeal to this old rule of the sacredness of property rights to retain in the hands of a limited number the fruits of the labor of many.

We have never been willing to face this problem, to line it up with the basic underlying beliefs in democracy and to set our actions side by side with the actual example of the Christ-like way of living.

Thus, within our nation there are many who do not understand the values of democracy, and we have been unable to spread these values throughout the world, because as a people we have been led by the gods of Mammon from the spiritual concepts and from the practice of carrying-out of these concepts conceived for our nation as a truly free and democratic people.

The Moral Basis of Democracy, 1940

National Sharecroppers Week

CONTEST FOR HIGH SCHOOL STUDENTS

Prizes: $50.00

TO BE AWARDED BY MRS. FRANKLIN D. ROOSEVELT
on March 5, 1940

CONTEST I	CONTEST II
$15 - 1st Prize $10 - 2nd Prize	**$15 - 1st Prize $10 - 2nd Prize**
•	•

CONTEST I

1—Write a composition of 300-500 words, in the form of a letter to the editor of a newspaper, *describing* the *conditions* of *sharecroppers* in America.

2—Write or type on one side of paper only. Use 8 x 11 paper.

Write name, school, home address in upper left hand corner of each page.

3—You may enter only one of these contests.

•

To be mailed on or before February 26, 1940 to *High School Contest, National Sharecroppers Week*, 112 East 19th Street, New York City.

CONTEST II

1—Write a review, 300-500 words in length, of *one* of the following books. In your review, indicate what the book reveals as to the *conditions* of *sharecroppers* in America.

You Have Seen Their Faces
  by Erskine Caldwell and Margaret Bourke-White   1937.

A Southerner Discovers The South
  by Jonathan Daniels   1938.

Revolt Among The Sharecroppers
  by Howard Kester   1936.

The Sharecropper
  by Charlie May Simon   1937.

Cabin In The Cotton
  by H. H. Kroll   1931.

2—For rules, see items 2 and 3, under Contest I.

Auspices: EDUCATORS COMMITTEE NATIONAL SHARECROPPERS WEEK
112 East 19th Street, New York City

DR. MARY E. WOOLLEY   DR. ABRAM L. HARRIS

Notice of a New York civil rights event of 1940, at which Eleanor Roosevelt awarded prizes to competing high school students. The contestants wrote letters to editors or essays on recent books about sharecroppers.

"IF YOU ASK ME": RACE, PREJUDICE, AND EQUALITY

———

[Question from a reader] Do you believe that complete racial equality will ever be achieved? If so, how?

I do not know quite what you mean by complete racial equality. If you mean respect for the individual and equality as a citizen and in all social contacts, regardless of what race or creed you may belong to, I certainly expect it can be achieved, as we achieve a more perfect democracy and live up to our religious beliefs. The same God created all human beings and he certainly never intended that we should have less respect for any one of his creatures than for another. If we believe in religious teaching and in a real democracy, we shall give equal respect to human beings, and equal opportunity to live freely and participate in community life to every human being.

Do you approve of intermarriage of Negroes and whites?

At the present time I think that intermarriage between Negroes and whites may bring to both of the people involved great unhappiness, because of the social pattern in which we happen to live. If, of course, two people, with full realization of what they are facing, decide they still want to marry, that is their right and no one else can interfere, but it takes very strong characters to face the kind of situation in which they will find themselves in almost any part of the world. For those I love, I should dread the suffering which must almost certainly lie ahead.

Don't you feel that if the American government spent half as much time solving the problems of its own minority groups as it does meddling in European affairs, less of its people would turn to communism for a solution of their problems?

I think very few people in the United States are turning to communism as a solution to their problems. I am afraid that you will have to get over thinking that the United States is meddling in European affairs. The US has a vital interest in affairs all over the world now, because without that interest the world cannot be stabilized, and we cannot prosper in an unsettled world.

There is no reason, however, why the United States should not give proper attention to helping people at home to a solution of their prejudices. There are no minority problems existing here except those due to prejudice, and the people themselves have to overcome those prejudices. The government may help them by stimulating education on these subjects, by seeing that as a government there is equal administration of justice, and that equal opportunities are accorded to all people. These things will never become realities, however, except through the removal of prejudice from the hearts of all our people.

I realize that no person who has accomplished as much for the good of our nation as you have could help but step on a few toes. This is where the malicious rumor I am constantly hearing must have had its origin. It is generally believed in this part of the country that you are part Negro and that is why you are taking up for them. Could you manage to let them know the truth?

Anyone who cares to look into the genealogy of the Roosevelts—and I happen to be descended from the Theodore Roosevelt side of the family—can also look into the collateral branches and can find the answer to your question. As far as I know, I have no Negro blood; but I suppose if any of us could trace our ancestry back far enough we would find in the tribes from which we are all originally descended, all kinds of blood is mixed. It always seems quite foolish to me to begin to wonder what strains you might have beyond those you actually know about!

Last evening while conversing with some young women I have known for years, the subject of racial equality came up. To my dismay, several girls whom I had always considered fair and unprejudiced made such remarks as: "I don't believe in equal rights for colored

and white people." Similar remarks were made regarding Jewish
people. Will you kindly tell me how one goes about calmly trying to
convince people who consider themselves "nice people" but harbor
within their minds such prejudices? Every one of these girls is a
member of some church in our community.

I would suggest that the girls you mention be given a copy of *In
Henry's Backyard* to read as a starter. [Anthropologist Ruth Benedict's
book of 1948, *In Henry's Backyard: The Races of Mankind,* refuted
racism and celebrated kinship of all races.]

Sometimes I think we are a little too calm when we run up against this
type of prejudice. However, the best thing to point out is that one is
not asking for equal rights to begin with, but equal opportunities, and
then when those are obtainable the rights will take care of themselves.

One might suggest that democracy is today at the crossroads, and
unless we show some zeal in fighting for fundamental democratic
beliefs, we may find other beliefs in the ascendency.

We have found in a number of instances that states' rights had to be
subordinated to the good of the whole people. When we flout the
Constitution by an appeal to states' rights, we are, I think, courting
disaster. Sooner or later a nation has to make up its mind to be a
united nation or fall apart, and the attitude of these young ladies
is an attitude which will bring about dissolution, since we cannot
remove people who have been here long enough to become citizens.

I am a citizen of Holland. Is it true, as people say here, that colored
people in America have a hard life? Is it true that there are special
places where they must live just like the Indians? Do the Americans
lynch a Negro when he is trying to vote?

The colored people in America have in some ways a hard life because
they have been discriminated against in many ways in the United
States. They are not treated as some Indians are, who are placed on

reservations and treated as wards of the government. The Negroes are full-fledged citizens, freed by Abraham Lincoln's Emancipation Proclamation, but in large cities there are often sections which become almost entirely occupied by different groups of people— colored people, Italian people, Puerto Ricans, and so on.

Lynchings in the United States occur only very occasionally, and I do not think a lynching would occur in the majority of states because a Negro was trying to vote. It might in a few states be considered as a way to prevent the Negro from using the ballot.

Did you ever say in any of your public utterances that you believed in racial intermarriage?

I have no recollection of what I said on this subject, but it is quite obvious that racial intermarriage has been going on among many races on the face of the earth for many, many years, so my opinion for or against it would be completely useless.

I am a principal of a small Southern high school. In theory I have always been opposed to segregation, but I wonder whether you realize, Mrs. Roosevelt, the terrible problems this anti-segregation law [the Supreme Court's Brown v. Board of Education decision of 1954] confronts us with down here. It is all very well to pass the law, but who is going to help us make it work?

I think the Southerners themselves will gradually make the anti-segregation law work, with the aid of their deep religious feeling as well as with their real understanding of how you may eventually achieve a good relationship on an equal basis between peoples of different races. Segregation in itself means discrimination, and there-fore it must go, but I think the South can show us better than any other area of this country how good relationships can be achieved.

Ladies Home Journal, 1941–1949
McCall's, 1950–1954

RACE, RELIGION, AND PREJUDICE

It seems trite to say to the Negro, you must have patience, when he has had patience for so long; you must not expect miracles overnight, when he can look back to the years of slavery and say—how many nights he has waited for justice. Nevertheless, that is what we must continue to say in the interests of our government as a whole and of the Negro people; but that does not mean that we must sit idle and do nothing. We must keep moving forward steadily, removing restrictions which have no sense and fighting prejudice. . . . Above everything else, no action must be taken which can cause so much bitterness that the whole liberalizing effort may be set back over a period of many years.

The New Republic, 1942

THE FOUR EQUALITIES

A great many people believe that there should be no intermingling of races. Hitler has proved with bloody massacres that he holds this belief. Nevertheless, down through the ages, it has been proved over and over again that this is one of the questions which people settle for themselves, and no amount of legislation will keep them from doing so.

We would not have so many different shades of color in this country today if this were not so. This is a question, therefore, that I think we have to leave to individuals, not only all over the United States, but all over the world, to handle.

There is no more reason to expect that there will be more intermarriage if the four fundamental basic rights of citizens are granted to all people in this country than there will be if they are withheld. In fact, I think it is probable that there would be less.

An equal opportunity for education may raise economic standards as a whole—may make it possible for colored people to get equal pay, because they will have training equal to that of white people. There will be more self-respect; the dignity and pride of race will be enhanced and the bitterness of inferiority removed. . . .

We are fighting a war today so that individuals all over the world may have freedom. This means an equal chance for every man to have food and shelter and a minimum of such things as spell happiness to that particular human personality. If we believe firmly that peace cannot come to the world unless this is true for men all over the world, then we must know in our nation that every man, regardless of race or religion, has this chance. Otherwise we are fighting for nothing of real value.

So here at home I think we have to fight for these four simple freedoms.

Equality before the law, which assures us of justice without prejudice, for Jew or Gentile, for any race or color, as far as human beings can obtain justice.

Equality of education for everyone, because of the need for an equal opportunity in life.

Equality in the economic field, which means we are so organized in our communities and in our system of economics that all men who want to work will have work and that work will be suited to their capacity and will be rewarded without prejudice.

Finally, because we believe in the democratic and republican form of government, by which we are governed through the consent of the governed, we must give to all the citizens of a democracy a chance for equality of expression. We believe that there should be no impediment which prevents any man from expressing his will through the ballot.

The acceptance of these fundamental rights seems to me the only basis on which the men who fight this war can look forward into the future with real hope to a world organization which may gradually bring about a betterment of human conditions the world over.

The New Threshold, 1943

IF I WERE A NEGRO TODAY

———

If I were a Negro today, I think I would have moments of great bitterness. It would be hard for me to sustain my faith in democracy and to build up a sense of goodwill toward men of other races.

I think, however, that I would realize that if my ancestors had never left Africa, we would be worse off as "natives" today under the rule of any other country than I am in this country where my people were brought as slaves.

In a comparatively short period of time the slaves have become free men—free men, that is, as far as a proclamation can make them so. There now remains much work to be done to see that freedom becomes a fact and not just a promise for my people.

I know, however, that I am not the only group that has to make a similar fight. Even women of the white race still suffer inequalities and injustices, and many groups of white people in my country are the slaves of economic conditions. All the world is suffering under a great war brought about because of the lag in our social development as against the progress in our economic development.

I would know that I had to work hard and to go on accomplishing the best that was possible under present conditions. Even though I was held back by generations of economic inequality, I would be proud of those of my race who are gradually fighting to the top in whatever occupation they are engaged in. . . .

I would certainly go on working for complete economic equality and my full rights under a democratic government. I would decide which were the steps that I felt represented my real rights as a citizen and I would work for those first, feeling that other things such as social relationships might well wait until certain people were given time to think them through and decide as individuals what they wished to do.

I would not do too much demanding. I would take every chance that came my way to prove my quality and my ability and if recognition was slow, I would continue to prove myself, knowing that in the end good performance has to be acknowledged.

I would accept every advance that was made in the Army and the Navy, though I would not try to bring those advances about any more quickly than they were offered. I would certainly affiliate with the labor movement because there is the greatest opportunity for men to work side by side and find out that it is possible to have similar interests and to stand by each other, regardless of race or color.

I would try to remember that unfair and unkind treatment will not harm me if I do not let it touch my spirit. Evil emotions injure the man or woman who harbors them so I would try to fight down resentment, the desire for revenge and bitterness. I would try to sustain my own faith in myself by counting my friends and among them there would undoubtedly be some white people.

Negro Digest, 1943

ON SOCIAL EQUALITY:
LETTER TO ADDIE FRIZIELLE

———

[Response to a critic who objected to desegregation of restrooms in a Washington, DC, workplace and who alleged that ER endorsed "social equality."]

May 13, 1944

Dear Miss Frizielle:

I have not advocated social equality between colored and white people. This is a personal thing which nobody can advocate. Nobody can tell me whom I shall have inside my house, any more than I can tell others.

The only things which I have advocated are four basic rights which I believe every citizen in a democracy must enjoy. These are the right for equal education, the right to work for equal pay according to ability, the right to justice under the law, the right to participate in the making of laws by use of the ballot.

Questions beyond that are personal things and people must decide them for themselves.

I am sure it is true that here in Washington you have found some discourteous colored people. I have found colored people who were discourteous, and I have also found white people who were discourteous. As a matter of fact, I doubt if it does people anywhere any harm to tell them that you believe they are entitled to certain rights and you are willing to see them obtain those rights.

If you have to use the same toilets and wash basins where you work, then all of you must have to take physical examinations, in which case I think you are as safe as you would be in any place where a great many people are coming and going. If you are nervous, there are certain precautions you can always take.

Sincerely yours,
[ER]

Gilder Lehrman Collection, 1944

ER and Mary McLeod Bethune, left, join representatives from women's organizations at a conference "on building better race relationships," held under the auspices of the YWCA in Washington, DC, on February 13, 1944.

ON SOCIAL EQUALITY:
LETTER TO PAULI MURRAY

———

October 3, 1944

Dear Pauli,

I will give your letter which you sent me to the president. . . .

I will be glad when the election is over and I can assure you that though I do think it would be better for the country if the president were to continue in office for the next few years, I shall be equally happy if he is out because as far as my personal feelings go, I would like nothing better than to be free to do what I choose during the next few years.

Social equality to me does not mean at all what it seems to mean to certain people. I do not think you can legislate about the people with whom you have friendly relations and those people are your social equals. I think it is all important that every citizen in the United States have an equal opportunity and that is why I have emphasized the four basic things we should fight for [in "The Four Equalities"].

A number of people have been asking me to make a statement on segregation. I do not want to do it until we have achieved the four basic citizen rights because I do not think it wise to add any antagonism that we do not wish to have. Besides, I think if I made such a statement [that] it would be felt I was doing it purely for political reasons and I am much more interested in having good race relations than I am in the political situation.

In addition to this, I think that there will be a time which will come very soon after the war comes to an end, for those of us who really care that this question should be settled without bloodshed, will have to stand up and be counted and that will be the time when to make such a statement would have some effect and some meaning.

I believe, of course, that all public places should be open to all citizens of the United States, based entirely on behavior and ability to pay as individuals. I do not think this has anything to do with social equality which is concerned with one's personal relationships. I might be quite willing to sit next to someone in a streetcar or a bus whom I would not want in my own house but that person would have just as much right in the streetcar as I had and we should be judged entirely on our behavior. But any statements such as I am making in this letter will be much more effective when no campaign is going on and should only be made after we get our four basic rights accepted, unless the situation becomes such that in order to help people to be patient we have to give them the feeling that there are people with them who will help them, which may save us from bloodshed.

This letter is confidential and not for publication and that is said because of the way in which people have been publishing all that I have written lately.

Very sincerely,
[ER]

ER Papers, 1944

TOLERANCE IS AN UGLY WORD

I do not like the word tolerance. If you tolerate something, you do not like it very much.

I believe that what we have to do in this country is to stop disliking things and like them.

In the future the world is going to be tied together by airplanes and radio, and we are going to be near many people whom we have not had to know in the past. It is not going to be possible just to tolerate our neighbors. We are going to like them or they are not going to like us. Our neighbors are going to include people whose skins are yellow, brown, red, black and white. Their religions will be more varied than the color of their skins and our liking must come from understanding. Regardless of race or religion, human beings have certain things in common and we must discover that quickly.

We, in this country, are a highly mechanized people. We have inventive genius where machinery is concerned, and mechanical skills. Some of the things we have accomplished seem nothing short of miracles to other people.

Other people understand things, however, which we know little about. Our boys who have been in India are coming back to tell us about snake charmers and the people who make flowers grow before your eyes. These are powers we know nothing about.

So we have things to learn from other people just as they have things to learn from us, but we are not going to learn if we just "tolerate" each other.

I have an idea that we are going to find some fundamental traits, such as kindness and integrity and love of children, are present in many human beings.

If we can do away with fear, we begin to love. If we are not afraid of aggression among nations, either in the military sense or the economic sense, we may have peace. If we are not afraid of being dominated by those who are stronger than ourselves, then we will learn to like people and cooperate with them.

First we must cease to be afraid of our neighbors at home and take the word "tolerance" out of our vocabulary and substitute for it the precepts of, live and let live, cooperate in work and play, and like our neighbors. If we do this, we will soon find out that our basic needs and desires are the same, and that given the same opportunities for development, we develop in much the same way.

The problem is not to learn tolerance of your neighbors, but to see that all alike have hope and opportunity and that the community as a whole moves forward.

Coronet, 1945

Eleanor Roosevelt joined the board of directors of the NAACP in 1945. Here, in 1947, she shares a document with fellow board member Dr. James McClendon, front left. NAACP executive officers Walter White and Roy Wilkins, back row. and lawyer Thurgood Marshall, front right. Marshall, head of the NAACP Legal Defense and Education Fund, pursued legal strategies to end segregation from the 1930s onward.

Eleanor Roosevelt and Walter White accompany President Truman to a session of the 1947 NAACP convention at the Lincoln Memorial in Washington, DC. Urged to do so by ER, who spoke to the convention, Truman gave the closing speech; this was the first time any president addressed the NAACP.

FROM THE MELTING POT— AN AMERICAN RACE

In this country we have meant to be the great melting pot of the world. Wave after wave of immigration came to our shores. All of us, either ourselves or our ancestors, came from foreign lands. The only people who "belong" here are the Indians.

The variety of our backgrounds has been one of our great strengths. We owe our continued vigor over a long period of years to the adventurous blood which has been pumped into our veins. People who stay at home, too dispirited to get out and seek something better than they have known before, do not come to new worlds. For many generations we kept on adding pioneer strength and character that enriched our original stock.

Even the Negro slaves who came here against their will brought us a strong and adventurous spirit. It took not only health but character and a will to live to survive the conditions under which they were brought to this country, and their years of hardship and bondage. To find people of the Negro race emerging from slavery with the ability to adapt and improve themselves quickly is a sign that their ancestors who came originally were strong and vigorous, with latent powers far beyond what we might have expected. . . .

But our melting pot has not melted too successfully. Instead of all being welded together into one American race, we find, despite occasional intermarriage, settlements which retain the characteristics of the mother country. Little Italys; Little Polands or Irelands; districts where primarily Jewish people or Negro people are found; German cities; Norwegian and Danish settlements in rural areas. All these make us conscious of our differences; there is not that complete flowing together and obliteration of old lines of difference which we should like to see.

The most optimistic among us will have to agree that there are barriers which keep us from integrating and intermarrying as rapidly as possible.

Let us consider what these barriers are.

Perhaps by far the greatest is that of language. Children born here of foreign parents go to public school and learn English; sometimes this erects a greater barrier between them and their parents than the one which separates them from youngsters of different backgrounds. . . .

The second obstacle to amalgamation in the United States lies, of course, in the customs and habits in the home. School friendships will wipe out some of these differences. . . . The foreign customs will become Americanized as they fit into the new pattern. . . .

Probably the most difficult of barriers is the difference in religious beliefs. Our Constitution was based on the concept that we should practice our religious faiths in complete freedom. So it is peculiarly American to insist that even if people of different faiths marry, all of them shall have a right to practice their religion in the way they consider fitting.

This theory is so deeply ingrained in most Americans that even people wholly ignorant of certain religious tenets are still willing to concede others a right to religious freedom. I think the only real danger of our curtailing religious rights lies in the possibility that some of our church groups might come to wield too much influence in the nation's political and economic life. I think that would provoke very serious opposition because of the strong feeling in this country that the church should confine itself to spiritual matters, leaving affairs of government and economy entirely free from church influence or domination.

Looking at the factors which seem to be barring us from making one nation out of our curiously variegated background, I think we will find our real obstacles are few indeed.

Liberty Magazine, 1945

ER at a 1950s NAACP meeting. On the left, union leader Walter Reuther, founder of the United Auto Workers (UAW), UAW president from 1938 to 1970, and a highly visible spokesman for the UAW civil rights agenda. On the right Roy Wilkins, who succeeded Walter White in 1955 as executive secretary of the NAACP and served until 1977.

SOME OF MY BEST FRIENDS
ARE NEGRO

As I look back over the years that have given me so many opportunities for personal growth and understanding of peoples, I find that I count among my closest and oldest friends many Negro Americans.

It is neither unusual nor new for me to have Negro friends, nor is it unusual for me to have found my friends among all races and religions of people. . . .

Perhaps my first really close friendship with a Negro of about my own age started with a woman who is now a dear friend: Mrs. Mary McLeod Bethune. When I first met her I did not realize that the years would bring us so close together, but I was from the first meeting deeply impressed with her Christianity and intelligence. . . .

Perhaps she can recall our first meeting. She might have asked me down to her school or I may have first met her after her appointment in Washington. But it was in Washington that we really got to know each other very, very well. I have always marveled at her and thought it was wonderful that she could go through so many hardships and emerge so free of bitterness. . . .

Later she often came to the White House. I can't tell about any particular meal because there were so many—she came to so many things. And the National Council of Negro Women came. And a great many other colored women were in the other organizations which came.

In Washington, I think, we managed to break down the notion that we were doing anything out of the ordinary in entertaining Negro Americans as social equals. Gradually it became pretty well accepted. . . .

One of my finest young friends is a charming woman lawyer—Pauli Murray, who has been quite a firebrand at times but of whom I am very fond. She is a lovely person who has struggled and come through very well. I think there were times when she may have done foolish things. But now I think she is well ready to be of real use.

My relationship with Pauli is very satisfying. I notice I call her by her first name. . . . When they are younger it is quite easy for me to call them by their first names. . . .

But with people my own age I address them as Mr. or Mrs. It does not change the way I feel about them. It is just the way I was brought up. But these are not set rules of conduct. I simply call Walter White "Walter." And by the way, he calls me "Eleanor" which is very rare. . . .

For years my work has brought me in contact with Negroes and that is why I have made friends with them. Through my work at the UN I met one of the grandest people I know. His name is Ralph Bunche. He is always the senior adviser on colonial problems. . . .

On a more casual level I know A. Philip Randolph. I think he is serene, charming, and nice looking. I only have had the pleasure of seeing him at various labor dinners and on committees with labor people. . . .

Edith Sampson is a great friend of mine. I am very fond of her because she is a warm person. I like her very much but I realize that because she is so warm and so outgoing, she sometimes irritates people.

Two personalities have made a significant but different contribution to our United Nations delegation—Channing Tobias and Edith Sampson. He is a different kind of person. He is friendly and warm, but quiet and an intellectual. . . .

One of the odd things about my Negro friends is their consistent failure to invite me to their social gatherings. I am rarely invited to their weddings, musicals, or teas. I invariably invite them to my house, but the invitation is not returned. I suppose this is because they have an understanding of my busy schedule and are a little shy. . . .

In friendships and in inviting different people to your home, hostesses often worry about mixing—will the different kinds of personalities clash?

That is my only concern in inviting guests in. . . .

Once some of my neighbors and I were serving at a big buffet party. One of my neighbors found she was serving a Negro guest. Afterwards she told me she had never thought that she would serve and talk with a Negro. She said it did not bother her at all and she was glad that it did not.

I have never had any white person object. I value and enjoy my Negro friends equally with my white friends. . . .

[T]here were many strange and unreal rumors circulating against my husband and me in the South. I remember they had something they called "Eleanor Clubs." Negro members of these clubs were supposed to push white people on Thursdays or something really strange.

I asked my close Negro friends if they had ever heard of such a club. Of course they had not because they did not exist. Then Franklin had the Secret Service and FBI investigate. We found not one single "Eleanor Club" and we never found out who started the rumors. I do not personally mind being criticized because of my friends. But that was a time when criticism of me could have hurt my husband and because of that I was worried. . . .

Shortly after that, while we were in the White House, we began to hear another kind of story from some of my Negro friends. The story was that I had advised and encouraged the president in his awareness of the needs of Negroes in America. One of the versions of the story was that I was responsible for FEPC [the Fair Employment Practices Commission] and other things the president believed in. This is not true.

Franklin always had an awareness of the most important things he had to do. If he had to get the Southern vote in order to get something essential to the whole country, he could not take a stand that would upset the South. But he never said that I could not take a stand. Sometimes, after talks with my Negro friends and with their white friends too, I used to ask Franklin, "Do you mind if I do so and so." And he would answer: "I shall stand or fall on what I have been able to accomplish. You have a right to do what you think is right."

He did not know Negroes as individuals and as friends as well as I did. He was not able to get about easily. But I had the opportunity to do so and I made friends. I was never asked by him not to do anything I wanted to do with them or for them. Franklin had such a deep sense of justice and an overriding wish to see all Americans treated as equals that he never prevented me from taking any stand, even though I sometimes worried if my actions in regards to my friends would harm his campaigns.

I also think that we were privileged to start something in Washington that will be continued: the acceptance of Negroes as social equals and as friends. . . .

When more whites and Negroes become friends and lose whatever self-consciousness they started out with, we shall have a much happier world.

Ebony, 1953

A. Philip Randolph, president of the first all-black union, the Brotherhood of Sleeping Car Porters, and a leading civil rights activist. Randolph's achievements in the 1940s laid the groundwork for the civil rights movement in the 1960s. Above, with ER in 1946.

ON DESEGREGATION
OF PUBLIC SCHOOLS

New York, Monday—During the past week a case came before the Supreme Court of the United States affecting segregation on the grammar-school level. Thurgood Marshall presented the case against segregation; John W. Davis represented the side for separate but equal facilities. It has always seemed to me that there could be separate facilities, and technically they might offer the same opportunities for both colored and white. But the mere fact of segregation, which is not a voluntary act but an imposed one, makes equality impossible.

Some people rise above segregation but, by and large, it conditions most of them to a different approach to life.

There probably won't be a decision on this case for some time but when it is handed down it will be a momentous one. If the court sanctions segregation, then the fight for equality among the races will receive a setback not only in this country but throughout the world. It follows, then, that our leadership in the areas of the world where people are colored will be weakened. On the other hand, if the decision is that segregation in this country must come to an end, I think we will move forward a long way, both at home and abroad, in our battle to lead the world, spiritually and morally.

It is said that not only Gov. James S. Byrnes of South Carolina but others have made plans to close their public schools and do it in a way that would make it possible for the schools to reopen as private schools. How this juggling is to be done I do not know, but I am told it has been planned.

I cannot, however, believe that any part of this country will cease to be law-abiding. We have come a long way since Civil War days and we are much more mature. Even though we may not like certain policies, we have learned to grit our teeth and bear them and gradually grow accustomed to them.

That is what I expect to see happen in the North and in the South in the long run. It will make a great difference so far as we all are concerned because just as long as there is segregation there are people among us who are not completely emancipated.

"My Day," December 16, 1952

ER and Mary McLeod Bethune at the opening of a federally-built residence hall for black women government workers in May 1943.

THE *BROWN V. BOARD OF EDUCATION* DECISION

New York, Wednesday—While I was on the *Tex and Jinx Show* [Tex McCrary and Jinx Falkenburg hosted a popular TV talk show] I was given the news of the unanimous Supreme Court decision that wiped out segregation in the schools. I am delighted this was a unanimous decision because I think it will be difficult for the states with segregated school systems to hold out against such a ruling.

If it were not for the fact that segregation in itself means inequality, the old rule giving equal facilities might have gone on satisfying our sense of justice for a long time. It is very difficult, however, to ensure real equality under a segregated system, and the mere fact that you cannot move freely anywhere in your country and be as acceptable everywhere as your neighbor creates an inequality.

Southerners always bring up the question of marriage between the races and I realize that that is the question of real concern to people.

But it seems to me a very personal question which must be settled by family environment and by the development of the cultural and social patterns within a country. One can no longer lay down rules as to what individuals will do in any area of their lives in a world that is changing as fast as ours is today.

"My Day," May 20, 1954

ER with civil rights activists Rosa Parks, left, and Autherine Lucy before a civil rights rally at Madison Square Garden, New York City, in 1956. Rosa Parks, secretary of an NAACP chapter in Alabama, had refused in 1955 to give up her bus seat to a white passenger, an act that spurred the Montgomery bus boycott. She met ER in New York that year; both had connections to the Highlander School, an adult education institution in Tennessee, where Parks had attended a session and to which ER made donations. Autherine Lucy was the first black student to attend the University of Alabama in 1956.

CHAPTER 6

The UN
and Human Rights

Eleanor Roosevelt had opposed FDR's choice of Harry S. Truman as his
running mate in 1944; Truman distrusted ER as well. His appointment in 1945
of the former first lady as US representative to the United Nations marked
the start of a slowly improving relationship.

President Truman's choice of Eleanor Roosevelt as a US delegate
to the United Nations in 1945 involved a degree of risk. ER lacked
formal experience in diplomacy and foreign affairs; forthright,
independent, and voluble, she might blunder into controversial
topics (some foreign policy experts feared) or otherwise torpedo
debate. But, as Truman saw, the appointment promised far more

advantage than liability. To choose ER for the UN post harnessed the Roosevelt name to the Truman administration; it enabled the president to capitalize on ER's popularity, prestige, and political skill. Most important, the appointment gave the former first lady a focus for her humanitarian zeal and immense energy. The prospect of UN service catered to her sense of responsibility, her need to be "useful." Every citizen had "a noble obligation to work on public questions," as ER wrote in 1946. She accepted the UN position, she stated, "because it seemed as though I might be able to use the experiences of a lifetime and make them valuable to my nation and to the people of the world."

For Eleanor Roosevelt, the UN appointment launched an era of achievement. She chaired the UN commission of eighteen members that drafted the Universal Declaration of Human Rights, a document that the UN General Assembly approved on December 10, 1948. The declaration set forth in a preamble and thirty articles a vision of rights to which all human beings were inherently entitled, starting with life, liberty, and security of person. It enumerated, in ER's words, "certain protections which the individual must have if he is to acquire a sense of security and dignity in his own person." The document lacked legal force; it was not a treaty, international agreement, or statement of legal obligation, as ER explained. Rather it was "a declaration of basic human rights and freedoms." Shaped by ER, the declaration remains one of her major legacies. After its passage, the commission headed by ER worked on two covenants, legal agreements to bind the nations that ratified them, to enforce the declaration's goals. The General Assembly finally approved the covenants in 1966. Eleanor Roosevelt served in the UN until the start of the Eisenhower administration in 1953, when she resigned.

As US delegate to the UN, Eleanor Roosevelt defended and explained the human rights agenda. She promoted the rights of oppressed peoples, urged resettlement of refugees from communist states, and fielded attacks from her Soviet colleagues. Cold

War concerns prevailed. In the excerpts below, ER discussed her rationale for accepting the UN post and the challenges posed by her Russian counterparts. She shared her vision of the Declaration of Human Rights as an educational document; as a bolster to security, personal and global; and as "the international Magna Carta of all men everywhere." She responded to USSR charges against the United States, both by going on the offensive—citing obstacles to freedom in communist states—and on the defensive—rebutting claims of Soviet-bloc delegates about racism and bias against women in the United States. Her claims of progress in civil rights, to be sure, aggrieved her colleagues in the civil rights movement. Finally, she returned to her signature theme of "interdependence," in this instance on an international scale. She also asserted, characteristically, that the best defense against communism was to make democracy work at home. Or, as she explained in a UN publication in 1949, "Our first task in getting along with the communists is to find ways to make democracy do what it says it does."

AN INVITATION
FROM PRESIDENT TRUMAN

My Dear Mrs. Roosevelt:

I am pleased to inform you that I have appointed you one of the representatives of the United States to the first part of the first session of the General Assembly of the United Nations to be held in London in January 1946. . . .

You, as a representative of the United States will bear the grave responsibility of demonstrating the wholehearted support which this government is pledged to give to this United Nations organization, to the end that the organization can become the means of preserving the international peace and of creating conditions of mutual trust and economic and social well-being among all the peoples of the world. I am confident that you will do your best to assist the United States to accomplish these purposes in the first meeting of the General Assembly.

Harry Truman
December 21, 1945

ER Papers, 1945

AT LAST I ACCEPTED

In December of 1945 I received a message from President Truman . . . and he asked me if I would serve as a member of the United States delegation.

ER at a UN meeting in London, 1945.

"Oh, no! It would be impossible!" was my first reaction. How could I be a delegate to help organize the United Nations when I have no background or experience in international meetings?

Miss Thompson [Malvina Thompson, ER's secretary] urged me not to decline without giving the idea careful thought. I knew in a general way what had been done about organizing the United Nations. . . . I believed the United Nations to be the one hope for a peaceful world. I knew that my husband had placed great importance on the establishment of this organization.

At last I accepted in fear and trembling. But I might not have done so if I had known that President Truman could only nominate me as a delegate and that the nomination would have to be approved by the United States Senate, where certain senators would disapprove of me because of my attitude toward social problems and more especially youth problems. As it happened, some senators did protest to the president against my nomination but only one, Senator Theodore G. Bilbo [Mississippi], actually voted against me. . . . Anyway, my nomination was confirmed by the Senate, and I still marvel at it.

Autobiography, 1961

"IF YOU ASK ME":
GETTING ON WITH THE RUSSIANS

———

[Question from a reader] I am puzzled about what is going on at the UN. It seems to me that when the Americans or British make a proposal, the Russians ignore it or make a directly opposite one. I get the feeling that we will never be able to work with the Russians. Do you feel that way?

No, I do not feel that way. It seems to me quite possible to get on with the Russians, though I think it is going to take us a long while really to understand each other. There are fundamental differences that exist between us, in our backgrounds and in our points of view, which arise very largely from the fact that Russia is a very young nation—young and virile—but, nevertheless, insecure. We have more than 150 years behind us, and we have attained a good deal of the poise and security which come with maturity. . . .

ER listens to a UN session in 1946 with fellow US delegates John Foster Dulles and Adlai Stevenson. Dulles, who opposed ER's appointment, would become Secretary of State in 1953. Stevenson served as a US delegate to the UN in 1946 and 1947 before his successful campaign for governor of Illinois in 1948.

It is much easier to have confidence in people if you have a sense of security. We have gained it, and I think for that very reason we should perhaps be better able today to be generous about some of the very obvious moves which are made by the Russians, largely because of their lack of security. Only with confidence and trust can peace be a reality.

There is no question, for instance, that ultimately we will all have more security if we have a greater sense of interdependence, put more strength in the United Nations, and count less on our own individual strengths. Even we find that hard to accept, because it is such a new concept of living with other nations, and for the Russians, who have lived on the continent of Europe, where every nation has looked askance at every other nation for years, it is even harder than it is for us. . . .

When all this is considered, however, I think it is essential that the Russians also understand that the nations living around them, who have greater maturity, have set up certain standards, and that to live successfully with them the effort to understand those standards must be made. They will have to stop some of the practices which are relics of the past, and recognize eventually the basic difference between our two beliefs. We think the state must serve the individual, and they think the individual is subservient to the state. Gradually as our conceptions become clearer to each other, and as life becomes more worthwhile to every individual in his part of the world, we will, I believe, find a happier medium for working together and living together in peace and amity.

Ladies' Home Journal, 1947

THE RUSSIANS ARE TOUGH

I was leaving in the early morning by Army plane for Berlin. The argument on displaced persons had dragged itself out until a very late hour. When the vote was finally taken and adjournment was finally announced I made my way over to my opponent, Mr. [Andrei] Vishinsky, the delegate from the USSR. I did not want to leave with bad feeling between us. I said, "I hope the day will come, sir, when you and I are on the same side of a dispute, for I admire your fighting qualities." His answer shot back: "And I, yours."

That was February 1946. When I saw Mr. Vishinsky again, it was October, 1946. He came to join his delegation at the second session of the United Nations General Assembly in Flushing, New York. I realized that we might again have some acrimonious discussions. But I had no personal bitterness. I have never had any personal bitterness against any of the people in any of the Eastern European group. I have had, nevertheless, to argue at some length with them because we could not agree on fundamental problems. I have found that it takes patience and equal firmness and equal conviction to work with the Russians. One must be alert since, if they cannot win success for their point of view in one way, they are still going to try to win in any other way that seems to them possible.

For example, the Eastern European group has but one interest in the International Refugee Organization set up to deal with displaced persons in Europe: the repatriation of as many of their nationals as possible. We, on the other hand, while agreeing that repatriation is desirable, feel that there will be people who do not wish to return to their home countries. And our belief in the fundamental right of human beings to decide what they want to do must impel us to try to prevent any use of force against displaced persons. We must find the opportunity, if we possibly can, for people to carry out new plans for resettlement somewhere in the world.

I have worked over this and similar questions with the Russians at two meetings of the General Assembly at the United Nations. They are a disciplined group. They take orders and they carry them out. When they have no orders they delay—and they are masterful at finding reasons for delay. They are resourceful and I think they really have an oriental streak—which one finds in many people—which comes to the fore in their enjoyment of bargaining day after day.

When they find themselves outside their own country in international meetings or even in individual relationships, they realize they have been cut off from other nations. They are not familiar with the customs and the thinking of other peoples. This makes them somewhat insecure and, I think, leads them at times to take an exaggerated, self-assertive stand which other people may think

ER welcomes Soviet Minister Vyacheslav Molotov to Hyde Park in November 1946. In the center, USSR delegate to the UN Andrei Vishinsky, who seemed to ER a formidable foe in debate. "I trembled at the thought of speaking against the famous Mr. Vishinsky," she wrote in her *Autobiography*. "Well, I did my best."

somewhat rude. I think it is only an attempt to make the rest of the world see that they are proud of their own ways of doing things. . . .

I admire the Russians' tenacity, though it is slightly annoying to start at the very beginning each time you meet and cover the same ground all over again. I have come to accept this as inevitable. It means one hasn't convinced one's opponent that the argument presented was valid. It is perhaps only fair, therefore, that they should go on until they either decide it is useless to continue or one is able to convince them that the opposing stand has truth in it. . . .

We undoubtedly consider the individual more important than the Russians do. Individual liberty seems to us one of the essentials of life in peacetime. We must bear this is mind when we work with the Russians; we cannot accept their proposals without careful scrutiny. We know the fundamental differences which exist between us. But I am hoping that as time goes on, the differences will be less important, that we will find more points of agreement. . . .

Look, 1947

WE HAVE PUT INTO WORDS SOME INHERENT RIGHTS

As I look back at the work thus far of our Human Rights Commission I realize that its importance is twofold.

In the first place, we have put into words some inherent rights. Beyond that, we have found that the conditions of our contemporary world require the enumeration of certain protections which the individual must have if he is to acquire a sense of security and dignity in his own person. The effect of this is frankly educational. Indeed, I like to think that the Declaration [the Universal Declara-

ER addressed the first session of the committee that would draft the Universal Declaration of Human Rights at Lake Success, New York, June 1947.

tion of Human Rights] will help forward very largely the education of the peoples of the world.

It seems to me most important that the Declaration be accepted by all member nations, not because they will immediately live up to all of its provisions, but because they ought to support the standards toward which the nations must henceforward aim. Since the objectives have been clearly stated, men of goodwill everywhere will strive to attain them with more energy and, I trust, with better hope of success.

As the Convention is adhered to by one country after another, it will actually bring into being rights which are tangible and can be invoked before the law of the ratifying countries. Everywhere many people will feel more secure. And as the Great Powers tie themselves down by their ratifications, the smaller nations which fear that the great may abuse their strength will acquire a sense of greater assurance.

The work of the Commission has been of outstanding value in setting before men's eyes the ideals which they must strive to reach. Men cannot live by bread alone.

Foreign Affairs, 1948

<u>Preamble</u>

We, the Peoples of the United Nations, *unbelobang.*

Déclaration
des Droits
de l'Homme

1. - Considering that ignorance and contempt of human rights have
been among the principal causes of the sufferings of humanity and,
inparticular, of the massacres, which have polluted the World during
the World Wars; and

Preamble of
Sec. Draft

2. - Whereas there can be np peace unless human rights and freedoms
are respected; and there can be no human freedom or dignity, unless
war and the threat of war is abolished; and

Charter and
U.K. Draft

3. - Whereas the institution of conditions wherein human beings,
free to speak and believe, will be protected against fear and want
has been proclaimed as the supreme aim of the recent strife; and

Charter and
U.K Draft

4. - Whereas, in the Charter of June 26thy 1945, we have reaffirmed
our faith in fundamental human rights, in the dignity and worth of
of the human person and in equality of the rights of men and
women; and

U.K. Draft

5. - Whereas it is one of the purposes ofthe United Nations to
achieve international cooperation in promoting and encouraging respect
for human rights and fundamental freedoms for all without distinction
as to race, sex, language or religion; and

U.K. Draft

6. - Whereas the enjoyment of such rights and freedoms by all persons
must be protected by the Commonwealth of Nations and secured by
international as well as national laws;

Now, therefore, we the Peoples of the United Nations have resolved
to define in a solemn Declaration the essential rights a d fundamental
freedoms of man, so that this Declaration, being for ever present
to the minds of all members of the human community, ma constantly
remind them of their rights and duties and that the United Nations

First page of the draft preamble to the Universal Declaration of Human Rights,
1947, with ER's handwritten revisions.

WE MUST NOT BE CONFUSED ABOUT WHAT FREEDOM IS

The General Assembly, which opened its third session here in Paris a few days ago, will have before it the first fruit of the Commission's labors in this task, that is the International Declaration of Human Rights.

The Declaration was finally completed after much work during the last session of the Human Rights Commission in New York in the spring of 1948. . . .

The Declaration has come from the Human Rights Commission with unanimous acceptance except for four abstentions—the USSR, Yugoslavia, Ukraine, and Byelorussia. The reason for this is a fundamental difference in the conception of human rights as they exist in these states and certain other member states in the United Nations. . . .

We must not be confused about what freedom is. Basic human rights are simple and easily understood: freedom of speech and a free press, freedom of religion and worship, freedom of assembly and the right of petition, the right of men to be secure in their homes and free from unreasonable search and seizure and from arbitrary arrest and punishment.

We must not be deluded by the efforts of the forces of reaction to prostitute the great words of our free tradition and thereby to confuse the struggle. Democracy, freedom, human rights have come to have a definite meaning to the people of the world which we must not allow any nation to so change that they are made synonymous with suppression and dictatorship.

There are basic differences that show up even in the use of words between a democratic and a totalitarian country. For instance, "democracy" means one thing to the USSR and another to the USA. . . .

The USSR representatives assert that they already have achieved many things which we, in what they call the "bourgeois democracies" cannot achieve because their government controls the accomplishments of these things. . . .

For instance, the USSR will assert that their press is free because the state makes it free by providing the machinery, the paper, and even the money for salaries for the people who work on the paper. They state that there is no control over what is printed in the various papers that they subsidize in this manner; such, for instance, as a trade-union paper. But what would happen if a paper were to print ideas which were critical of the basic policies and beliefs of

ER in discussion at the United Nations in 1947. At the left, John Foster Dulles; in the center, next to ER, Secretary of State George Marshall; at the right, Vermont Senator Warren Austin, head of the US delegation to the UN.

the communist government? I am sure some good reason would be found for abolishing the paper. . . .

What are the differences, for instance, between trade unions in the totalitarian states and in the democracies? In the totalitarian state a trade union is an instrument used by the government to enforce duties, not to assert rights. Propaganda material which the government desires the workers to have is furnished by the trade unions to be circulated to their members.

Our trade unions, on the other hand, are solely the instrument of the workers themselves. They represent the workers in their relations with the government and with management and they are free to develop their own opinions without government help or interference. The concepts of our trade unions and those in totalitarian countries are drastically different. There is little mutual understanding. . . .

I have great sympathy with the Russian people. They love their country and have always defended it valiantly against invaders. They have been through a period of revolution, as a result of which they were for a time cut off from outside contact. They have not lost their resulting suspicion of other countries and the great difficulty is today that their government encourages this suspicion and seems to believe that force alone will bring them respect.

We, in the democracies, believe in a kind of international respect and action which is reciprocal. We do not think others should treat us differently from the way they wish to be treated. It is interference in other countries that especially stirs up antagonism against the Soviet government. If it wishes to feel secure in developing its economic and political theories within its territory, then it should grant to others that same security. We believe in the freedom of people to make their own mistakes. We do not interfere with them and they should not interfere with others.

Speech, 1948

PRESENTING THE DECLARATION TO THE GENERAL ASSEMBLY

Guided into existence by ER, the Universal Declaration of Human Rights represents a prime achievement of her six-year UN term.

In giving our approval to the Declaration today, it is of primary importance that we keep clearly in mind the basic character of the document. It is not a treaty; it is not an international agreement. It is not and does not purport to be a statement of law or of legal obligation. It is a declaration of basic principles of human rights and freedoms, to be stamped with the approval of the General Assembly by formal vote of its members, and to serve as a common standard of achievement for all people of all nations.

We stand today at the threshold of a great event both in the life of the United Nations and in the life of mankind, that is the approval by the General Assembly of the Universal Declaration of Human Rights. . . . This Declaration may well become the international Magna Carta of all men everywhere. We hope its proclamation by the General Assembly will be an event comparable to the proc-

The General Assembly approves the Universal Declaration of Human Rights on December 10, 1948.

lamation of the Declaration of the Rights of Man by the French people in 1789, the adoption of the Bill of Rights by the people of the United States, and the adoption of comparable declarations at different times in other countries.

Department of State Bulletin, 1948

TO MAKE DEMOCRACY MEAN WHAT WE SAY IT DOES

We know that the USSR and the communist parties are making promises for communism that sound very attractive to the downtrodden peoples of the world. We know that we should recognize that the fight today is in Asia, in Africa and in the islands of the Pacific among the peoples who have felt that they are looked down upon by the white race. One cannot observe the United Nations in action . . . without realizing that the white race is a minority race in the world, and that there are more peoples believing in other religions than there are Christians.

Our first task in finding ways to get along with the communists is to find ways to make democracy mean what we say it does. And we have to make democracy work in our own country where other peoples can see it function. They can't see inside Russia but here they can see everything that happens, and can see that freedom of information is in itself one of our first advantages.

This country can, and must, show that democracy isn't just a word, but that it means regards for the rights of human beings; that it means that every human being, regardless of race or creed or color, has equal dignity and equal rights; that it means that we care about the kind of freedom which allows people to grow, and allows them to develop their own potentialities and their own interests; that we recognize that democracy, as a basis for government, has to assume certain basic obligations to its citizens.

United Nations World Magazine, 1949

THEY NEVER OFFER
ANYBODY FREEDOM

———

Another thing . . . is that all through the Declaration the value of economic and social rights is emphasized. The USSR delegation fought for those and many of their suggestions are included in those Articles, but they still abstained on the whole of the Declaration. They fought for those economic and social rights because to them these are the really important things. They never offer anybody freedom and I have often wondered whether those who listened to their promises ever noticed that freedom was left out.

The interesting thing is that they are quite safe in doing so because many of the peoples to whom they talk don't know the meaning of freedom as we know it. . . .

Now I am going to read you just one article, because it will explain to you why it was impossible for the USSR to vote in favor of this document [the Universal Declaration of Human Rights], and it will show you the cleavage in thought which somehow, some day, we have to bridge. We are not going to bridge it right away. It is going to take time, but the understanding of it is necessary before we can begin to decide how we can work.

The article is one on movement. It reads:

> Everyone has the right to freedom of movement and residence within the borders of each State. Everyone has the right to leave any country, including his own, and to return to his country.

The amendment they wanted to [use instead of] that was:

> Everyone has the right to leave any country, including his own, and to return to his country according to the laws of his country.

That would have meant that the law said you couldn't leave your country without permission of the government.

Naturally in discussion it was brought out that many countries have regulations. I have to pay my income tax; I have to take the little piece of paper from my doctor saying when I was vaccinated. I must have been vaccinated within the last three years or I can't come back. But when that is done, I can leave and come back, and I can move anywhere within my own country and I can do it when I wish, and I can settle where I wish.

After the defeat of the amendment, I went over to talk to Mr. [Alexei] Pavlov [USSR delegate to the UN], and I said: "Mr. Pavlov," (I should say that he speaks French very well), "do you see no difference between the regulations which my country puts on freedom of movement, and the regulations of the USSR which forbid a citizen to leave without permission from his government, and to give no permission?" He looked at me and he said: "All regulations just the same." Now, that is a very interesting thing because that is a good illustration of where we think differently.

Now, I don't expect that gulf to be bridged for a long while. But I do feel that we can reach the point where we can live in the same world, but I think the only way we will reach it is if we show in the democracies that our beliefs are as strong; that we intend to crusade just as much as they do, and that we are as determined that all human beings shall eventually have the rights and freedoms set forth in this document, and that we are not going to be intimidated; neither are we going to be despondent.

USSR delegate Alexei Pavlov, left, next to delegate Charles Malik of Lebanon, ER's ally. Pavlov tried ER's patience at committee meetings. The Soviet delegates "could be very thorough," she wrote, at "seeking out American weakness or in distorting the picture of our country by citing some isolated fact to support their propaganda."

I think they count on wearing out our patience, on making us feel that it is hopeless, on getting us discouraged to the point where we will give up and decide that there is no way to live in the same world. The day we do that we have lost, and I hope, therefore, that we will concentrate on making our own selves, our own communities, our own country, the real democracy that we have given lip service to for so many years. [*Applause*] And in doing that, that we will be the spearhead and the spiritual and moral leader of all the other democracies that really want to see human rights and human freedoms make the foundation of a just and peaceful world. [*Applause*]

Phi Beta Kappan, 1949

EXCERPT FROM LETTER
TO PRESIDENT TRUMAN

———

[December 14, 1950]

The race question has become a very vital one since much of the feeling is that of the colored race against the white race. We are classed with the Colonial Powers [as] having exploited them because our businessmen in the past have exploited them, so we have no better standing than the United Kingdom or any other Colonial Power. I think we have to reckon with this in our whole world outlook because we will need friends badly and it is surprising how few we have in spite of all we have done for other peoples in the past.

I realize I sound like Cassandra, but I think this situation should be better understood by our people as a whole and we should be bending every effort to correcting it as soon as possible.

ER Papers, 1950

REPLY TO CHARGES
AGAINST THE US

T his statement is a reply to the views expressed by Byelorussia [Belarus], Czechoslovakia, Poland, the Ukraine, and the USSR concerning the United States in this Committee. My observations in this statement accordingly relate to these five countries.

I am interested that these five countries place so much stress on the unity of the provisions of the Universal Declaration of Human Rights in our debates here. In 1948 those five countries did not vote for the Declaration. At that time they were critical of it. Now they cite it for their own purposes. They seem to praise the Declaration one time and minimize its importance another time, so that I must question the sincerity of their reliance on the Declaration at this point. . . .

The speakers from these five countries insist over and over again that a condition of perfection exists in their countries. It always seems to me when things are so absolutely perfect that it would almost shine out and you would not have to express it so frequently.

I can only say that I wish it were possible for all of us to be allowed to go to the Soviet Union, for example, to see for ourselves the actual conditions which exist there. It would be very helpful if even some impartial observers were allowed to report to us on the actual conditions existing there.

Now let me turn to the charge made by some of the delegates of these five countries that the United States is disregarding the interests of the Negroes in our country. Unfortunately there are instances of American Negroes being victims of unreasoning racial prejudice in my country. However, we do not condone these acts in the United States. We do everything possible to overcome and eliminate such discrimination and racial prejudice as may still exist.

Racial discrimination in my country is irreconcilable with the fundamental principles of humanity and justice which are embodied in our Bill of Rights.

Affirmative steps are continually being taken to combat racial discrimination. Recently the president of the United States [Harry S Truman] issued an executive order to ensure protection against racial discrimination in employment under government contracts.

The president has on several occasions established advisory commissions to provide evaluations of the progress being made in the United States. The recommendations of these commissions have served to spur further action to obtain the equality we are seeking in my country. . . . Some of the recommendations and reports of those commissions were quoted here [at the UN] which show that we do not hide anything that is wrong.

Acts of prejudice and discrimination by private individuals or groups in my country are more than merely deplored by the government and by the vast majority of the people of the United States. Not only through the laws but also by the process of education and in many other ways, efforts are constantly being made to eliminate racial discrimination. It is the official policy of the US government, as expressed on many occasions by President Truman, that the remaining imperfections in our practice of democracy, which result from the conduct of small groups of our people, must be corrected as soon as possible.

Increased activity in the political life of our country has been characteristic of Negro Americans. They have become a vital factor in the life of our local, state, and national government. A reflection of this is seen in the number of Negroes holding government civil service appointments. In 1938 there were 80,000 Negroes holding such appointments; this number has increased to 270,000. Not only has there been an increase in the number of such appointments,

Eleanor Roosevelt with lawyer and judge Edith S. Sampson, the first African American US delegate to the United Nations, who served from 1950 to 1953. Like ER, Sampson was an appointee of President Truman.

but also they are constantly assuming more and more responsible positions in the government.

Negroes in the United States are voting in increasing numbers in all sections of our country.

It was suggested here that in certain places they were still having difficulty under the poll-tax laws. These laws are rapidly being changed and in many parts of the country where it was not possible it is now possible for Negro citizens to vote.

In addition, the years from 1940 to the present have seen the election of Negro citizens to a number of important local, state, and national offices.

At the same time I wish to point out we do not claim to have reached perfection. We feel that our recognition of how much more yet remains to be done is a source of strength to us because it serves as a stimulant to press ahead with our task in this respect.

It so happens that the very countries which are criticizing the United States in this Committee are not themselves progressing in the fields of human rights and fundamental freedoms in their own countries. That may be only because of the difficulty of communication, but it seems to us that there is a great silence among the people of those countries. It is the silence of a people shut up behind an Iron Curtain where human rights and life are being stifled.

Department of State Bulletin, 1952

THESE SAME OLD, STALE CHARGES

———

This is the seventh year in which I have heard these same old, stale charges hurled against the United States. On several previous occasions I have replied to these charges, point by point, with the true facts. But, after all, no one ever expects replies to Soviet slanders to have any effect whatsoever on their representatives. Each year I present the facts about the situation in the United States; and then the next year these representatives offer up the same old distortions of fact.

. . . I should like merely to summarize what I have said on six previous occasions, knowing full well it will not prevent this group of representatives from saying the whole thing all over again next year.

First, the US government and the American people do not want another world war; they are not preparing for another world war; they are doing, and will do, everything in their power to maintain international peace and security and to resist aggression.

Second, social conditions in the United States are not perfect and the standard of living of large numbers of the American people are far from satisfactory. It does not require this annual shower of crocodile tears by this group of representatives to make me aware of the defects in American life. I am fully aware of these defects, for I have spent the better part of my life fighting to help correct them.

Third, despite the fact that the standards of health, education, social welfare, housing, and race relations are not so high in the United States as we Americans would desire, they are much higher than the distinguished delegate of the Soviet Union and her colleagues would lead the Committee to believe. . . .

Fourth, despite all the imperfections in our American society and despite all I have heard about the perfect paradise that exists in the Soviet Union, Poland, Byelorussia [Belarus], and in certain other countries—I am sure every person with decent instincts still prefers to live in imperfect freedom than in a propaganda paradise without freedom. For the last twenty years in this country, the Republican Party, a majority of our newspapers, and millions of our citizens have been criticizing and denouncing the government; and for the next four years, the Democratic Party, many of our newspapers, and millions of our citizens will be criticizing and denouncing the new administration. Yet not one Republican politician or diplomat has been imprisoned or hanged for his opposition to the government in power. Not one newspaper has been suppressed. Not one citizen has been shipped off to a slave-labor camp. Nor will anything of this kind happen in the next four years to any American who happens to disagree with the Republican administration.

In conclusion, Mr. Chairman, we in the United States know better than these critics the many things that are lacking in our country. We have done much in the past, and we are doing much today, to correct these injustices and these low standards. We would be doing even more today if we were not compelled by the aggression in Korea and by the threat of aggression elsewhere to help strengthen the free world and to preserve the peace.

Department of State Bulletin, 1953

ER listening to a session at the United Nations in 1950.

ON THE POLITICAL RIGHTS
OF WOMEN

A s most of you know, the subject of this convention [a state-ment of women's rights to vote, to be eligible for office, and to hold public office, "all on equal terms with men, without dis-crimination"]—equal suffrage for women—is very close to my heart. I believe in active citizenship, for men and women equally, as a simple matter of right and justice. I believe we will have better government in all of our countries when men and women discuss public issues together and make their decisions on the basis of their differing areas of experience and their common concern for the welfare of their families and their world.

In the United States, and in most countries today, women have equal suffrage. Some may feel that for that reason this convention is of little importance to them. I do not agree with this view. It is true, of course, that the first objective of this convention is to encourage equal political rights for women in all countries. But its significance reaches far deeper into the real issue of whether in fact women are recognized fully in setting the policies of our governments.

While it is true that women in forty-five of our sixty member nations vote on the same terms as men, and in seven more already have partial voting rights, too often the great decisions are originated and given form in bodies made up wholly of men, or so completely dominated by them that whatever of special value women have to offer is shunted aside without expression. Even in countries where for many years women have voted and been eligible for public office, there are still too few women serving in positions of real leadership. I am not talking now in terms of paper parliaments and honorary appointments. Neither am I talking about any such artificial balance as would be implied in a 50-50, or a 40-60 division of public offices. What I am talking about is whether women are sharing in the direction of the policy making in their countries; whether they have opportunities to serve as chairmen of important committees and as cabinet ministers and delegates to the United Nations.

We are moving forward in my country in this regard, for we have had women in all these posts, but not enough of them, and they do not always have a full voice in consultation. I do not expect that there will ever be as many women political leaders as men, for most women are needed in their homes while their children are small and have fewer years in which to gain public recognition. But, if we are honest with ourselves, we know that all countries have a long way to go on these matters. I believe it is this situation, far more than the continual denial of equal suffrage in a few countries, which has spurred interest in this convention and brought it before our Committee today. This situation cannot be changed entirely by law, but it can be changed by determination and conviction. I hope we will use this discussion to deepen these convictions in ourselves. . . .

A question does arise, however, as to whether the term "public office" is intended to include military service. My delegation believes it is not so intended. Almost all countries make some distinctions in the kinds of military duty they regard as suitable for women. The most usual distinction, and a natural and proper one, is that women are not used as combat troops and are not appointed to certain posts which might involve the direction of combat operations. . . .

This convention on political rights of women is not in itself an answer to the problems of modern government. But it points up, I believe in useful ways, how governments can expand their resources by taking full advantage of the energy and experience of their women citizens.

Department of State Bulletin, 1953

DEFENDING RIGHTS IN THE US FROM ATTACK

I want first to say just a little about the statements which the distinguished delegate of the Soviet Union and several of her colleagues have made on the situation of women in the United States. . . .

We were struck, for instance, with the distinction the distinguished delegate of Byelorussia [Belarus] made Saturday afternoon. She said, I believe, that one of the great values in the provision of crèches and nursery schools in the Soviet Union was that it permitted a woman to fulfill her role as mother and at the same time share in the public life of her country. We do not think of the "role of mother" in our country as separating women or denying women a full share in our public life. We feel rather that it is the family which is the center for men and women alike, and for their children, and we try to make it possible for the father of the family to earn enough so that the woman can stay home and care for their children if she wishes. At the same time, as you all know, American women participate fully in all professions and public activities, and more than half our employed women are married women. . . .

The distinguished representatives of Czechoslovakia and the Soviet countries have spoken also of the situation of Negro voters in the United States. As you know, great progress has been made in recent years in ensuring Negro voters full security in casting their votes. Many more Negroes voted in this past election than ever before in our Southern states as well as Northern. The figures these delegations quoted seemed to be somewhat out of date in this regard. It was implied that the difficulty Negro women have experienced in regard to suffrage is connected with the existence

The slogan on the bottom of the poster reads: "Hail the Equality of Soviet Women." The smaller type on top states: "Women have the right to vote and be elected equally with men, section 137 of the Constitution of the USSR."

of a poll tax in some of our Southern states. The poll tax is a per capita tax, once usual in many countries, but it is now being replaced almost everywhere by other forms of taxation. It now exists in only five of our states. It applies equally to all people, whites as well as Negroes. However, since it applies equally to men and women, I do not see how any provision on the poll tax could be included in this convention without its resulting in discrimination against men.

I have been glad to hear that Soviet women hold many public offices and participate widely in public life. I have been glad to note this year that the Soviet Union, the Ukraine, and Byelorussia have included women on their delegations to the General Assembly. There have been very few women on these delegations in the past—in fact, I do not recall any since the first General Assembly in 1946. I hope that this convention may lead to greater participation by women in the true organs of power in the Soviet Union, such as the Presidium and the Secretariat of the Central Committee of the Communist Party, in which I understand no women are now included. The experience women have achieved in the more formal and subsidiary bodies throughout the Soviet Union should entitle them to recognition also in bodies which determine the major policies of their government. . . .

I have not answered certain charges against the United States as to the economic situation of women—Negro women especially—because this is a convention on political rights, and I have not wanted to take the time of this Committee for irrelevant matters. [The Convention on the Political Rights of Women was adopted on March 31, 1953.]

Department of State Bulletin, 1953

Children at the UN International Nursery School in New York in 1950
examine a poster on the Universal Declaration of Human Rights.

WHERE DO
HUMAN RIGHTS BEGIN?

———

Where, after all, do universal human rights begin? In small places, close to home—so close and so small they cannot be seen on any maps of the world. Yet they *are* the world of the individual persons; the neighborhood he lives in; the school or college he attends; the factory, farm, or office where he works. Such are the places where every man, woman, and child seeks equal justice, equal opportunity, equal dignity without discrimination. Unless these rights have meaning there, they can have little meaning anywhere. Without concerned citizen action to uphold them close to home, we shall look in vain for progress in the larger world.

ER Papers, 1958

CHAPTER 7

Postwar Politics

ER discusses the United Nations with Democrats in Philadelphia
in December 1953.

FDR's death in 1945 might have reduced Eleanor Roosevelt's impact on public life; instead the reverse occurred. ER's importance surged. Her years at the UN from 1946 to 1953 thrust her into the arena of Cold War politics. Her leadership in human rights, her support for world peace, and her grasp of international affairs made her an admired player on the world stage. Facing the intransigence of Soviet delegates bolstered her stance as an anti-communist. Free of her obligation to serve the interests of successive FDR administrations, a commitment that had both empowered and constrained her, she forged an independent role in Democratic politics. From the start of her UN career until her death in 1962, ER grew exponentially as a diplomat, politician, power broker, and beacon of postwar liberalism.

ER declined to run for political office, although, pressed to do so, she clearly weighed the possibility. Instead she wielded influence as a leader of liberal Democrats. During the 1948 presidential campaign, ER rejected her old friend, one-time secretary of agriculture and former vice president Henry A. Wallace, who, she claimed, lacked foreign policy experience, underrated USSR leaders, and chose feeble advisers ("people as inept politically as he is himself"). A critic of President Truman as well, ER supported the president in 1948 only with reluctance and at the last minute. After the election (as before), she directed at Truman a slew of commentary, advice, and complaint. She pressed the president to step up support for civil rights and to endorse permanent fair employment practices legislation; she also challenged policies she disliked, such as Truman's executive order to impose loyalty tests on federal employees. Though sometimes privately caustic, Truman remained responsive and deferential. In the 1950s ER traveled widely to promote US interests and boost international cooperation. A supporter of Israel, founded in 1948 and "the only Democratic regime in the whole of the Middle East," she urged funding to resettle Arab refugees in Arab nations. An early foe of Senator Joseph McCarthy's anti-communist crusade, "a bad day for democracy," ER strongly backed Americans for Democratic Action, founded by leading liberals in 1947, a bastion of the anti-communist left. Not least, she admired and counseled Democratic candidate Adlai Stevenson in his two bids for the presidency in 1952 and 1956.

Support for civil rights and the labor movement most explicitly defined ER's brand of liberalism. A board member of the NAACP and CORE, ER endorsed integration of the armed forces in the 1940s, school integration in the 1950s, and freedom riders in the early 1960s. Race discrimination in the US, ER argued, undercut America's preeminence in the world. She denounced the Taft-Hartley Act of 1947 and right-to-work laws; gave a keynote speech at the first AFL-CIO convention in 1955, when the two labor federations merged; and, spurred by A. Philip Randolph, joined the National Farm Labor Advisory Committee, which sought labor standards for migrant workers. In her last years, ER seized the chance to serve some of the causes that had shaped her career. She testified to Congress in 1959 on the needs of migrant labor; voiced support in 1961 for young civil rights workers just starting sit-ins to protest segregation; and finally, at the end of her career, served as chair of John F. Kennedy's Presidential Commission on the Status of Women. The commission report of 1963, in retrospect, marked a step toward the women's movement of the next decade. Whenever possible, ER explained her postwar policies as what FDR would have wanted. More accurately, she brought her own liberal agenda to a new generation and built a groundwork for reform movements of the years ahead.

WHY I DO NOT CHOOSE TO RUN

There has been some curiosity as to why I am not knocking at the door of the members of my political party, who make up the slates for candidates for office, in order to obtain a nomination for some elective office.

At first I was surprised that anyone should think that I would want to run for office, or that I was fitted to hold office. Then I realized that some people felt that I must have learned something from my husband in all the years that he was in public life! They also knew that I had stressed the fact that women should accept responsibility as citizens.

I heard that I was being offered the nomination for governor or for the United States Senate in my own state, and even for vice president. And some particularly humorous souls wrote in and suggested that I run as the first woman president of the United States!

The simple truth is that I have had my fill of public life of the more or less stereotyped kind. I do believe that every citizen, as long as he is alive and able to work, has an obligation to work on public questions and that he should choose the kind of work he is best fitted to do.

Therefore, when I was offered an opportunity to serve on the United Nations organization, I accepted it. I did this, not because I really wanted to go to London last January, but because it seemed as though I might be able to use the experiences of a lifetime and make them valuable to my nation and to the world at this particular time. I knew, of course, how much my husband hoped that out of the war, an organization for peace would really develop.

It was not just to further my husband's hopes, however, that I agreed to serve in this particular way. It was rather that I myself had always believed that women might have a better chance to bring about the understanding necessary to prevent wars if they could serve in sufficient number in these international bodies.

The plain truth, I am afraid, is that in declining to consider running for the various public offices which have been suggested to me, I am influenced by the thought that no woman has, as yet, been able to build up and hold sufficient backing to carry through a program. Men and women both are not yet enough accustomed to following a woman and looking to her for leadership. If I were young enough it might be an interesting challenge, and we have some women in Congress who may carry on this fight.

However, I am already an elderly woman and I would have to start in whatever office I might run for as a junior with no weight of experience in holding office behind me. It seems to me that fairly young men and women should start holding minor offices and work up to the important ones, developing qualifications for holding these offices as they work.

I have been an onlooker in the field of politics. In some ways I hope I have occasionally been a help, but always by doing things which I was particularly fitted by my own background and experience to do. My husband was skilled in using people and, even though I was his wife, I think he used me in his career as he used other people. I am quite sure that Louis Howe, who was one of the most astute politicians as well as one of the most devoted of friends, trained me and used me for the things which he thought I could do well, but always in connection with my husband's career.

In the last years of his life, Louis Howe used to ask me if I had any ambitions to hold political office myself. I think he finally became convinced that though I understood the worst and the best of politics and statesmanship, I had absolutely no desire to participate in it.

For many years of my life I realized that what my husband was attempting to do was far more important than anything which I could possibly accomplish; and therefore I never said anything, or wrote anything, without first balancing it against the objectives which I thought he was working for at the time. We did not always agree as to methods, but our ultimate objectives were fortunately very much the same.

Never in all the years can I remember his asking me not to say or to write anything, even though we occasionally argued very vehemently and sometimes held diametrically opposite points of view on things of the moment.

I think my husband probably often used me as a sounding board, knowing that my reactions would be the reactions of the average man and woman in the street.

My husband taught me that one cannot follow blindly any line which one lays down in advance because circumstances will modify one's thinking and one's actions. And in the last year since his death I have felt sure that our objectives would remain very much the same. But I have known that I was free and under compulsion to say and to do the things which I, as an individual, believed on the questions of the day. In a way it has lifted a considerable weight from my shoulders, feeling that now, when I speak, no one will attribute my thoughts to someone holding an important office and whose work may be hurt and not helped thereby. If people do not like what I say nowadays, they can blame me, but it will hurt no one else's plans or policies.

There is a freedom in being responsible only to yourself which I would now find it hard to surrender in taking a party office. I believe that the Democratic Party, at least the progressive part of the Democratic Party, represents the only safe way we have of moving forward in this country. I believe that the liberal-minded Democrats hold to the only international policy which can bring us a peaceful world. . . .

Many people will think that these are all very inadequate answers and that when you are told that you might be useful, you should accept the judgment of others and go to work. All I can say in reply is that during a long life I have always done what, for one reason or another, was the thing which was incumbent upon me to do without any consideration as to whether I wished to do it or not. That no longer seems to be a necessity, and for my few remaining years I hope to be free!

Look, 1946

THE TAFT-HARTLEY BILL
IS A BAD BILL

New York, Monday—I suppose it is impossible for any congressional bill to be put into language which the people can understand! It will be difficult for the average worker to understand the legal language of the Taft-Hartley labor bill passed by Congress last week.

In many ways I think labor leaders have themselves to blame for some of their present difficulties—John L. Lewis [president of the United Mine Workers of America and former president of the CIO, 1938–1940] chief among them, because the people as a whole have come to dread what he can do to our economy. And there are certain union rules which irk the people and which I do not think really help organized labor. These regulations have made the relations between the public and the unions increasingly unsympathetic, and should have been studied and corrected long ago. . . .

The Congress of Industrial Organizations should have got rid of communist leaders wherever they existed. The people of this country are more than willing to try to work with the Russians if they recognize on the part of the Russians a willingness to work side by side with other forms of governments and ways of life. However, the constant activity of American communists, who evidently get their financial support as well as their political direction from Russia, creates suspicion and antagonism here and in some other countries as well.

If the Russian government still hopes for world revolution brought about by representatives in other countries guided from Russia, it cannot be honest in trying to work cooperatively with other governments as they now exist. I am more than willing to believe that circumstances may modify the way of life and the forms of existing governments in many countries in the years to come, but the changes must come from the free will of the people, not from infiltration of ideas through the influence of outside governments. This is why union leaders known to be communists should not have been allowed in our labor movement. . . .

Nevertheless, the Taft-Hartley bill is a bad bill, even in its modified form. I think it will make the work of the National Labor Relations Board practically impossible, and it opens a wide field of labor activities to federal injunctions. I see nothing gained by taking the Conciliation Service [the office designed to reconcile sides in a labor dispute] out of the Department of Labor. It seems to me that this bill is weighted in favor of the employer. For instance, the bill requires the NLRB to obtain federal injunctions against certain union practices, but there is no provision that the board obtain injunctions against employer practices.

I have not room here to go into this bill in detail, but analyses of it are available and people should study it. I was in complete accord with the labor-reform suggestions made in the president's message, but this bill goes so far beyond that and is so weighted in favor of the employer that I feel that, if it becomes law, it will affect adversely the lives of many people.

"My Day," June 10, 1947

PLAIN TALK ABOUT WALLACE

So Henry Wallace is really going to head a third party and run for president in 1948! What strange things the desire to be president makes men do! He has probably forgotten but I remember his coming to see me in the summer of 1945 in Washington. At that time, I felt very strongly that it would be good for the country if Henry Wallace, whom we all believed in and admired, would leave active politics and become the leader of the independents of the country. Their vote had increased greatly in the years between 1929 and 1945, but they needed leadership and organization. . . .

At that time, Henry Wallace told me he believed it was his duty to stay and work in the Democratic Party. I knew then, as I know now, that he was doing what he thought was right. But he never has been a good politician, he never has been able to gauge public opinion, and he never has picked his advisers wisely.

All of these things might have been less important if he had been a disinterested, nonpolitical leader of liberal thought, but as a leader of a third party he will accomplish nothing. He will merely destroy the very things he wishes to achieve. . . .

I read with great care Henry A. Wallace's speech in Chicago Monday. Affirmatively, he stands for "a positive peace program of abundance and security, not scarcity and war. We can prevent depression and war if we only organize for peace in the same comprehensive way we organize for war."

There is no country in the world where the people would not agree they wished to organize for peace and abundance and security. But in this speech Mr. Wallace oversimplified the problems that face us today. . . .

To begin with, let us take the political situation which a third party faces. No one in this country wants a third party as much as the communists do. All over the world they are working for confusion because that is the way to create economic chaos and political weakness, and this is the one hope of defeating democracy in the world and proving that communism is the only thing people can turn to.

The American communists will be the nucleus of Mr. Wallace's third party. I know all the old arguments in favor of working with people who want the same objectives as you do. But I have worked rather more steadily and closely with the representatives of the USSR than has Mr. Wallace. I like all those I know and I hope we can get on with them in a peaceful world, but I know that our only approach is an economic approach . . . they understand strength, not weakness. . . .

A totalitarian government, whether it is fascist or communist, has certain earmarks. Secret police is one of them. Another is benefits to the people but no freedom. We live, in fact, in a much more complicated world than Mr. Wallace seems to understand. . . .

Oh, Mr. Wallace, if you were president you would not have such pat sentences to offer us! You would find it harder to act constructively than you suggest in your speeches!

Democratic Digest, 1948

ER preferred Henry Wallace to Harry Truman as FDR's running mate in 1944, but the Democratic Party favored Truman. Here, ER greets Wallace at a celebratory event in January 1945. By 1948, ER had changed her stance. When Wallace ran for president on the Progressive Party ticket that year, ER denied him her support; late in the campaign, with reluctance, she finally endorsed Truman.

After becoming president in 1945, Truman deftly handled ER's continuous barrage of advice, argument, and critique; they often disagreed. Truman's loyalty program, an executive order of March 21, 1947, required investigation of and loyalty oaths by federal employees. Designed to rebut charges that government offices employed communists, the policy drew criticism from civil libertarian ER.

ON LOYALTY TESTS

As a liberal, I don't like loyalty tests at all. I have a feeling that it's much more important for us to find out why we believe in democracy and really to know why we believe in it, and to put as much into it as the USSR puts into its Communism, because I have always found that you get a great deal more out of the things you can be positive about. I don't think we should have in the government people whose loyalty we really question handling documents which should be secret documents. I think that would be terrible. But, on the other hand it doesn't seem to me quite democratic to brand people as disloyal before you give them a chance to bring witnesses and answer their accusers. And so with all the feeling I have that we must not have disloyalty, I am also torn as to whether we really are building up our democracy and doing the positive things we ought to be doing, or whether we're just letting our democracy down.

The Christian Register, 1948

TO AMERICANS
FOR DEMOCRATIC ACTION

———

There's one thing that always frightens me, and that is that our communist representatives in the United Nations never talk about liberty. They never mention it. . . . But we must think about liberty because that is really one of the basic reasons why we prefer democracy to communism.

And somehow we must keep ourselves free from fear and suspicion of each other. . . . I sit with people who are representatives of communist countries, and to sit with them is a lesson in what fear can do. Fear can take away from you all the courage to be an individual. You become a mouthpiece for the ideas that you have been told you must give forth. I have no feeling of real antagonism toward these representatives because, poor things, they can do no other. They must do that; their lives depend on it.

Now it seems to me that the ADA [Americans for Democratic Action] is an organization that has thinking people in it. And we must preserve the right to think and to differ in the United States. We must be able to disagree with people and to consider new ideas and not to be afraid. The day that I am afraid to sit down in a room with people that I do not know because perhaps five years from now someone will say: "You sat in the room and five people were communists, you are a communist"—that day will be a bad day. It will be a bad day for democracy.

So I am grateful that the ADA prods us to think, that it has an opportunity to bring before us the ideas that seem important, that it also has the opportunity of backing people in elections who promise to be good public servants. . . . [W]e must come together, and consult together, and get other people to help us where we need help. . . . There must be no one who fights the battle of good government, of freedom of thought, of real democracy, with the sense of doing it alone. That is the value of ADA. You do not have to be alone.

The Congressional Record, 1950

ER and Minnesota senator Hubert Humphrey, left, view an Americans for Democratic Action award presented to former Democratic candidate Adlai Stevenson in 1960. Founded in 1947, ADA provided a forum for liberals and a voice on the anti-communist left. ER's close friend, labor leader Walter Reuther, was one of its founders, as were Humphrey, economist John Kenneth Galbraith, and historian Arthur Schlesinger, Jr.

ON A PROPOSED EQUAL
RIGHTS AMENDMENT

———

New York, Tuesday—Year by year various women's groups in the United States have been making efforts to induce the Congress to pass an amendment to the Constitution declaring that in every way men and women shall be equal. For a long time I felt that this proposed amendment was completely foolish.

Men and women can be equal but they cannot be identical. They always will have different functions, and even though they do the same things they often will do them differently. That is the real value of having men and women working together. Just as you need a father and a mother in the family, you need men and women citizens to get the best results in the government.

While women in industry were not very well organized, it seemed to me unwise to pass an amendment that might remove some of them from protective laws passed for their benefit. Today, however, women can be as well organized as men and are certainly able to fight for their rights.

I still think that in our country we really might have achieved more if we had determined in every state to remove such laws from the statute books as placed any disabilities on women. It is usually the state laws that really affect their daily lives.

Nevertheless I can see that perhaps it does add a little to the position of women to be declared equal before the law and equal politically and in whatever work a woman chooses to undertake.

This position is upheld by the resolutions passed during the last meeting of the United Nations Commission on the Status of Women. This group adopted a draft convention on political rights for women. . . . [I]t should bring about great changes throughout the world.

There are many parts of the world where women are not entitled to vote or to hold public office under the same conditions as men. It is quite possible, of course, that these conditions will remain as many states will not ratify this covenant at once. Nevertheless, the knowledge that there is such a covenant may well be used by women as a lever to move forward wherever they feel oppressed. . . .

There is one thing to remember, however, and that is that when you have put things on paper you haven't actually accomplished anything. The people have to accept changes, and when you are changing age-old customs this is sometimes difficult of accomplishment. In a police state an edict may be enforced, but under other forms of government the people have to be persuaded and convinced and that takes time and education. So, even if governments think over these resolutions seriously, it will be the people who will have to bring about these changes.

It is well to get started, however, and I am happy that this consideration is being given to the conditions and opportunities of women throughout the world.

· · · · ·

I was a little shocked the other day to read in a column . . . an account of some of the resolutions passed by the National Woman's Party in their three-day convention in Washington.

[The column] reports that they reaffirmed their complete "devotion" to the task of "freeing American women from the position of chattels."

I don't think many American women will identify themselves in that category. . . .

An equal rights amendment, to which these dear ladies of the National Woman's Party have been devoting themselves these past several years, can be passed or not be passed without much good or much harm being done. I think we have reached a point where women are well enough organized in industry so that they can protect themselves. The arguments that I have felt valid for many years—that women needed protection in industry—seem to me no longer very important.

"My Day," May 25, 1951 and June 7, 1951

ISRAEL REMAINS
A BASTION OF DEMOCRACY

[LETTER OF JUNE 15, 1951,
TO SAMUEL SCHNEIDERMAN,
ISRAELI JOURNALIST]

Dear Mr. Schneiderman,

In answer to your telegram, I am very anxious to clear up any confusion which may have resulted from the discussion on my television program devoted to peace in the Middle East. . . .

Those people who have watched the rise of Israel since 1948 cannot but be impressed with the magnificent way in which the people of Israel have made immense sacrifices to make room for the hundreds of thousands of Jewish immigrants from all over the world. Despite the fact that Israel fought a bitter war to maintain its independence and that at best its resources at that time were incapable of maintaining the then-existing population, the doors of Israel were thrown wide to needy Jews from dozens of countries. An outstanding achievement was the emptying of Displaced Persons camps in Germany and Austria, thus giving to these unfortunate people a home and a freedom that had for so long been denied to them.

At first opposed to Zionism, the movement to create a Jewish state, ER changed her mind in 1947, while representing the US at the UN. She supported Israel with enthusiasm from its start in 1948 for the rest of her life. Here, in 1955, with youngsters, at a French camp for prospective Jewish immigrants to Israel.

These people might even today be an international charge, with our government bearing the major share of their upkeep. In addition, Jews in countries where they had been discriminated against and allowed the privilege only of second- or third-class citizens, found in Israel a country that gave a new meaning to life and a new opportunity to develop as normal and constructive human beings.

The Jewish community of the United States has made notable voluntary contributions through the United Jewish Appeal to assist in the transfer of the Jewish refugees and immigrants from Europe and Asia to Israel. I am proud to have been chosen as chairman for the month of June for the New York campaign of the United Jewish Appeal. . . .

I do not believe that there is another chapter in modern history that can compare to this achievement in Israel. It has within three years established the only democratic regime in the whole of the

Middle East, serving as an example to all the other countries in the area. In this context, and since we are trying as a government to aid the Arab nations with their problems, I think it is important that the United States give some recognition in the form of a grant to the State of Israel to help that new democracy achieve economic stability and thus strengthen its determined resolve to protect liberty and democracy in the Middle East against aggression. The bill now before Congress asking for $150,000,000 has just come to my attention and is one that will assist in ensuring that Israel remains a bastion of democracy and will continue to offer hope and freedom for those Jews who today find themselves under intolerable conditions. I hope in time a comprehensive plan covering the whole Middle Eastern area may be worked with the cooperation of all those countries, but peace must come about first.

In Israel in 1955, with her secretary Maureen Corr, second from left, and friend Trude Lash, right. "I think Franklin would have found Israel a rather exhilarating spot," ER wrote to former president Truman on March 26, 1955.

ER visits an Arab community in El Gabya, Israel, in 1959.

The problems of refugees is one in which I have been interested for a long time. I know that Israel is prepared to make a generous payment toward the resettlement of the Arab refugees in Arab countries within the framework of a general peace treaty. I feel and I know my government feels a responsibility to all the poor people who have lost their homes through the misfortunes of war. I hope the Arabs will be willing soon to sit down with Israel and work out peace treaties so that all these problems of human suffering can be solved and peace once more restored to the Middle East.

Very sincerely yours
[ER]

ER Papers, 1951

ON SENATOR McCARTHY

Hyde Park, Thursday—I have a rather interesting letter from a lady today and I would like to answer it in my column. She says: "In view of your past record of sponsoring organizations with communist leanings, some of which even booed your late husband, I cannot conceive of your making a speech against a red-blooded American like Senator McCarthy. He has earnestly tried to free our government of communists. What have you done in that line?"

First, I would like to point out that I have not yet made a speech against Senator McCarthy.

The only organization I ever sponsored which had any degree of communist control was the American Youth Congress of the early thirties. There was a very good reason for working with those young people and the bulk of the membership was not then, and never was later, communistic.

A group among them were communists then and perhaps may have remained so—that I do not know. But I would like to remind people in general and especially my correspondent that this was a particularly difficult period for young people.

They were coming out of college in great numbers and finding no jobs. Democracy was failing them and many of the most intelligent thought communism would solve their problems.

Sooner or later many of them found out how intolerable communist control was and they became better citizens of our democracy than ever before. They did not inform against their former colleagues, they simply gave up communism and went to work as citizens of our democracy.

They were the more valuable because they knew what was wrong with communism and they understood and cherished the democratic form of government and the democratic way of life.

Back in the thirties, however, these young people—even those who booed the president—needed friends. They were rude, true, but also desperately unhappy and frustrated. It was fortunate that the White House understood this.

My devotion to my country and to democracy is quite as great as that of Senator McCarthy. I do not like his methods or the results of his methods and I would like to say to my correspondent that I think those of us who worked with young people in the thirties did more to save many of them from becoming communists than Senator McCarthy has done for his fellow citizens with all his slurs and accusations.

At the end of the UN's spring session in 1952, ER traveled extensively through South Asia and the Middle East. Here, in Bombay, India, in March 1952.

I know the danger of communism. I know it perhaps better than many other American citizens because for nearly five months of every year for the last six years, I have sat in meetings with the communist representatives of the USSR.

I despise the control they insist on holding over men's minds. And that is why I despise what Senator McCarthy has done, for he would use the same methods of fear to control all thought that is not according to his own pattern—in our free country!

"My Day," August 29, 1952

On a trip to promote democracy in Japan in the spring of 1953, ER met with Emperor Hirohito, government officials, students, teachers, women's associations, and people who had been injured by the US use of the atomic bomb in 1945.

Facing page: ER airmailed the text for a "My Day" column from Morocco in the spring of 1957 to her secretary, Maureen Corr, in New York. The events mentioned here were included in her published column of April 11, 1957.

"IF YOU ASK ME": QUESTIONS ON COMMUNISM, SECURITY, AND CIVIL LIBERTIES

You said recently that a congressional investigation of schools and colleges won't accomplish anything except scare everybody to death. Does this mean you don't think any communists are teaching in our schools? Please explain yourself.

I have no idea how many communists may or may not be teaching in our schools and colleges, but I think the congressional investigation is likely to be much less effective than a careful survey by the heads of school systems and colleges and universities themselves. They are certainly better fitted to do this kind of housecleaning than the members of the Un-American Activities Committee, and they are less likely to create mistrust and suspicion. When a teacher is called to testify before a congressional committee nowadays it has a demoralizing effect on other faculty members and on students. . . .

One of my grandson's professors tells his classes that the Committee on Un-American Activities is ruining our reputation in the rest of the world. First, Mrs. Roosevelt, do you think there's any truth in this? Secondly, should a man be permitted to say such things in the classroom?

Yes, I think this professor's statement is absolutely correct. As for his right to make the statement, if it is proper for an individual to hold opinions it seems to me proper for him to state them in the classroom, as long as they are not directed against the welfare of the country and do not advocate the overthrow of the government by force.

I read recently that even after you knew the American Youth Congress was communist-dominated you went right on entertaining them and being friendly with them. I know you're not a communist,

Mrs. Roosevelt, but would you mind telling me why you did a thing like that?

When the American Youth Congress voted to oppose the United States' stand against Hitler, after the Hitler-Stalin alliance, I wrote them that I could no longer work with a group that had obviously fallen under the spell of communist leadership. I did contribute a small sum of money at that time for work being done for the sharecroppers in Missouri, but the American Youth Congress was not entertained in the White House again.

After Germany declared war on Russia and the Youth Congress decided to back the Allies, they wrote me asking if I would work with them again. I told them no, pointing out that they had lied to me. When I had asked them, one after another, at a meeting in my sitting room in the White House, whether they were pro-Soviet or had any connections with organizations favorable to the Soviets, each one had assured me that he had not.

I still believe that the majority of the young people in the Youth Congress were not communists, though they did fall under the spell of communist leadership and were led to take certain stands that I do not think they later would have endorsed or upheld.

How would you feel about an investigation of communists among the clergy?

I would feel it outrageous.

If you had your choice of a Republican senator to take McCarthy's place as chairman of the Senate Investigating Committee, who would it be?

I would far prefer to see the Senate Investigating Committee done away with, and everything possible done to strengthen the FBI in its functions.

ER visits the Highlander School, an adult education institution that trained labor protesters and other activists, in Tennessee in 1959.

Did the late President Roosevelt ever express to you any suspicion or alarm about communists in the State Department?

I don't remember my husband ever expressing suspicion about people in the State Department. If he were suspicious of anyone he would not have spoken to me but to Secretary [Cordell] Hull.

As for alarms, if my husband thought a situation was dangerous he immediately took the steps he considered necessary. He did not indulge in expressing alarms or fears.

In your opinion what group or groups in the US are putting up the best fight against communism?

Labor, the liberals and all those who understand that communism is fed by misery and despair and are working to prevent that kind of misery and despair from spreading in the world.

If you were asked to testify publicly about a friend who had once been a member of the Communist Party but was now a loyal Amer-

ican, and you knew such testimony would cost him his job, what
would you do?

Ordinarily, if I knew a man had once been a communist I would
not hesitate to say so—and to add that I knew he was now a loyal
citizen. But if I were dealing with such a hysterical situation that
a statement of this kind would cost this man his chance to earn a
living, and if I knew of no overriding reason for giving such testimony, I would refuse to give it.

McCall's, 1953

FOR ADLAI STEVENSON IN 1956

———

I went to the first meeting [of the United Nations] in London to
organize the UN and that is where I first came to know Adlai
Stevenson. . . .

Adlai Stevenson told us about the people in the other delegations.
He really made a study of the people we would deal with, and what
the setup would be and background information. This made all the
difference in our ability to work with the others. I watched Adlai
Stevenson from then on. . . . Some people gain respect and others lose
respect when you are working with them. Adlai Stevenson gained. . . .

I remember after the 1952 elections Adlai Stevenson went on a trip
around the world. I followed him in most places and particularly in
Asia. Always I was told "We like your Mr. Stevenson—he listened to
what we had to say." This taught me a lesson. If you want to learn, it
is a good idea to listen. I discovered that we Americans have a reputation for doing all the talking. If you don't know much about the
people and their background, doing all the talking and not finding
out their ideas is not a wise thing to do. One difficulty, of course,

is that we have become the leaders of the free world and possibly this came without our wanting it and without much preparation, so we need to learn. Adlai Stevenson took his trip to Africa—not only because it was the one place I had not already been as he joking[ly] said—because he had not seen this continent which he realized was one area where our problems would lie in the next few years, and he felt obliged to learn about these people. I like that kind of a mind, and a person must take the trouble to learn what he needs to know if you are going to solve new problems in new ways.

How about things happening at home? There is hardly a domestic problem that doesn't touch on international problems. Civil rights is an example. We must use patience. We can't do everything at once, nor as quickly in every place, but we must move and we must show that we really intend that every citizen shall have equality of opportunity, recognition as a citizen and live without feeling he is not an equal of every other citizen in our democracy. If this doesn't happen and we show that we are not in earnest, it will hurt in our

"I think we were against impossible odds," ER wrote to former president Truman on November 6, 1952, just after Illinois governor Adlai E. Stevenson lost his bid for the presidency. A strong admirer of Stevenson, ER supported his second campaign for president four years later. Here, with Stevenson at the opening of Congress in 1957.

world leadership. We must bear in mind that two-thirds of the world's population is colored, and we are the minority race. We have often exploited the people of other races, but this is not wise. Today they long for freedom in all areas of the world. We are the people who lead in the struggle for freedom and we can't afford to let people see any exploitation here at home. That is not the example of a nation that says everyone is created free and equal!

Speech, 1956

ARGUMENT TO EXTEND
THE MINIMUM WAGE

———

I am very happy to have the opportunity to talk to you gentlemen this morning, because the bill before you (S. 1046) is one about which I have very strong feelings and convictions. I was eighteen years old when I first went for the Consumers League into sweatshops in New York City. (By the way I am speaking to you today for the National Consumers League of which for many, many years I have been a vice-president.) For the first time in my life I saw conditions I would not have believe existed—women and children working in dark, crowded, dirty quarters, toiling, I was told, all day long and way into the night, to earn a few pennies, carding safety pins or making little things of feathers.

These conditions I can never forget. So some twenty years ago, when the Congress passed and my husband signed the Fair Labor Standards Act, I rejoiced. At last we had tackled on a national scale the basic problem of poverty—the non-living wage. The minimum wages established in 1938 were low. . . . But low as they were, they provided a floor below which in those Depression days no worker, covered by the Act, could legally be paid. That was a tremendous step forward and a firm foundation on which to build. . . .

I have always believed that in a democracy it is the obligation of the government to give to its citizens the protection and care they need for the benefit of the individual, the family, and the nation as a whole. Comparatively few workers earning less than $1.25 an hour today belong to labor unions. Therefore, they are in a very poor position to bargain individually with their employers for higher wages. For them the state and the federal governments have an obligation to set a floor below which no employer may go in setting wages. I believe a minimum wage law is a protection for decent businessmen as well, men who recognize the need and wisdom of paying adequate wages, but who must meet the competition of less conscientious employers who use wage cutting as a means of gain. Moreover, our entire economy would benefit if millions of workers at the minimum level

ER at a meeting of the National Advisory Committee on Farm Labor in 1959. Behind ER, labor leader A. Philip Randolph and actress Helen Gahagan Douglas. Seated, on left, next to ER, Dr. Frank Graham, president of the University of North Carolina, and on the right, labor secretary James Mitchell.

The Amalgamated Clothing Workers of America expanded under the leadership of Jacob Potofsky in the 1950s. Students at an ACWA training institute join ER at Val-Kill in 1957.

were enabled by a 25 cent increase in the hourly minimum wage to buy more food, clothing and medical care they so badly need. . . .

I want to say an urgent word for a group of workers which is always left out when social legislation is written. They are the expendables. The ones who are bargained out of a piece of social legislation as the price of getting something else in. I am speaking of farm laborers, including the migratory agricultural workers and their families. Today they compare economically to the workers in the industrial sweatshops of the early 1900s. . . .

I am a member of the National Advisory Committee on Farm Labor, and have had ample opportunity to know of the misery and destitution of farm workers and their families. . . .

The New York Women's Trade Union League, which ER had joined in the 1920s, endured until 1950. NYWTUL alumnae gathered in 1958. Next to ER, at left, front, is her old friend Rose Schneiderman. On the right, economist Isador Lubin, FDR adviser, head of the US Bureau of Labor Statistics from 1933 to 1946, and New York State's industrial commissioner, from 1955 to 1958.

Much needs to be done for these people. They should be covered by unemployment and workmen's compensation laws. The application of the Social Security Act to farm workers should be improved. Better housing, medical care, education for their children should be provided. But the most immediate need is a minimum wage law that will ensure decent wages to these hardworking, neglected American citizens. . . .

I thank you, gentlemen, for this opportunity to talk to you about these serious matters which are before you, and to congratulate you on your efforts to find effective ways to reduce the extent of our social and economic problems.

ER Papers, 1959

ON CORE AND SIT-INS

New York.... The Congress of Racial Equality, on which serve such people as Roger N. Baldwin, Algernon B. Black, Grenville Clark, Martin Luther King and many others, is backing the non-violent movement of students in the South against segregated lunch counters. In Raleigh, N.C., this spread to a variety of stores a few days ago.

The example of these Carolina students will probably be followed by students in other places. Students simply file in and out and stand or sit quietly at the counters. They are not being served and the action is merely a protest against segregation in eating places against which there is no law, though, of course, the owner of the store has the right to refuse to sell to customers if he wishes to do so.

Of course, if stores close, it means loss of money to the owners, and the hope is that in time people will realize that it does no real harm to serve all nationalities without regard to race or color.

Lunch counters should not be so difficult to integrate, since in most places people have grown accustomed to sitting next to people of almost every color. This also holds good for public transportation vehicles in a good many parts of the country now as well.

"My Day," February 18, 1960

ON CIVIL RIGHTS LEGISLATION

New York—It is a good thing that the Senate has finally passed the civil rights bill after an eight-week fight with forty-two Democrats and twenty-nine Republicans in favor. This is only the second civil rights legislation to pass the Senate since the Reconstruction Era. The first civil rights act of 1957 was also a voting rights measure. Already those who want a really fair bill giving the Negroes their full rights are denouncing this bill, and I am quite sure that it will continue to be denounced. But I hope that it is at least a step in the right direction.

All of us in the Democratic Party, I think, owe Senator Johnson a vote of thanks. He has risked repercussions among his Southern colleagues and among his own constituents. He has made it possible for the Democrats to claim equal, if not more, responsibility for the passage of the bill which of course should never have had to be passed—for the right to vote should be something which every citizen of this country enjoys without any question. Since it was necessary to pass the bill, however, we are fortunate to have had a parliamentary leader with the skill of Senator Johnson.

My one fear is of intimidation which I feel sure will be tried to prevent Negro citizens in the South from registering and voting. I hope the attorney general can find ways of protecting the registration and of preventing retaliation when the Negro citizens of the South exercise their constitutional right.

"My Day," April 11, 1960

"IF YOU ASK ME": ON INTEGRATION AND SEGREGATION

[Question from a reader] I don't see why all discrimination against Negroes is blamed on the South. What about the discrimination in housing throughout the North? Don't you think it is just as bad to keep Negroes out of certain communities and certain neighborhoods as it is to keep them out of certain schools?

I have repeatedly said that the North has one essential step to take in complying with the Supreme Court decision. It will, of course, take time, but discrimination in housing must be wiped out and such communities as are completely segregated in our big cities must disappear. The South has many steps to take, and perhaps the most important is permitting Negroes to register and to vote. The drive the communists are making to induce Asian and African peoples to join with them is frequently based on their claim that all people are brothers and that we in the United States do not acknowledge or believe in the International Declaration of Human Rights. The moral impact of this document on the world has been considerable, and we who voted in favor of the resolution accompanying it have an obligation to try to live up to its standards. Both the North and the South must keep moving forward toward equality and justice for all our people.

Let's face it—aren't Negroes, except in schools, segregated in New York? Most of them live in one area by themselves, in Harlem; they have their own newspapers and magazines; they're almost never seen in any "white" restaurants; and they are employed in only the most menial jobs. Where do Northerners get off, talking so much about desegregation?

You are right as far as housing is concerned, although great strides are being made in integration, particularly in government-subsidized housing. However, there is marked progress in integration in many other areas of life. All Negroes are not, any longer, employed in menial jobs. Many move at ease in professional and financial circles, and you will often now see Negroes in parties at what you call white restaurants. The change is gradual, but I don't think Negroes need feel any shame in the progress they are making, and I hope they will continue to progress steadily. I realize we in the North have much less to do than the South in desegregation, and therefore we should have more understanding of the greater problems that exist in the South.

Is there any chance that efforts to integrate the South by legislation could fail—as, for example, Prohibition did?

None whatsoever. Integration can take a shorter or longer time, depending on the cooperation or resistance of certain groups, but eventually the barriers must fall, and real equality must emerge. However, equality does not necessarily mean any substantial amount of intermarriage, as so many people seem to fear. In France, for example, whites and Negroes have long had equality, and there has been very little intermarriage.

McCall's, 1959–1962

ER with President John F. Kennedy on March 1, 1961. Initially, each had misgivings about the other. JFK resented ER's support for Adlai Stevenson in 1956, when Kennedy first tried a run for the Democratic nomination. ER had an unfavorable opinion of JFK's father, Joseph P. Kennedy, who had served briefly as ambassador to Great Britain during the war and whose isolationism and defeatism alienated FDR.

ON THE FIRST
KENNEDY-NIXON DEBATE

September 27, 1960

Dear Senator Kennedy:

I watched with great interest the debate last night, and I had a number of interesting people with me. Senator Benton [William Benton of Connecticut], whom you know, thought it a simply wonderful performance. He thought you were both very good and that on the whole you did better than Mr. Nixon. I am so prejudiced against Mr. Nixon that I dare not trust my own opinion, but I am going to tell you how some people felt.

One person said to me that he felt you spoke a little too fast and had not yet mastered the habit of including your audience at every point by saying "I hope you agree with me, or don't you agree with me, or my feeling is that you, the people to whom I am speaking, will feel, etc."

Someone else said they thought you appeared a little too confident. I did not agree with this, but thought I should tell you.

It was felt that Nixon would appeal to the pity for the underdog which is prevalent in the American people, by seeming to be "humbler." I never have this feeling about Nixon, so I am a bad judge in this particular case.

On the whole, I think it was a milestone for TV and a really good way to campaign because it reaches so many people and gives them a chance to evaluate the ideas, the knowledge, and the personalities of the candidates. Unfortunately, however, television does not give the impression one gets from really talking to the individual himself, and this is perhaps one of the reasons why campaigning in person is still important. But, on the whole, I think these debates, judging by the first one, are definitely an advantage to you.

I am looking forward to seeing you.

Very sincerely yours,
[ER]

ER Papers, 1960

Appointed in 1961 by President Kennedy as the chair of the President's Commission on the Status of Women, ER commented, "This is the last thing I will ever do." Working for two years, the thirty-five-member commission, led by presidential adviser Esther Peterson, made its final report in 1963, after ER's death. JFK intended the commission to compensate for his administration's paucity of women's appointments. Here, ER and JFK join commission members in the Oval Office in February 1962.

THE KENNEDY COMMISSION ON THE STATUS OF WOMEN

———

Paris—Before coming over here my last two days in the United States were spent largely in Washington, D.C., and I want to tell about them before writing about my current month-long trip.

On last Monday morning in the White House the president opened the first meeting of the Commission on the Status of Women. . . .

After the morning session we had lunch in a downstairs restaurant that did not exist in my day there. . . . A guide showed us around the White House, telling us about certain things that have been changed under Mrs. Kennedy's direction and which she explained to the American people over two television networks this week.

The basement floor and the first floor for entertaining have certainly been made far more attractive than ever before. Mrs. Kennedy has

Commission members at work in a session at Hyde Park in June 1962. Esther Peterson, at center, next to ER.

succeeded in having presented to the White House some really very beautiful pieces of furniture and decorative pictures, which add enormously to the interest of these rooms.

We kept ourselves strictly on schedule all day and opened our afternoon meeting promptly at two o'clock at 200 Maryland Avenue, below the Capitol, where the Commission on Women's Status will have its permanent office.

We soon began to discuss the best way to organize to achieve the maximum of work not only on the six points laid down in the president's directive to the commission but in other situations which will certainly arise. The commission will try to make its influence felt concerning women's problems not only in the federal area but in state and local areas and in industry as well as in women's [unclear] home responsibilities.

Labor leader and presidential adviser Esther Peterson, President Kennedy's highest-level woman appointee, took on the leading role in the Commission on the Status of Women and shaped its conclusions. With ER in January 1962.

New York governor Nelson Rockefeller, at far left, and ER watch President Kennedy address an International Ladies Garment Workers Union (ILGWU) rally in May 1962. The union president, David Dubinsky, is at the far right.

The effort, of course, is to find how we can best use the potentialities of women without impairing their first responsibilities, which are to their homes, their husbands and their children. We need to use in the very best way possible all our available manpower—and that includes womanpower—and this commission, I think, can well point out some of the ways in which this can be accomplished. . . .

The vice president and Mrs. Johnson gave a delightful reception at their home in the late afternoon for the members of the commission.

"My Day," February 16, 1962

CHAPTER 8

Lessons from Life

ER at Hyde Park, 1951

Eleanor Roosevelt prized the role of teacher. Her zeal for education dated back to the turn of the century, to her formative years as a top student at Allenswood and to the influence of Mlle Souvestre. It surged into prominence again in the 1920s at the Todhunter School, where she taught history and current events, and again in the 1930s, when she organized the community school at Arthurdale. Familiar with the works of philosopher John

Dewey, as was common among educators of her generation, ER absorbed and applied the precepts of progressive education—at Todhunter, at Arthurdale, and in her writing. She neither relied on Dewey uncritically nor endorsed his educational philosophy as a panacea. "I have never thought it wise to accept one theory and consider it perfect," ER declared in a "My Day" column of March 28, 1958; in her opinion, parts of Dewey's educational theory might work well in practice or not. But the main axiom of progressive education—to learn through experience—was central to her credo. So was Dewey's tenet that learning meant a continual process of restructuring and reorganizing, or in ER's formulation, "readjustment." To ER, as to Dewey, the gist of education involved learning how to learn.

Over the decades, ER returned often to the ongoing process of learning and to the theme of learning from experience. She looked back continually, if selectively, to the people and circumstances that had shaped her development. Her mission as educator merged easily with yet another stance she adopted, that of advice-giver; the role of counselor flourished in her postwar magazine columns, where, as in much that she wrote, her life experience was salient. Whenever the subject permitted, in all of her columns and articles, ER turned to early memories or to other facets of her past for illustration. As she showed her readers again and again, she never stopped learning from experience. She imparted, in turn, an ongoing series of lessons from life.

ER stressed the power of mind over circumstances. She told her readers that self-esteem ("friendship with oneself") was imperative, that curiosity ensured interest in life, that it was crucial to look forward not backward, and that engagement with others enabled an individual to "forget about yourself." Her directives urged readers to seek challenge, vault obstacles, defy adversity, and acclimate to changing situations. "The learning process must go on as long as we live," ER reminded her audience. "Life is interesting only so long as it is a process of growth." Two books of her last years recapitulated her educational precepts, positive outlook, and democratic convictions. In *You Learn by Living*, a bestseller of 1960, ER tackled learning from experience through anecdote and analysis. Mental outlook prevailed, independent of any particular situation: "Nothing ever happens to us except in our minds," ER observed. In a final book, *Tomorrow Is Now*, published posthumously in 1963, ER summed up the transformations of the twentieth century—economic, political, and social—that had shaped her experience, culminating with the battle for civil rights. Familiarity with history, ER contended, bolstered prospects for democracy; nations, like people, could learn from experience. She pressed her readers to nurture awareness, exert initiative, engage with public issues, and, as ever, to adjust to continuous change.

WHAT I HOPE
TO LEAVE BEHIND

I personally have never formulated exactly what I would like to leave behind me. I am afraid I have been too busy living, accepting such opportunities as came my way and using them to the best of my ability, and the thought of what would come after has lain rather lightly in the back of my mind. . . .

Unconsciously our characters shape themselves to meet the requirements which our dreams put upon our life. . . .

Most women dream first of a happy family. The instinct for reproduction is inborn in most of us. If we have known happy homes, we want to reproduce the same type of thing we have had; and even though we may always be critical of some things in our past, time nearly always puts a halo around even a few of the disagreeable things, and most women dream, as they rock their babies or busy themselves in household tasks, that their daughters will do the same things someday.

In some intangible way it satisfies our hunger for eternity. We may not actually figure it out, but the long time that we see streaming down uncounted years, going back of us and going on beyond us, comes to mean for us immortality.

For a number of years it took too much vitality to keep the home going, and that home represented so many different kinds of activities that none of us had any urge to go outside of this sphere. . . .

When the care of the children ceases to be entirely in one person's hands, then in the past, as in the present, women have turned to other things. Some have changed the map of the world, some of them have influenced literature, some have inspired music. Today we are dreaming dreams of individual careers.

I find I have a sense of satisfaction whenever I learn that there is a new field being opened up where women may enter. A woman will rejoice in her freedom to enter on a new career. She will know that she has to make some sacrifice as far as her own life is concerned, and for that reason you will find more and more women analyzing what are the really valuable things in human life, deciding whether a job of some kind will be worthwhile for them from several points of view, whether it will give them sufficient financial return to provide for the doing of certain household things better than they could do themselves, and whether the job they will do will give them more satisfaction and make them better-rounded people and, therefore, more companionable and worthwhile in their associations with the human beings who make up their home life.

What is the real value of a home? To me the answer is that the value lies in human contacts and associations—the help which I can be to my children, which my husband and I can be to each other, and what the children can be to us. These are the real values of home life. A sense of physical comfort and security can be produced quite as well by well-trained servants.

I feel that if holding a job will make a woman more of a person, so that her charm, her intelligence, and her experience will be of greater value to the other lives around her, then holding a job is obviously the thing for her to do. Sometimes a woman works not only to make money and to develop her personality, and be more of a person in herself, but also because she is conscious that she wishes to make some kind of contribution in a larger field than that of her home surroundings.

In all the ages there have been people whose hearts have been some-how so touched by the misery of human beings that they wanted to give their lives in some way to alleviate it. We have some examples of women like this today: Lillian Wald and Mary Simkhovitch in New York, Jane Addams in Chicago [the three women were leaders of the social settlement movement]. They were none of them actu-ated, when they started out on their careers, by any small personal ambitions. They have achieved great personal success, but that is simply as a by-product; for what they set out to do and have done was to alleviate some of the trials of humanity in the places where they were able to work. . . .

There is no doubt that we women must lead the way in setting new standards of what is really valuable in life. . . .

With advancing years I feel I must give this question of what I want to leave behind me greater thought, for before long I shall be moving on to fields unknown, and perhaps it may make a difference if I actually know what I would like to bequeath to a new generation.

Perhaps the best I can do is to pray that the youth of today will have the ability to live simply and to get joy out of living, the desire to give of themselves and to make themselves worthy of giving, and the strength to do without anything which does not serve the interests of the brotherhood of man. If I can bequeath these desires to my own children, it seems to me I will not have lived in vain.

Pictorial Review, 1933

With FDR and his assistant, Missy LeHand, in 1929.

IN DEFENSE OF CURIOSITY

——————

I think, at a child's birth, if a mother could ask a fairy godmother to endow it with the most useful gift that gift should be curiosity.

When I was young I was taught, as all children were, that curiosity was a fault. Curiosity seemed to mean a kind of ugly prying into other people's affairs, something which "nice, well brought-up" people refrained from. That is a kind of curiosity which, to this day, I detest. The desire to know the secrets which others may wish to hide seems, to me, cruel. Every human soul has its own secrets and its own right to keep them buried if it wishes. An idle curiosity to furnish later idle gossip is not only cruel but a despicable trait of human nature.

I think, however, that I was born with an interest in people, for I well remember at five years of age being taken by my father to serve Thanksgiving dinner for the Newsboys' Club which my grandfather had established in New York City. I at once acquired a tremendous interest in some of the little boys who ate so much and seemed so merry in spite of their ragged clothes and their lack of all the things that I looked upon as part of my daily security.

I was abroad at school and nearly grown up when I identified this interest with curiosity. One evening, Mlle Souvestre, the head of the school, who was already seventy years old, gathered her pupils in her library, and after reading to us for a while, let us all enter into a discussion. I heard for the first time that night a new definition of curiosity. She turned to us and said, "You must cultivate curiosity, for only through curiosity can you learn, not only what there is in books, but what lies around you in the world of things and people." Then she showed us, one by one, how narrow our backgrounds had been, and gave us little glimpses of what we did not know, and what we might already know if we had had the curiosity even in our past limited environments. All of us went away from that room with a new idea of what curiosity might do for us. . . .

In its simplest form, curiosity will help you to an all-around educa-tion. That is why little children are so often living question marks. They naturally desire to know about the rest of the world in which they live, and if they lose that curiosity, it is usually because we grown people are so stupid. . . .

The thoroughness with which a child will pursue a subject until it has been completely mastered, going over it again and again, until it becomes so thoroughly familiar that you think it must be tiresome, is something which we should all respect, and, instead of trying to curb and stop this type of curiosity, we should always encourage it. . . .

What we talk of as personality is nothing more than the effect of experience and knowledge, filtering through the emotional system of an individual until it becomes part of his inner consciousness and radiates from it in what we recognize as personality. If we feel a person has a negligible personality, it usually means that that person has lacked the curiosity to see life and really understand it. It is quite easy to see a great many things and yet to be so lacking in curiosity and understanding that one does not know what they mean. . . .

A few years ago, when I was conducting a class in the study of city government, we took up one of the functions of the government— namely public health. This is closely allied to housing, so I suggested that our group visit some of the different types of tenements. There was considerable concern among some of the mothers, for fear some illness might be contracted. It apparently never occurred to them that hundreds of young people lived in these tenements all the time, nor that, very likely, there entered into their sheltered homes daily people who served as delivery boys, servants, and workmen, who spent much of their time in tenements; so, even if the sheltered children did not visit them, the tenement home radiated out all that was good in it and all that was bad in it and touched the home on Park Avenue. No home is isolated, remember, so why should we not have a curiosity about all the homes that must in one way or another affect our own? . . .

Lack of curiosity among these young people meant lack of imagination and complete inability to visualize any life but their own, and, therefore, they could not recognize their responsibility to their less fortunate brothers and sisters. . . .

The great experiences of life are the same wherever you live and whether you are rich or poor. Birth and death, courage and cowardice, kindness and cruelty, love and hate, are no respecters of persons, and they are the occasions and emotions which bring about most of the experiences of life. You cannot prevent unhappiness or sorrow entering into any life—even the fairy godmother of the legend could not give freedom from these experiences—but curiosity will ensure an ever-recurring interest in life and will give you the needed impetus to turn your most baleful experience to some kind of good service.

Saturday Evening Post, 1935

With FDR and daughter Anna in Washington in January 1934.

HOW TO TAKE CRITICISM

What about criticism? I am always being asked if it troubles me or makes me angry, or hurts me. Should we be affected by criticism regardless of its source? . . .

One of the things which my critics most frequently stress is the fact that I am not elected to any office, therefore, I can have no sense of responsibility, they say, since no one elected or appointed me to any office, so it is clear that I must be seeking publicity.

Let me disabuse them of that idea. People who live in a goldfish bowl cannot escape publicity. It is obvious that the president's wife is not an elected official, but she has certain obligations. First, there is the obligation to run the president's house, his official house, the White House, paying due attention to all the rules and regulations which custom and the law lay down for the running of that house, which belongs to the people of the United States. This is an obligation on which there is little difference of opinion and if I confined myself to giving parties, even in wartime, my critics would be few, I imagine, though one cannot be sure!

The differences arise in regard to other activities. As the president's wife, a great many people throughout the United States think that you can get information for them which they cannot get themselves, or help them to accomplish certain things which they cannot accomplish themselves. In both of these situations, they are quite correct sometimes in appealing to you, and you are without any impropriety to give them information. . . . A good many people think that because of your husband's position, you can exert influence to obtain favors which they could not obtain on their own merits. If you did this, you would rightly be criticized. . . .

In the natural course of events, however, you get to know a good deal about the country and its people. . . . This gives you an opportunity perhaps to be of service and here is where criticism centers.

Should the president's wife, who is not elected to any office, be interested in working conditions, for instance? She can have rare opportunities for knowing about them if she has eyes, ears and understanding. Should she be blind, deaf and dumb?

There is no question about it—all criticism is entirely permissible. There are no laws as to your conduct, you are a citizen, free like any other, so you live by your own judgment, tastes and conscience. Hence the question is "How much attention should the individual criticized pay to criticism?"

No human being enjoys being disliked so it would be normal to try to avoid actions which bring criticism. . . .

In the last analysis you have to be friends with yourself twenty-four hours of the day. If you run counter to others now and then, you have enemies, but life would become unbearable if you thought about it all of the time, so you have to ignore the critics. You know quite well when you face audiences and are among crowds of people, that perhaps everybody present dislikes you cordially. Then you do your best to make others see your point of view, but if you cannot win them over, you still must go on your way because each human being has an obligation to do what seems right according to his own conscience. If you are honest, you will always be your own most severe critic. . . .

Friendship with oneself is all important because without it, one cannot be friends with anyone else in the world.

Ladies' Home Journal, 1944

At the Val-Kill cottage, Hyde Park, with Fala and Tamas, in 1948.

BACKGROUND KNOWLEDGE

I think background knowledge, when we really want to build wisely for the future, is very important. . . .

I think it very important for the future that our young people remember that twice in twenty-five years the Germans started world wars. I think it very important that they know what lies back of the starting of those wars. But above everything else, I think it important that they have the background knowledge which clearly shows that we arrive at catastrophe by failing to meet situations—by failing to act where we should act. Our consciences are not tender enough. We can always find good excuses why the present moment is not the moment in which to take a stand. Background knowledge would make us review every step—and the many steps where we really knew that things were happening that we didn't approve of, but we first didn't say so because we could always make ourselves believe that something worse might happen if we took a stand. If we did anything, if we said anything, something worse might happen! We might have a war! And we ended up by having the war because we did nothing. I think this is the most important thing that we should learn from background knowledge—that one should not hesitate to stand for the right as one sees it because if one does not, the opportunity passes and the next situation is always more difficult than the last one.

I hope very much that out of the background which some people have acquired and out of the knowledge of what this war has brought to people in Asia and in Europe we are going to get the necessary purpose to make us work hard in the days to come for an organization, a really functioning organization, of United Nations. The idea that we can do as we did with the League [of Nations] and take a distant interest only is, I think, part of our background knowledge. We know it doesn't work. So I hope we have learned that we really have to work if we want the United Nations to achieve anything.

Annals of the American Academy
of Political and Social Science, 1946

PEOPLE WHO
SHAPED MY LIFE

———

What you are in life results in great part from the influence exerted on you over the years by just a few people. . . .

The personalities of my husband and mother-in-law, I am sure, exerted the greatest influence in my development.

My mother-in-law was a lady of great character. She always knew what was right and what was wrong. She was kind and generous and loyal to the family through thick and thin. But it was hard to differ with her. She never gave up an idea she had, whether it was for herself or for you. And her methods of achieving her own ends at times seemed a bit ruthless if you were not in accord. She dominated me for years.

But I finally developed within myself the power to resist. Perhaps it was my husband's teaching me that there was great strength in passive resistance. Perhaps it was that, having two such personalities as my husband and his mother, I had to develop willy-nilly into an individual myself.

Both wanted to dominate their spheres of life, though they were enough alike to love each other dearly. My husband was just as determined as his mother, but hated to hurt people and never did so unless they really angered him. She won even with him sometimes, but usually he simply ignored any differences in their point of view.

His illness finally made me stand on my own feet in regard to my husband's life, my own life, and my children's training. The alternative would have been to become a completely colorless echo of my husband and mother-in-law and be torn between them. I might have stayed a weak character forever if I had not found that out.

In some ways my husband was a remarkable teacher. His breadth of interests made him always a stimulating person to be with, and you could not live with him and fail to learn many things. This happened not only to me but also to his children and many of his close associates.

For instance, it was he who taught me to observe. Just sitting with him in the observation car at the end of a train, I learned how to watch the tracks and see their condition, how to look at the countryside and note whether there was soil erosion and what condition the forests and fields were in, and as we went through the outskirts of a town or village I soon learned to look at the clothes on the wash line and at the cars and to notice whether houses needed painting. Little by little, I found I was able to answer my husband's questions, after I had taken a trip alone, and give him the information he would have gathered had he taken the trip himself.

Though I had always loved the country, I had no real knowledge of forestry or flood control. But I could not live with my husband and not learn about those things.

I not only learned what was before my eyes in my own country, but I learned what had happened in other countries of the world centuries ago and through their whole history, and why conditions were as they were in various countries throughout the world.

My husband opened the windows of the world for me. As I think it over, he was perhaps the greatest teacher of the many who contributed to my education.

The last person, probably, to have influenced me much as an individual was Louis Howe, my husband's adviser. He pushed me, not for my own sake but for my husband's, into taking an interest in public affairs.

With cadets at West Point in 1951.

This was a field I had carefully shunned, feeling that one member of the family with a knowledge of politics was all that one family could stand. But, little by little, I found myself beginning to understand why certain things were done and how they came about. Before I realized it, I was at least interested in the fields of domestic and foreign affairs. . . .

Look, 1951

WHERE I GET MY ENERGY

My uncle Theodore Roosevelt was known for his remarkable energy. He preached the gospel of the strenuous life and as a child I heard much of his wonderful physical prowess—his hunting, exploring, riding, and polo playing. No matter how busy his life became, he always read prodigiously and still found time to spend with his children.

What was the source of his immense energy and his huge capacity for work and play? Today people ask me the same questions. I decided long ago that we must have some very sturdy ancestors. When I am told that I have extraordinary vitality for a woman of seventy-four, I feel that a good part of the credit must go to my ancient forebears. . . .

From my mother's side of the family—the Halls and the Livingstons—as well as the Roosevelts—I also have a heritage of good health and good living. Though both of my parents died young, I had many aunts, uncles, and cousins who managed to live to a ripe and vigorous old age. . . .

To be able to regulate your life and your habits in a sensible way is perhaps even more important as you grow older than when you are young. I was fortunate in learning self-discipline early. My grandmother who brought me up from the time I was seven was much more severe with me than she had ever been with her own sons and daughters. . . .

Social life was very important in my grandmother's world and her social code demanded a great deal of self-discipline—particularly of women. Social obligations were sacred—no matter how you felt, the show must go on. If you were depressed, you certainly did not air your sadness in public. Even in showing appropriate emotions, like pleasure or polite regret, you were decorous and subdued. If there were social obligations to be met, my grandmother believed it was incumbent on me to see that I felt well. She had no sympathy with a headache, for instance. She simply felt irritated that I had not avoided whatever had caused it.

This rather stern code has stood me in good stead on many occasions when more serious responsibilities made it absolutely necessary for me to stay well. . . .

Today, of course, there is little reason why I should not organize my life just to suit myself since I live alone. . . .

I like a regular routine. . . . My engagement book tells me what is to be done every half-hour, and if I ever were to lose it, I would soon be in a terrible situation.

For instance, this was my schedule on last October 17:

6:45 A.M. Got up a bit earlier than usual; had a quick breakfast and made two urgent phone calls.

7:30 A.M. Took taxi to La Guardia Airport.

8:10 A.M. Off by plane to Washington; got my paper read en route.

9:30 A.M. My son Franklin met me at National Airport, drove me to his new office to meet his new associates.

10:30 A.M. Back to hotel for conference with Mr. Carl Stover at the Brookings Institution. I agreed to give a talk at the Institution next spring. Mr. Seth Jackson, whom I met on my last trip abroad, came to call and to seek advice about his plans.

11:30 A.M. To reception of the Democratic Central Committee of the District of Columbia, at the Mayflower Hotel.

1:15 P.M. Spoke at Committee luncheon.

2:00 P.M. Mrs. Anna S. Miller of the Washington, D.C. Housing Association drove me to the airport and invited me to address her group in May which I will do.

2:30 P.M. Took plane back to New York.

3:45 P.M. Took taxi home.

4:15 P.M. Got to work with my secretary on my correspondence which I usually do right after breakfast. Read my mail and dictated replies; also dictated my column.

5:30 P.M. Guests for tea who left just in time for me to have a very quick tub and change to evening dress.

6:30 P.M. Not quite dressed when a friend arrived to go with me to the Overseas Press Club.

8:30 P.M. Spoke at dinner given in my honor.

10:45 P.M. Home again to work on my correspondence.

1:30 A.M. October 18. To bed.

Sometimes, I must confess, I look with apprehension at a schedule like this one. Yet I know that if my schedule were not busy, I would feel less alive. . . .

With Frank Sinatra at the Girls' Town ball in Florida in 1960.

At present I look like Methuselah but I feel no older than my youngest friends. I am sure that I am no more exhausted at the end of a busy day than many who are half my age. When you know that there is so much to be done that is not yet accomplished you are always looking forward instead of backward. This is one of the secrets of having strength and energy. As you grow older too, it becomes easier to think about other people and to forget about yourself. Thus you have many interests and these, I think, give you the capacity to do whatever really needs to be done.

Harper's, 1959

LEARNING FROM EXPERIENCE

LEARNING TO LEARN

What I have learned from my own experience is that the most important ingredients in a child's education are curiosity, interest, imagination, and a sense of the adventure of life. You will find no courses in which these are taught; and yet they are the qualities that make all learning rewarding, that make all life zestful, that make us seek constantly for new experience and deeper understanding. They are also the qualities that enable us to continue to grow as human beings to the last day of our life, and to continue to learn.

By learning, of course, I mean a great deal more than so-called formal education. Nobody can learn all he needs to know. Education provides the necessary tools, equipment by which we learn how to learn. The object of all our education and all the development which is a part of education is to give every one of us an instrument which we can use to acquire information at any time we need it.

I remember certain milestones in learning how to learn. As far as training memory was concerned, that began very young. I loved poetry and I would often learn it while I was dressing and undressing. When I was quite young I had a French teacher who made us learn by heart a good part of the New Testament in French. This was helpful later when I was in a French school in England. The French mistress had us listen to her read a French poem, of perhaps eight lines, and repeat it after the first reading. At first I could not do it, but gradually I was able to manage fairly well.

She taught us history, and, though we were only fifteen or sixteen, I imagine her methods were more like those of a college professor. We sat on little chairs on either side of her fireplace, over which maps were hung. She would turn to the map of the area of the world we were learning about and tell us to remember our geography because it affected history. Then she would give us a list of books to read and take up the particular point we were studying, giving us as many different lights on the period as she thought we could understand. Our requirement was to do our reading and then write a paper on the assignment.

The English girls were apt to remember what she had said and repeat it in their papers. I can still see her, as one of the girls was reading her paper aloud, standing over her with a long ruler in her hand, taking away the paper, and tearing it up.

"You are giving me back what I gave you," she said, "and it does not interest me. You have not sifted it through your own intelligence. Why was your mind given you but to think things out for yourself?"

It became a challenge for me to think about all the different sides of a situation and try to find new points that Mlle Souvestre had not covered, points that had not even been covered in our books. It was rather exciting to have these questions come to my mind as I read and I can remember now how pleased I was when she would ask me to leave my paper with her and later return it with the comment, "Well thought out, but have you forgotten this or that point?"

That was an imaginative method of education and most valuable.

We obtain our education at home, at school, and, most important, from life itself. The learning process must go on as long as we live. Nothing alive can stand still, it goes forward or back. Life is interesting only so long as it is a process of growth; or, to put it another way, we can grow only so long as we are interested.

. . . . .

FEAR—THE GREAT ENEMY

Fear has always seemed to me to be the worst stumbling block which anyone has to face. It is the great crippler. Looking back, it strikes me that my childhood and my early youth were one long battle against fear.

I was an exceptionally timid child, afraid of the dark, afraid of mice, afraid of practically everything. Painfully, step by step, I learned to stare down each of my fears, conquer it, attain the hard-earned courage to go on to the next. Only then was I really free.

Of all the knowledge that we acquire in life this is the most difficult. But it is also the most rewarding. With each victory, no matter how great the cost or how agonizing at the time, there comes increased confidence and strength to help meet the next fear. . . .

I can remember vividly an occasion when I was living in my grandmother's house on Thirty-seventh Street in New York City. One of my aunts was ill and asked for some ice, which was kept in the icebox out of doors in the back yard.

I was so frightened that I shook. But I could not refuse to go. If I did that, she would never again ask me to help her and I could not bear not to be asked.

I had to go down alone from the third floor in the dark, creeping through the big house, which was so hostile and unfamiliar at night, in which unknown terrors seemed to lurk. Down to the basement, shutting a door behind me that cut me off from the house and safety. Out in the blackness of the back yard.

I suffered agonies of fear that night. But I learned that I could face the dark and it never again held such horror for me. . . .

The encouraging thing is that every time you meet a situation, though you may think at the time it is an impossibility and you go through the tortures of the damned, once you have met it and lived through it you find that forever after you are freer than you ever were before. If you can live through that you can live through anything. You gain strength, courage, and confidence by every experience in which you really stop to look fear in the face.

You are able to say to yourself, "I lived through this horror. I can take the next thing that comes along."

The danger lies in refusing to face the fear, in not daring to come to grips with it. If you fail anywhere along the line it will take away your confidence. You must make yourself succeed every time. *You must do the thing you think you cannot do.*

· · · · ·

READJUSTMENT IS ENDLESS

Readjustment is a kind of private revolution. Each time you learn something new you must readjust the whole framework of your knowledge. It seems to me that one is forced to make inner and outer readjustments all one's life. The process never ends. And yet, for a great many people, this is a continuing problem because they appear to have an innate fear of change, no matter what form it takes: changed personal relationships, changed social or financial conditions. The new or the unknown becomes in their minds something hostile, almost malignant. . . .

I have known many cases where, because people had been able to adjust to changing conditions as they went along, they were able to make huge readjustments when it became necessary.

One reason for this ability to cope with disaster is that *nothing ever happens to us except what happens in our minds.* Unhappiness is an inward, not an outward, thing. It is as independent of circumstances as is happiness. Consider the truly happy people you know. I think it is unlikely that you will find that circumstances have made them happy. They have made themselves happy in spite of circumstances. . . .

Like countless women, I have had to face the future alone after the death of my husband, making the adjustments to being by myself, to planning without someone else as the center of my world. Long before, of course, I had learned that the process of adjustment never stops.

. . . . .

HOW TO GET THE BEST
OUT OF PEOPLE

If you approach each new person you meet in a spirit of adventure, you will find that you become increasingly interested in them and endlessly fascinated by the new channels of thought and experience and personality that you encounter. I do not mean simply the famous people of the world, but people from every walk and condition of life. You will find them a source of inexhaustible surprise because of the unexpected qualities and interests which you will unearth in your search for treasure. But the treasure is there if you will mine for it.

If such a search is to be successful, however, you will need two qualities which you can develop by practice. One is the ability to be a good listener. The other is the imaginative ability to put yourself in the other person's place; to try to discover what he is thinking and feeling; to understand as far as you can the background from which he came, the soil out of which his roots have grown, the customs and beliefs and ideas which have shaped his thinking. . . .

It was by sitting and talking with miners' wives that I came really to know what they thought and felt, what it was like to be a min-

Dorothy Height, president of the National Council of Negro Women, presents ER with the Mary McLeod Bethune Human Rights Award on November 12, 1960.

er's wife. This awareness did not come at once. It never does. But countless times during the years of the Great Depression I sat in their small kitchens, sometimes with their husbands, sometimes without them, but always with a group of children too young to go to school hanging around their mother's skirts. Often a sick child lay on the only bed and when I asked where the others slept the mother would point out a little closet with no outside windows and with sacking on the floor as the only bedding.

Listening to such a woman talk, taking in the surroundings, one finds oneself, little by little, coming to understand the feelings of that other human being. Intellectually, one may have known for years that certain needs exist, but until one sees with one's own eyes and comes to feel with one's own heart, one will never understand other people.

You Learn by Living, 1960

THE PRACTICAL APPLICATION OF DEMOCRATIC PRINCIPLES

We can no longer oversimplify. We can no longer build lazy and false stereotypes: Americans are like this, Russians are like that, a Jew behaves in such a way, a Negro thinks in a different way. The lazy generalities—"You know how women are. . . . Isn't that just like a man?"

The world cannot be understood from a single point of view. . . .

One thing is certain: in this modern world of ours we cannot afford to forget that what we do at home is important in relation to the rest of the world. The sooner we learn this, the sooner we will understand the meaning of our social revolution.

It is not too much to say that our adjustment to our own social revolution will affect almost every country in the world. Nor is it too much to say that we should be able to make our adjustment with comparative ease. What is required of us is infinitesimal compared to the adjustments that are to be made in the backward nations—in prejudice, in superstition, in ignorance in habits and customs. They are coming out of the bush; we have only to come out of the darkness of our own blind prejudice and fear into the steady light of reason and humanity.

You will tell me, perhaps, that to cope successfully with our social revolution we must bring about a revolution in the mentality of the American people. While there is much truth in this, it is well to remember that, in many respects and in many areas of the United States, that revolution has been fought—and won. In his first inaugural my husband said, "We do not distrust the future of essential democracy."

The ensuing years, up to the Second World War, revealed that, when they had taken a wrong turning, the American people were willing to shift their position, to look freshly at conditions, and to find new methods of tackling them. And they were able to do this within the framework of the American system; they were able to find a middle course that upheld the capitalistic system at a time when most of the world seemed to have adopted the policy of extremes—either the extreme right of Nazism or the extreme left of Communism.

What we have failed too often to do is to appeal to this capacity for flexibility in the people.

The revolution in our social thinking appears, in capsule form, to my eyes, in one family I know well—my own. My mother-in-law belonged to the established world of the last century. She accepted its shibboleths without questioning. To her these things were true.

When she died, in September 1941, my husband felt strongly this ending of an unshakable world behind him. And yet, he told me, it was probably as well for his mother to leave us at that time. She was immersed in her old world and the new one was alien to her. The adjustment for her would have been impossible.

In using the term, I do not mean adjustment to the dramatic and obvious physical changes: to modern transportation and electrical gadgets and all the scientific inventions that have transformed our world. . . .

No, the basic change in the social revolution has been the change in values. To my mother-in-law, for instance, there were certain obligations that she, as a privileged person, must fulfill. She fed the poor, assisted them with money, helped them with medical expenses. This was a form of charity required of her.

The point of view that she simply could not accept was my husband's. He believed—as I trust most civilized people believe now—that human beings have rights as human beings: a right to a job, to

Four presidents, past, present, and future, at ER's funeral on November 10, 1962.

education, a right to health protection, a right to human dignity, a right to a chance of fulfillment.

This is the inevitable growth in our thinking as a nation—the practical application of democratic principles. No one today would dare refer to the mass of the people, as Alexander Hamilton once did, as "that great beast." And that, perhaps, is a minor victory in the long battle for human rights.

Tomorrow Is Now, 1963

NOTES

CHAPTER 1
BECOMING ER

5   **Ambition** Joseph P. Lash, *Eleanor and Franklin* (New York: Signet, 1971), 110. [Draft of essay from the 1890s in the Franklin Delano Roosevelt Library (FDRL), Joseph P. Lash Papers, Box 12]

6   **I Became a Much More Ardent Citizen and Feminist** *This Is My Story* (New York: Harper, 1937), 296-297. Courtesy of the Eleanor Roosevelt Estate.

7   **Why I Am a Democrat** "Why I Am a Democrat,"*Junior League Bulletin* 10, no. 2 (November 1923), 18-19. Courtesy of the Junior League Bulletin.

8   **I Am a Democrat** *Women's Democratic Campaign Manual, 1924* (Washington, DC: The Democratic National Committee, 1924), 85. Courtesy of the Eleanor Roosevelt Estate.

9   **How to Interest Women in Voting** "How to Interest Women in Voting," *Women's Democratic Campaign Manual, 1924,* 102-103. Courtesy of the Eleanor Roosevelt Estate.

10   **What I Want Most Out of Life** "What I Want Most Out of Life," as told to Catharine Brody, *Success* 11 (May 1927), 16-17, 70. Courtesy of the Eleanor Roosevelt Estate.

14   **How to Vote for President in 1928** "As a Practical Idealist," *North American Review* 224 (November 1927), 472-475. Courtesy of the Eleanor Roosevelt Estate.

15   **Shall Aristocrats Rule?** "Jeffersonian Principles the Issue in 1928," *Current History* 28, no. 3, 355-356. Reprinted with permission from *Current History* magazine (June, 1928). © 2017 Current History, Inc.

17   **The Modern Wife's Difficult Job** "The Modern Wife's Difficult Job," *The Literary Digest* (August 30, 1930), 18. Courtesy of the Eleanor Roosevelt Estate.

22   **Education and Citizenship** "Good Citizenship: The Purpose of Education," *Pictorial Review* 31 (April 1930), 4, 94, 97. Courtesy of the Eleanor Roosevelt Estate.

25   **Building Character** "Building Character," *The Parents Magazine* 6 (June 1931), 17. Courtesy of the Eleanor Roosevelt Estate.

26   **Ten Rules for Success in Marriage** "Ten Rules for Success in Marriage," *Pictorial Review* 33 (December 1931), 4, 36. Courtesy of the Eleanor Roosevelt Estate.

29   **Today's Girl and Tomorrow's Job** "Today's Girl and Tomorrow's Job," *Woman's Home Companion* 59 (June 1932), 11-12. Courtesy of the Eleanor Roosevelt Estate.

35   **The Political Wife** "Wives of Great Men," *Liberty* 9, no. 40 (October 1, 1932), 13-14. Courtesy of the Eleanor Roosevelt Estate.

38   **We Women Have Great Opportunity for Usefulness** "Passing Thoughts of Mrs. Franklin D. Roosevelt," *Women's Democratic News* 8, no. 10 (February 1933), 6. Courtesy of the Eleanor Roosevelt Estate.

CHAPTER 2
ON WOMEN, WORK, AND POLITICS

44   **Women Must Learn to Play the Game as Men Do** "Women Must Learn to Play the Game as Men Do," *Red Book Magazine* 50 (April 1928), 78–79, 141–142. Courtesy of the Eleanor Roosevelt Estate.

47   **What Ten Million Women Want** "What Ten Million Women Want," *The Home Magazine* 5, no. 3 (March 1932), 19–21, 86. Courtesy of the Eleanor Roosevelt Estate.

51   **A Place for Women in Politics** "Today's Girl and Tomorrow's Job," *Woman's Home Companion* 59 (June 1932), 12. Courtesy of the Eleanor Roosevelt Estate.

52   **ER's First White House Press Conference** "Press Conference of March 6, 1933," Furman Transcription, in Maurine Beasley, ed., *The White House Press Conferences of Eleanor Roosevelt* (New York: Garland Publishing, Inc., 1983), 7. Courtesy of the Eleanor Roosevelt Estate.

54   **On the National Woman's Party, Women Workers, and the ERA** "Press Conference of July 6, 1933," Furman Transcription, in Beasley, ed., *White House Press Conferences*, 13. Courtesy of the Eleanor Roosevelt Estate.

55   **Women and Working Conditions** *It's Up to the Women* (New York: Frederick A. Stokes Company, 1933), 229–232. Courtesy of the Eleanor Roosevelt Estate.

57   **Women in Public Life** *It's Up to the Women*, 210–213. Courtesy of the Eleanor Roosevelt Estate.

58   **ER to Lorena Hickok: Two Letters** Letters of May 23, 1934, and May 13, 1935, in Rodger Streitmatter, ed., *Empty without You: The Intimate Letters of Eleanor Roosevelt and Lorena Hickok* (New York: The Free Press, 1998), 109, 152–153. [Lorena Hickok Papers, FDRL]

62   **When Will a Woman Become President?** "Simmons Company Radio Broadcast of September 4, 1934," in Stephen Smith, ed., *The First Lady of Radio: Eleanor Roosevelt's Historic Broadcasts* (New York and London: The Free Press, 2014), 48–49. [ER Papers, Speech and Article File, 1917–1962, FDRL, Box 1400]

64   **Advice to Women in Politics** *Democratic Digest* (July 1936), p. 3, quoted in Blanche Wiesen Cook, *Eleanor Roosevelt: Volume 2, 1933–1938* (New York: Viking, 1999), 372. Courtesy of the Eleanor Roosevelt Estate.

64   **Should Wives Work?** "My Day," July 24, 1937. MY DAY © Eleanor Roosevelt. Reprinted by permission of ANDREWS MCMEEL SYNDICATION for UFS. All rights reserved.

66   **For Some People, Work Is Almost a Necessity** "Press Conference of June 16, 1938," Strayer Transcript, in Beasley, ed., *White House Press Conferences*, 52–54. Courtesy of the Eleanor Roosevelt Estate.

68   **Working Women in the Depression** "Press Conference of October 10, 1938," Strayer Transcript, in Beasley, ed. *White House Press Conferences*, 58–59. Courtesy of the Eleanor Roosevelt Estate.

70   **Plenty of Capable Women** "Press Conference of December 27, 1938," Strayer Transcript, in Beasley, ed., *White House Press Conferences*, 66. Courtesy of the Eleanor Roosevelt Estate.

70 **Working Wives** "My Day," June 16, 1939. MY DAY © Eleanor Roosevelt. Reprinted by permission of ANDREWS MCMEEL SYNDICATION for UFS. All rights reserved.

71 **Women in Politics** "Women in Politics," *Good Housekeeping* 110, no. 4 (April 1940), 45, 201–203. Courtesy of the Eleanor Roosevelt Estate.

76 **To Fight the Amendment: ER to Rose Schneiderman** Letter of February 11, 1944, ER Papers, FDRL, Selected Digitized Correspondence of ER, 1933–1945, Rose Schneiderman File (4), p. 13.

78 **On the ERA** "My Day," May 14, 1945. MY DAY © Eleanor Roosevelt. Reprinted by permission of ANDREWS MCMEEL SYNDICATION for UFS. All rights reserved.

79 **I Do Not Support the Equal Rights Amendment** ER to Nora Stanton Barney, November 25, 1946, in Allida Black et al., eds., *Eleanor Roosevelt Papers,* (Detroit: Thomson Gale, 2007), vol. 1 405–406.

CHAPTER 3
HUMANIZING THE NEW DEAL

83 **The Feeling That We Are Responsible for Each Other** *Democratic News* (December 1932), cited in Joseph P. Lash, *Eleanor and Franklin* (New York: W. W. Norton, 1971), 507.

84 **The Bright Side of the Depression** Manuscript for *Liberty* Magazine, in George M. McJimsey, ed. *Eleanor Roosevelt: The Role of the First Lady* (n.p.: Congressional Services Inc., 2003), Document 13, pp. 26–28. [ER Papers, Speech and Article File, FDRL, Box 1401] Courtesy of the Eleanor Roosevelt Estate.

86 **Depression Menus** *It's Up to the Women* (New York: Frederick A. Stokes, 1933), 64–65, 67–69, 70–71. Courtesy of the Eleanor Roosevelt Estate.

88 **Fair Working Conditions** "The State's Responsibility for Fair Working Conditions," *Scribner's Magazine* 93 (March 1933), 40. Courtesy of the Eleanor Roosevelt Estate.

90 **On Starting Arthurdale** "Passing Thoughts of Mrs. Franklin D. Roosevelt," *Women's Democratic News* 9, no. 1 (September 1933), 6. Courtesy of the Eleanor Roosevelt Estate.

92 **Defending Arthurdale** "Press Conference of April 11, 1934," Furman Typescript, in Maurine Beasley, ed. *The White House Press Conferences of Eleanor Roosevelt* (New York: Garland Publishing, Inc., 1983), 20. Courtesy of the Eleanor Roosevelt Estate.

94 **The Homestead Program** Untitled manuscript of 1935 for *Liberty* magazine, in McJimsey, ed. *Eleanor Roosevelt*. Document 106, pp. 289–94, 299. [ER Papers, Speech and Article File, FDRL, Box 1403]

97 **Whether the Depression is Half Over** "Press Conference of February 27, 1935," Thompson Transcript, in Beasley, ed., *White House Press Conferences*, 28–29. Courtesy of the Eleanor Roosevelt Estate.

100 **The First Lady's Dictionary** Attachment to letter, ER to Bess Furman, April 13, 1935, ER Papers, FDRL, Selected Digitized Correspondence, Bess Furman (Armstrong) file (1), pp. 19–22.

103 **The Unemployed Are Not a Strange Race** "The Unemployed Are Not a Strange Race," Address to Washington Conference of the Women's and Professional Projects of the WPA, *Democratic Digest* 13 (June 1936), 19. Courtesy of the Eleanor Roosevelt Estate.

104 **Are You Free If You Cannot Vote?** "My Day," December 8, 1938. MY DAY © Eleanor Roosevelt. Reprinted by permission of ANDREWS MCMEEL SYNDICATION for UFS. All rights reserved.

105 **Defining Democracy** "Press Conference of January 17, 1939," Furman Transcript, in Beasley, ed., *White House Press Conferences*, 70. Courtesy of the Eleanor Roosevelt Estate.

105 **On the American Youth Congress** "Keepers of Democracy," *The Virginia Quarterly Review* 15, no. 1 (Winter 1939), 3–4. Courtesy of the Eleanor Roosevelt Estate.

107 **Children and Community** "The Responsibility of the Individual and the Community," *Proceedings of the White House Conference on Children in a Democracy, Washington D.C., January 18-20, 1940*, United States Department of Labor, Children's Bureau Publication No. 266 (Washington, DC: Government Printing Office, 1940), 83–84.

109 **Insuring Democracy** "Insuring Democracy," *Collier's* 105 (June 15, 1940), 70, 87–88. Courtesy of the Eleanor Roosevelt Estate.

111 **This Is No Ordinary Time: Address to the Democratic Convention** "Address to the 1940 Democratic Convention of Mrs. Franklin D. Roosevelt," July 18, 1940, Press Release, Papers of the National Committee of the Democratic Party, Women's Division, in McJimsey, ed., *Eleanor Roosevelt,* Document 193, 660–661.

114 **Memo for FDR** "Memo for the President," Significant Documents, FDRL, ER-9, Memorandum, ER to FDR re: Blacks in the Military, c. September 1940.

115 **High Ideals: Address to Workers at the Leviton Strike** "Address to Local 3 of the International Brotherhood of Electrical Workers at Leviton Manufacturing Company Strike Headquarters, 1941," in *American Federationist* (March 1941), 14–15. Courtesy of the Eleanor Roosevelt Estate.

118 **To Me, Organization of Labor Seems Necessary** "My Day," March 13, 1941. MY DAY © Eleanor Roosevelt. Reprinted by permission of ANDREWS MCMEEL SYNDICATION for UFS. All rights reserved.

120 **On Democracy** *The Moral Basis of Democracy* (New York: Howell, Soskin & Co., 1940), 76–77. Courtesy of the Eleanor Roosevelt Estate.

CHAPTER 4
THIS IS NO ORDINARY TIME: WORLD WAR II

126 **Why Wars Must Cease** "Because the War Idea is Obsolete," in Rose Emmet Young, ed. *Why Wars Must Cease* (New York: Macmillan, 1935), 27–28. Courtesy of the Eleanor Roosevelt Estate.

127 **We Would Like to Stay Out of War** "My Day," June 28, 1941. MY DAY © Eleanor Roosevelt. Reprinted by permission of ANDREWS MCMEEL SYNDICATION for UFS. All rights reserved.

128   **We Know What We Have to Face: On Pearl Harbor** "Pan American Coffee Bureau Program #11," December 7, 1941, in Stephen Drury Smith, ed., *The First Lady of Radio* (New York and London: The New Press, 2014), 191–192. [ER Papers, FDRL, Speech and Article File, Box 1411]

131   **The Greatest Test This Country Has Ever Met** "My Day," December 16, 1941. MY DAY © Eleanor Roosevelt. Reprinted by permission of ANDREWS MCMEEL SYNDICATION for UFS. All rights reserved.

132   **Starvation and Horror Live with Them Day by Day** "My Day," September 25, 1942. MY DAY © Eleanor Roosevelt. Reprinted by permission of ANDREWS MCMEEL SYNDICATION for UFS. All rights reserved.

133   **What We Are Fighting For** "What We Are Fighting For," *The American Magazine* 134 (July 1942), 16–17, 60–62. Courtesy of the Eleanor Roosevelt Estate.

136   **The Right of Survival of Human Beings** "My Day," August 13, 1943. MY DAY © Eleanor Roosevelt. Reprinted by permission of ANDREWS MCMEEL SYNDICATION for UFS. All rights reserved.

137   **To Undo a Mistake Is Always Harder Than Not to Create One Originally: On Internment** "To Undo a Mistake Is Always Harder Than Not to Create One Originally," Draft of an article written after a visit to the Gila River Relocation Center in Arizona, 1943, FDRL, published in Jeffery F. Burton, et al., eds. *Confinement and Ethnicity: An Overview of World War II Japanese American Relocation Sites* (Tucson: Western Archeological and Conservation Center, National Park Service, United States Department of the Interior, 2000), chap. 2.

141   **"If You Ask Me": Wartime Questions** "If You Ask Me," *Ladies Home Journal* (March, April, May, July, August, September, and December, 1942; May, July, and December, 1943). Courtesy of the Eleanor Roosevelt Estate.

147   **We Know in the End We Will Win: On D-Day** "Invasion Day—Radio Speech, June 6, 1944," in McJimsey, ed., *Eleanor Roosevelt,* Document 241, p. 891. [ER Papers, FDRL, Speech and Article File, Box 1415]

150   **To Women in Unions** Draft of untitled article for *Ammunition* [AUW/CIO publication] in McJimsey, ed., *Eleanor Roosevelt*, Document 242, p. 892. Courtesy of the Eleanor Roosevelt Estate.

152   **Women in the Postwar World** "Women in the Postwar World: Forward," *Journal of Educational Sociology* 17, no. 8 (April 1944), 449–450. Courtesy of the Eleanor Roosevelt Estate.

154   **How about Women at the Peace Conference?** First page of draft of article for *Reader's Digest*, in McJimsey, ed., *Eleanor Roosevelt,* Document 237, p. 861. [ER Papers, FDRL, Speech and Article File, Box 1415]

155   **Letter to Rose Schneiderman: On a Fourth Term** ER to RS, August 5, 1944, ER Papers, FDRL, Selected Digitized Correspondence, Rose Schneiderman File (4), p. 29.

156   **Excerpt from the Final White House Press Conference, April 12, 1945** "Press Conference of April 12, 1945," Furman typescript, in Beasley, ed., *White House Press Conferences,* 334–35. Courtesy of the Eleanor Roosevelt Estate.

158   **On FDR's Death,** "My Day," April 17, 1945. MY DAY © Eleanor Roosevelt. Reprinted by permission of ANDREWS MCMEEL SYNDICATION for UFS. All rights reserved.

160 **Are We Learning Nothing?** "My Day," April 30, 1945. MY DAY © Eleanor Roosevelt. Reprinted by permission of ANDREWS MCMEEL SYNDICATION for UFS. All rights reserved.

161 **Radio Broadcast of May 8, 1945: On V-E Day** "Radio Message—V-E Day, May 8, 1945," in Smith, ed., *The First Lady of Radio,* pp. 239–240. [ER Papers, FDRL, Speech and Article File, Box 1416]

162 **On the A-Bomb: This Discovery Must Spell the End of War** "My Day," August 8, 1945. MY DAY © Eleanor Roosevelt. Reprinted by permission of ANDREWS MCMEEL SYNDICATION for UFS. All rights reserved.

163 **Radio Broadcast of August 14, 1945: On V-J Day** "Radio Message—V-J Day, August 14, 1945" in Smith, ed., *The First Lady of Radio*, pp. 242–243. [ER Papers, FDRL, Speech and Article File, Box 1415]

CHAPTER 5
CIVIL RIGHTS AND DEMOCRACY

168 **We Go Ahead Together or We Go Down Together** "Address of Mrs. Franklin D. Roosevelt," National Conference on Fundamental Problems in the Education of Negroes, May 11, 1934, in McJimsey, ed., *Eleanor Roosevelt*, Document 35, p. 90. [ER Papers, FDRL, Speech and Article File, Box 1399]

169 **Correspondence with Walter White on the Anti-Lynching Campaign** Walter White to ER, January 10, 1935; ER to Walter White, c. March 1935; November 23, 1934; c. March, 1935; March 16, 1936, and March 19, 1936, ER Papers, FDRL, Selected Digitized Correspondence, Walter White files (2), p. 10; (1), p. 100, (2), p. 54; (3), pp. 36, 41.

173 **You Cannot Expect People to Change Overnight** "The Negro and Social Change," An Address at the Baltimore Celebration of the 25th Anniversary of the Urban League, *Opportunity: A Journal of Negro Life* 14 (January 1936), 22–23. Courtesy of the Eleanor Roosevelt Estate.

175 **ER to Pauli Murray on Her Rejection from the University of North Carolina** ER to Pauli Murray, December 19, 1938, ER Papers, FDRL, Selected Digitized Correspondence, Pauli Murray file, p. 2.

177 **Resigning from the DAR** "My Day" February 27, 1939. MY DAY © Eleanor Roosevelt. Reprinted by permission of ANDREWS MCMEEL SYNDICATION for UFS. All rights reserved.

178 **Press Conference after ER's Resignation from the DAR** Furman Transcript,February 27, 1939 in Maurine Beasley, ed., *The White House Press Conferences of Eleanor Roosevelt*, (New York: Garland Publishing, 1983), 92–93. Courtesy of the Eleanor Roosevelt Estate.

180 **Keepers of Democracy** "Keepers of Democracy," *The Virginia Quarterly Review* 15, no. 1 (Winter 1939), 2–3, 4–5. Courtesy of the Eleanor Roosevelt Estate.

184 **We Have Never Been Willing to Face This Problem** *The Moral Basis of Democracy* (New York: Howell, Soskin, & Co., 1940), 41–43. Courtesy of the Eleanor Roosevelt Estate.

186 **"If You Ask Me": Race, Prejudice, and Equality** "If You Ask Me," *Ladies Home Journal* (July 1941; December 1946; August 1947; March 1948; May 1948; May 1949). *McCall's* (July 1950; October 1954).

190 **Race, Religion, and Prejudice** "Race, Religion, and Prejudice," *The New Republic* 106, no. 19 (May 11, 1942), 630. Courtesy of *The New Republic*.

190 **The Four Equalities** "The Four Equalities: The First Lady Outlines Principles to Supplement the Four Freedoms," *The New Threshold* (August 1943), 81–83. Courtesy of the Eleanor Roosevelt Estate.

192 **If I Were A Negro Today** "Freedom: Promise or Fact," *Negro Digest* 1 (October 1943), 8–9. Courtesy Johnson Publishing Company, LLC. All rights reserved.

194 **On Social Equality: Letter to Addie Frizielle** ER to Addie Frizielle, May 13, 1944, Gilder Lehrman Collection. Courtesy of the Eleanor Roosevelt Estate.

196 **On Social Equality: Letter to Pauli Murray** ER to Pauli Murray, October 3, 1944, ER Papers, FDRL, Selected Digitized Correspondence, Pauli Murray file, pp. 121–122.

197 **Tolerance Is an Ugly Word** "Tolerance Is an Ugly Word," *Coronet* 18 (July 1945), 18. Courtesy of the Eleanor Roosevelt Estate.

200 **From the Melting Pot—An American Race** "From the Melting Pot—An American Race," *Liberty Magazine* (July 14, 1945), 17, 89. Courtesy of the Eleanor Roosevelt Estate.

203 **Some of My Best Friends Are Negro** "Some of My Best Friends Are Negro" *Ebony* 9 (February 1953), 17–20, 24–26. Courtesy EBONY Media Operations, LLC. All rights reserved.

207 **On Desegregation in Public Schools** "My Day," December 16, 1952. MY DAY © Eleanor Roosevelt. Reprinted by permission of ANDREWS MCMEEL SYNDICATION for UFS. All rights reserved.

209 **The *Brown v. Board of Education* Decision** "My Day," May 20, 1954. MY DAY © Eleanor Roosevelt. Reprinted by permission of ANDREWS MCMEEL SYNDICATION for UFS. All rights reserved.

CHAPTER 6
THE UN AND HUMAN RIGHTS

213 **An Invitation from President** Truman Harry S. Truman to ER, December 21, 1945, *ER Papers,* vol. 1, document 68, p. 158.

214 **At Last I Accepted** *Autobiography* (New York: Harper, 1961), 299. Reprinted by permission of HarperCollins Publishers.

215 **"If You Ask Me": Getting On with the Russians** "If You Ask Me," *Ladies' Home Journal* (January 1947), in *ER Papers,* vol. 1, 511–512. Courtesy of the Eleanor Roosevelt Estate.

218 **The Russians Are Tough** "The Russians Are Tough," *Look* (February 18, 1947), 511–512. Courtesy of the Eleanor Roosevelt Estate.

220 **We Have Put into Words Some Inherent Rights** "The Promise of Human Rights," *Foreign Affairs* 26, no. 3 (April 1948), 477. Republished with permission of *Foreign Affairs*. Permission conveyed through Copyright Clearance Center, Inc.

223 **We Must Not Be Confused about What Freedom Is** "The Struggle for Human Rights," Address, the Sorbonne, Paris, September 28, 1948, *ER Papers,* vol. 1, Document 379, p. 900 [ER Papers, FDRL, Speech and Article File, Box 1418]

226 **Presenting the Declaration to the General Assembly** "General Assembly Adopts Declaration of Human Rights: Statement," by Mrs. Franklin D. Roosevelt, *Department of State Bulletin* 19, no. 494 (December 19, 1948), 751–752.

227 **To Make Democracy Mean What We Say It Does** "What I Think of the United Nations," *United Nations World Magazine* 3, no. 8 (August 1949), 41, 48.

228 **They Never Offer Anybody Freedom** "Making Human Rights Come Alive," Transcript of a speech to the Second National Conference of UNESCO, Cleveland Ohio, April 4, 1949, *Phi Beta Kappan* 31, no. 1 (September 1949), 27–28. Courtesy of the Eleanor Roosevelt Estate.

231 **Excerpt from Letter to President Truman** Significant Documents Collection, FDRL, ER-18, Letter, ER to Harry S. Truman re: the UN and race issues, December 14, 1950.

232 **Reply to Charges against the US** "Reply to Attacks on US Attitude toward Human Rights Covenant," *Department of State Bulletin* 26, no. 655 (January 14, 1952), 59–61.

235 **These Same Old, Stale Charges** "Soviet Attacks on Social Conditions in the US," *Department of State Bulletin* 28, no. 78 (January 19, 1953), 116–117.

237 **On the Political Rights of Women** "UN Deliberations on the Political Rights of Women," Statement of December 12, *Department of State Bulletin* 28, no. 706 (January 5, 1953), 29–31.

239 **Defending Rights in the US from Attack** "UN Deliberations in the Political Rights of Women," Statement of December 15, *Department of State Bulletin* 28, no. 706 (January 5, 1953), 31–32.

242 **Where Do Human Rights Begin?** "Challenges in a Changing World," Remarks to the UN Commission on Human Rights, March 27, 1958, cited in Cook, *Eleanor Roosevelt: Volume 1*, 503. [ER Papers, FDRL, Speech and Article File, Box 3058]

CHAPTER 7
POSTWAR POLITICS

247 **Why I Do Not Choose to Run** "Why I Do Not Choose to Run," *Look* 10 (July 9, 1946), 25. Courtesy of the Eleanor Roosevelt Estate.

251 **The Taft-Hartley Bill Is a Bad Bill** "My Day," June 10, 1947. MY DAY © Eleanor Roosevelt. Reprinted by permission of ANDREWS MCMEEL SYNDICATION for UFS. All rights reserved.

252 **Plain Talk about Wallace** "Plain Talk about Wallace," *Democratic Digest* 25 (April 1948), 2. Courtesy of the Eleanor Roosevelt Estate.

255 **On Loyalty Tests** "Liberals in this Year of Decision," *The Christian Register* (June 1948), in Black, ed., *ER Papers*, vol. 1, 828, 829. Courtesy of *The Christian Register.*

256 **To Americans for Democratic Action** "Remarks to the Americans for Democratic Action on Individual Liberty," *The Congressional Record*, (April 1, 1950).

258 **On a Proposed Equal Rights Amendment** "My Day," May 25, 1951 and June 7, 1951. MY DAY © Eleanor Roosevelt. Reprinted by permission of ANDREWS MCMEEL SYNDICATION for UFS. All rights reserved.

260 **Israel Remains a Bastion of Democracy** ER to Samuel Schneiderman [an Israeli Journalist] June 13, 1951, in Black, ed., *ER Papers*, vol. 2, 628–629. Courtesy of the Eleanor Roosevelt Estate.

264 **On Senator McCarthy** "My Day," August 29, 1952. MY DAY © Eleanor Roosevelt. Reprinted by permission of ANDREWS MCMEEL SYNDICATION for UFS. All rights reserved.

268 **"If You Ask Me": Questions on Communism, Security, and Civil Liberties** "If You Ask Me," *McCall's* (July 1953). Courtesy of the Eleanor Roosevelt Estate.

271 **For Adlai Stevenson in 1956** "Campaign Address for Adlai Stevenson," October 1956, Charleston, West Virginia. [ER Papers, FDRL, Speech and Article File, Box 1422]

273 **Argument to Extend the Minimum Wage** "Statement on Behalf of the National Consumers League Before the Subcommittee on Labor and Public Welfare, US Senate, May 14, 1959." [ER Papers, FDRL, Speech and Article File, Box 1423]

277 **On CORE and Sit-Ins** "My Day," February 18, 1960. MY DAY © Eleanor Roosevelt. Reprinted by permission of ANDREWS MCMEEL SYNDICATION for UFS. All rights reserved.

277 **On Civil Rights Legislation** "My Day," April 11, 1960. MY DAY © Eleanor Roosevelt. Reprinted by permission of ANDREWS MCMEEL SYNDICATION for UFS. All rights reserved.

278 **"If You Ask Me": On Integration and Segregation** "If You Ask Me," *McCall's* (June 1959; November 1960; November 1962). Courtesy of the Eleanor Roosevelt Estate.

281 **On the First Kennedy-Nixon Debate** ER to Senator John F. Kennedy, September 27, 1960 re: The First Televised Debate, Significant Documents Collection, ER-25, FDRL.

283 **The Kennedy Commission on the Status of Women** "My Day," February 16, 1962. MY DAY © Eleanor Roosevelt. Reprinted by permission of ANDREWS MCMEEL SYNDICATION for UFS. All rights reserved.

CHAPTER 8
LESSONS FROM LIFE

289 **What I Hope to Leave Behind** "What I Hope to Leave Behind," *Pictorial Review* 34 (April 1933), 4, 45. Courtesy of the Eleanor Roosevelt Estate.

293 **In Defense of Curiosity** "In Defense of Curiosity," *Saturday Evening Post* 208, no. 8 (August 24, 1935), 8–9, 64–66. In Defense of Curiosity © SEPS licensed by Curtis Licensing Indianapolis, IN. All rights reserved.

296 **How to Take Criticism** "How to Take Criticism," *Ladies' Home Journal* 61 (November 1944), 155, 171. Courtesy of the Eleanor Roosevelt Estate.

298 **Background Knowledge** "The Importance of Background Knowledge in Building for the Future," *Annals of the American Academy of Political and Social Science* 246, no. 1 (July 1946), 9, 10–11. Republished with permission conveyed through Copyright Clearance Center, Inc.

300 **People Who Shaped My Life** "Seven People Who Shaped My Life," *Look* 15 (June 19, 1951), 54–56, 58. Courtesy of the Eleanor Roosevelt Estate.

302 **Where I Get My Energy** "Where I Get My Energy," *Harper's* 218 (January 1959), 45–47. Courtesy of the Eleanor Roosevelt Estate.

306 **Learning from Experience** *You Learn By Living: Eleven Keys for a More Fulfilling Life* (New York: Harper & Row, Publishers, 1960), 4–6, 25, 26–27, 29–30, 78, 82–83, 136–137. Reprinted by permission of HarperCollins Publishers.

312 **The Practical Application of Democratic Principles** *Tomorrow Is Now* (New York: Harper & Row, 1963), 62, 63–65. Courtesy of the Eleanor Roosevelt Estate.

BIBLIOGRAPHY

BOOKS ABOUT
ELEANOR ROOSEVELT

Beasley, Maurine Hoffman. *Eleanor Roosevelt and the Media: A Public Quest for Self-Fulfillment.* Urbana and Chicago: University of Illinois Press, 1987.

Beasley, Maurine Hoffman, Holly Cowan Shulman, and Henry R. Beasley, eds. *The Eleanor Roosevelt Encyclopedia.* Westport, Conn.: Greenwood Press, 2001.

Bell-Scott, Patricia. *The Firebrand and the First Lady: Portrait of a Friendship: Pauli Murray, Eleanor Roosevelt, and the Struggle for Social Justice.* New York: Knopf, 2016.

Black, Allida M. *Casting Her Own Shadow: Eleanor Roosevelt and the Shaping of Postwar Liberalism.* New York: Columbia University Press, 1996.

Cook, Blanche Wiesen. *Eleanor Roosevelt:* Volume 1, *1884–1933.* New York: Viking, 1992.

_____*Eleanor Roosevelt:* Volume 2, *1933–1938.* New York: Viking, 1999.
_____*Eleanor Roosevelt:* Volume 3, *1938–1962.* New York: Viking, 2016

Glendon, Mary Ann. *A World Made New: Eleanor Roosevelt and the Quest for Universal Human Rights.* New York: Random House, 2001.

Goodwin, Doris Kearns. *No Ordinary Time: Franklin & Eleanor Roosevelt: The Home Front in World War II.* New York: Simon & Schuster, 1994.

Hickok, Lorena. *Reluctant First Lady.* New York: Dodd, Mead, 1962.

Hoff-Wilson, Joan, and Marjorie Lightman, eds. *Without Precedent: The Life and Career of Eleanor Roosevelt.* Bloomington: Indiana University Press, 1984.

Lash, Joseph P. *Eleanor and Franklin: The Story of Their Relationship Based on Eleanor Roosevelt's Private Papers.* New York: W. W. Norton, 1971.

_____ *Eleanor: The Years Alone.* New York: W. W. Norton, 1972.

O'Farrell, Brigid. *She Was One of Us: Eleanor Roosevelt and the American Worker.* Ithaca, N.Y.: Cornell University Press, 2010.

Quinn, Susan. *Eleanor and Hick: The Love Affair That Shaped a First Lady.* New York: Penguin Press, 2016.

Ward, Geoffrey C., and Ken Burns, *The Roosevelts: An Intimate History.* New York: Knopf, 2014.

Ware, Susan. *Beyond Suffrage: Women in the New Deal.* Cambridge, Mass. Harvard University Press, 1981.

COLLECTIONS
OF ELEANOR ROOSEVELT'S WORKS

Beasley, Maurine Hoffman, ed. *White House Press Conferences of Eleanor Roosevelt.* New York: Garland, 1983.

Black, Allida M. ed. *Courage in a Dangerous World: The Political Writings of Eleanor Roosevelt.* New York: Columbia University Press, 1999.

_____*What I Hope to Leave Behind: The Essential Essays of Eleanor Roosevelt.* Brooklyn, N.Y.: Carlson Publishing, Inc., 1995.

_____ *Eleanor Roosevelt Papers: The Human Rights Years,* vol. 1, *1945–1948,* and vol 2, *1949–1952.* Detroit: Thomson Gale, 2007.

Emblidge, David, ed. *My Day: The Best of Eleanor Roosevelt's Acclaimed Newspaper Columns, 1936–1962.* N.p.: Da Capo Press, 2001.

McJimsey, George T., ed. *Documentary History of the Roosevelt Presidency.* Bethesda, Md.: University Publications of America, 2001–, *Eleanor Roosevelt: The Role of the First Lady,* vol. 20. N.p.: Congressional Information Service, Inc., 2003.

Neal, Steve. *Eleanor and Harry: The Correspondence of Eleanor Roosevelt and Harry S. Truman.* New York: Scribner, 2002.

Smith, Stephen Drury, ed. *The First Lady of Radio: Eleanor Roosevelt's Historic Broadcasts.* New York and London: The New Press, 2014.

Streitmatter, Rodger, ed. *Empty without You: The Intimate Letters of Eleanor Roosevelt and Lorena Hickok.* New York: The Free Press, 1998.

SELECTED BOOKS
BY ELEANOR ROOSEVELT

It's Up to the Women. New York: Frederick A. Stokes, 1933.

This Is My Story. New York: Harper and Bros., 1937

The Moral Basis of Democracy. New York: Howell, Soskin & Co., 1940.

If You Ask Me. New York: D. Appleton-Century Company, 1946.

This I Remember. New York: Harper, 1949.

You Learn by Living. New York: Harper, 1960.

Autobiography. New York: Harper, 1961.

Tomorrow Is Now. New York: Harper and Row, 1963.

PHOTO CREDITS

INDEX

PAGE NUMBERS IN *ITALICS* INDICATE PHOTOGRAPHS OR REPRODUCTIONS OF DOCUMENTS. PAGE NUMBERS IN **BOLDFACE** INDICATE ER'S OWN WORDS.

A

Abzug, Bella Savitzky, *119*
ADA. *See* Americans for Democratic Action (ADA)
Addams, Jane, 291
AFL-CIO, 246–247
African Americans, 109–110. *See also* civil rights; school desegregation
  and American melting pot, 200–201
  and communism, 180–181
  ER on conditions in 1943, **192–193**
  ER's civil rights work, 166
  ER's memo to FDR on integration of military, **114–115**
  and New Deal voting coalition, 82
  during WWII, 125, 134–135, 143
Allen, Florence, 48, 50
Allenswood, vii, *vii, viii,* 287
"Ambition" (ER school essay), **5**
America First, 133–134
American Friends Service Committee, xv
American Newspaper Guild, 83
American Youth Congress, *106,* 264–265, 268–269
  ER's early contacts with, xi
  Virginia Quarterly Review article, **105–107**
Americans for Democratic Action (ADA), 106, 246, 256–257, *257*
Anderson, Marian, *165,* 165–166, 178, *181, 183*
Anderson, Mary, 43
anti-communism, 245. *See also* McCarthy, Joseph
anti-lynching campaign, 166, **169–173,** *170*
Arthurdale, West Virginia, xii, xv, 82–83, *93, 96*
  and civil rights, 166
  ER on origins of, **90–91**
  ER's defense of, **92–93**
  and progressive education, 287, 288

atomic bomb, **162–163**
Austin, Warren, *224*

B

background knowledge, **298–299**
Baldwin, Roger N., 277
Barney, Nora Stanton, 79
Benedict, Ruth, 188
Benton, William, 281
Bethune, Mary McLeod, xi, *195, 203, 209*
Bilbo, Theodore G., 215
Black, Algernon B., *53,* 277
Black, Ruby, 82
Bora Bora, *148*
Brotherhood of Sleeping Car Porters, 207
Brown v. Board of Education, 167, 189, **209–210**
Bugbee, Emma, *53*
"Building Character" (ER), **25**
Bunche, Ralph, 204
Bye, George T., xv, xvi
Byrnes, James S., 173, 208

C

Camp Tera, *100*
Campobello Island, *16*
CCC. *See* Civilian Conservation Corps
charitable giving, xv
Chiang Kai-shek, Madame, *152*
child labor, 110
children, 109–110
  and community, **107–108**
  education for minorities, **168–169**
  poverty's effect on, 174
Christman, Elizabeth, 76
Churchill, Clementine, *147, 151*

CIO. *See* Congress of Industrial
    Organizations
citizenship, **22–25**
Citizenship Act (1924), 145
civil liberties
    "If You Ask Me" column on communism,
        security, and civil liberties, **268–271**
    loyalty tests and, **255–256**
    during WWII, xii, 124, 125, 131–132
civil rights, xi, 165–210, 247. *See also*
        integration; school desegregation
    address at celebration of 25th
        anniversary of Urban League,
        173–175
    children and, 109–110
    comments in *New Republic* on race,
        religion, and prejudice, **190**
    correspondence with Walter White on
        anti-lynching campaign, **169–173**
    ER's activism in 1940s-1950s, 246–247
    ER's liberalism and, 82
    ER's 1934 speech, xv
    ER's work as delegate to UN, 213
    ER's WWII activism, xii
    as foreign relations issue, 272–273
    "The Four Equalities," **190–192**
    "From the Melting Pot—An American
        Race," **200–202**
    as goal in postwar US, **160**
    "If You Ask Me" column on integration
        and segregation, **278–280**
    "Keepers of Democracy," **180–183**
    letter to Addie Frizielle on social
        equality, **194–195**
    letter to Pauli Murray on rejection by
        University of North Carolina, **175–
        177,** *176*
    letter to Pauli Murray on social equality,
        196–197
    letter to Truman on, **231**
    memo to FDR on integration of military,
        114–115
    "My Day" column on *Brown v. Board of
        Education*, **209–210**
    "My Day" column on civil rights
        legislation, **277–278**
    "My Day" column on CORE and sit-ins, **277**
    "My Day" column on desegregation of
        public schools, **207–208**
    "My Day" column on resignation from
        the DAR, **177**

National Sharecroppers Week poster, *185*
press conference after ER's resignation
    from DAR, **178–179**
readers' reactions to ER's stance, xvi
"Some of My Best Friends Are Negro,"
    203–206
Soviet opposition to Universal
    Declaration of Human Rights,
    232–235
state of African Americans in 1943,
    192–193
"Tolerance Is an Ugly Word," **197–199**
US's unwillingness to face problem of,
    184–185
"We go ahead together or we go down
    together" speech, **168–169**
during WWII, 125, 131–132, 134–135
civil rights movement, xvii, 167
Civil Works Administration (CWA), 85
Civilian Conservation Corps (CCC), xi,
    85, 99
civilian defense, 124
Clapp, Elsie, 96
Clark, Grenville, 277
Cold War, 212–213, 245. *See also* Soviet
    Union
College Settlement, 2
Commission on the Status of Women,
    xviii, 247, *282, 283,* **283–285,** *284*
Committee on Un-American Activities.
    See House Un-American Activities
    Committee
communism
    and American Youth Congress, **105–107,**
        264–265, 268–269
    and civil rights, 180–181, 186–187
    ER's defense of Arthurdale, **92–93**
    ER's work as delegate to UN, 213
    "If You Ask Me" column on communism,
        security, and civil liberties, **268–271**
    opposing by improving US democracy,
        227–228
    "Plain Talk About Wallace," 253–254
    and US labor movement, 251–252
Communist party, American Youth
Congress and, **105–107**
community, children and, **107–108**
Conciliation Service, 252
Congress, U.S., 48–49, 169–173
Congress of Industrial Organizations
    (CIO), *155,* 180, 251

Congress of Racial Equality (CORE), 167, 246, **277**
conscientious objectors, 143–144
Constitution Hall, 165, 178
Cook, Nancy, 3, *4, 16,* 20, 33
CORE. *See* Congress of Racial Equality
Cornell University, New York State College of Home Economics, 86
Corr, Maureen, *262,* 266
Costigan-Wagner bill, 169, 171, 172
Cox, Lucy, *6*
Craig, May, 67
criticism, how to take, **296–297**
Cummings, Homer S., 172–173
curiosity, **293–295**
CWA (Civil Works Administration), 85

D

D-Day radio broadcast, **147–149**
Dall, Curtis, *37*
Daughters of the American Revolution (DAR), 165–166, **177–179,** *179,* 180
Davis, John W., 207
Declaration of Human Rights. *See* Universal Declaration of Human Rights
defense industry, women in, 124–125
democracy
civil rights and, **184–185**
education's importance to, **168–169**
ER on, **227–228**
ER's definition of, **105**
liberty and, 256–257
practical application of democratic principles, **312–315**
"What We Are Fighting For," **133–135**
Democratic Convention (1940), *111,* **111–113,** *113*
Democratic National Committee, 2
Democratic Party
ER on, **15–17**
ER's faith in, 250
Henry Wallace and, 253, 254
"Why I Am a Democrat," **7–8**
desegregation. *See* integration; school desegregation
Dewey, John, 287–288
Dewson, Molly (Mary W.), xi, 3, *50,* 114
Dickerman, Marion, 3, *4, 16,* 20, 33
Dies, Martin, 180
Douglas, Helen Gahagan, *274*

Dubinsky, David, *118, 285*
Ducas, Dorothy, *53*
Dulles, John Foster, *216, 224*

E

Eastern Europe, 218
Economy Act (1933), 42
education
civil rights and, **168–169,** 191
ER and, 287–288
learning from experience, 288–289, **306–312**
Pictoral Review article, **22–25**
Eisenhower, Dwight, *314*
Eleanor and Franklin (Lash), 106
"Eleanor Clubs," 166, 205
election of 1920, viii, *6*
election of 1924, 2
election of 1928, x, 2, 14–15, *24*
election of 1932, x–xi, *41*
election of 1936, xi
election of 1940, **111–113,** *113*
election of 1944, 254
election of 1948, 246, 252–254
election of 1952, 272
election of 1956, 271–273
election of 1960, 281–282
Emancipation Proclamation, 189
employment. *See* labor
equal rights amendment (ERA), xvii–xviii, 55
ER's opposition to, 42
letter to Nora Stanton Barney, **79**
letter to Rose Schneiderman, **76–77**
"My Day" column about, **78**
"My Day" column on, **258–260**
press conference on, **54**
equalities, four, **190–192**
experience, learning from, xviii, 288–289, **306–312**

F

Fair Employment Practices Commission (FEPC), 206
fair housing laws, 167
Fair Labor Standards Act (1938), xvii, 83, 273
Falkenberg, Jinx, 209
family, in ER's values, 289–290

Farley, James, xi, 111–112, *114*
Farm Security Administration, 96
fascism, xix–xx, 124
FBI, 137–138, 205
fear
    effect on learning, 308–309
    effect on liberty, 256
FEPC (Fair Employment Practices
        Commission), 206
First International Congress of Working
        Women, *10*
"first lady's dictionary," **100–102**
Fish, Hamilton, 127
food (Depression menus), 82, **86–88**
"The Four Equalities" (ER), **190–192**
freedom
    ER on Soviet attitudes towards, **228–231**
    ER's speech on nature of, **223–225**
freedom of religion, 200–201
freedom of the press, 142
French language, 307
Frizielle, Addie, 194–195
"From the Melting Pot—An American
        Race" (ER), **200–202**
Fry, Varian, 124
Furman, Bess, 41, *53*, 81, 93, 100–102, 178

G

Galbraith, John Kenneth, 257
Germany, 156–157, 160, 162
Gila River, Arizona, internment camp, 125,
        140
Good Housekeeping, 43
Graham, Frank, *274*
Grauer, Ben, xiv–xv
Great Depression, xi–xii. *See also* New
        Deal
    ER on bright side of, **84–85**
    press conference on New Deal, **97–99**
    "The Unemployed Are Not a Strange
        Race," **103**
    and women's place in the workforce,
        42–43, *65*
    working women in, **68–69**

H

Hall, Anna Livingston Ludlow (ER's
        mother), vi

Hall, Mary Livingston Ludlow (ER's
        grandmother), vi, 30
Halsey, William, *150*
Harmon, Ernest, *150*
Height, Dorothy, *311*
Helm, Edith, 69
Hickok, Lorena, *58, 59*
    ER's first meeting with, xi
    ER's letters to, **59–60,** *61*
    and press conferences, v, 1, 42
Highlander School (Tennessee), 210, *270*
Hill, Herbert, 114
Hirohito (emperor of Japan), 266
Hiroshima. *See* atomic bomb
Hitler, Adolf, 269
Hobby, Oveta Culp, *147*
homestead program, **94–97**. *See also*
        Arthurdale, West Virginia
House Un-American Activities Committee,
        106, 180, 268
"How to Interest Women in Voting" (ER), **9**
"How to Take Criticism" (ER), **296–297**
Howe, Louis M., *13,* 43
    death of, xv
    and election of 1920, 6
    and ER's journalism, x, xiii, 3
    influence on ER, ix, 2, 249, 301
Hull, Cordell, 270
human rights, 211–243. *See also* Universal
        Declaration of Human Rights
    letter to Truman on civil rights, **231**
    making democracy mean what we say
        it does, **227–228**
    origins of, **242–243**
    response to Soviet bloc criticisms of
        US, **235–236**
    speech on nature of freedom, **223–225**
    UN deliberations on political rights of
        women, **237–241**
Human Rights Commission, 220–221, 223
Humphrey, Hubert, *257*
Hunter College, 119, 175
Hyde Park, New York, 3, *219, 283, 287, 298*

I

Ickes, Harold, 93
"If You Ask Me" (ER magazine column), xvi
    on communism, security, and civil
        liberties, **268–271**

on integration and segregation, **278-280**
on race, prejudice, and equality, **186-189**
on Russia's actions in UN, **215-217**
on World War II questions, **141-147**
ILGWU (International Ladies' Garment
　　Workers Union), 118, *285*
"In Defense of Curiosity" (ER), **293-295**
*In Henry's Backyard: The Races of
　　Mankind* (Benedict), 188
"Insuring Democracy" (ER), **109-110**
integration. *See also* school desegregation
　　"If You Ask Me" column on, **278-280**
　　of military, **114-115**
　　"My Day" column on, **277**
interdependence, xix, 125
Interior Department, US, 95
International Brotherhood of Electrical
　　Workers, *116*
International Ladies' Garment Workers
　　Union (ILGWU), 118, *285*
International Refugee Organization, 218
International Youth Assembly, *146*
internment camps. *See* Japanese
　　American internment camps
interracial marriage, 186, 189, 209-210
Israel, 246, **260-263,** *262, 263*
It's Up to the Women (ER), xvi, 42
　　Depression menus, 82, **86-88**
　　women and working conditions, **55-56**
　　women in public life, **57-58**

J

Jackson, Robert, *146*
Japan, 162, *266. See also* V-J Day
Japanese American internment camps,
　　125, **137-140,** *138, 139, 140*
Jews
　　and Israel, 260-263
　　during WWII, 136-137
Johnson, Lyndon B., 278, 285, *314*

K

Kameny, Aaron, 170
"Keepers of Democracy" (ER), **180-183**
Kennedy, Jacqueline, 283-284
Kennedy, John F., *280, 282, 285, 314*
　　Commission on the Status Of Women,
　　　　xviii, 247, **283-285**

ER's letter about Nixon-Kennedy
　　debates (1960), **281-282**
Kennedy, Joseph P., 280
Kennedy Commission on the Status of
　　Women. *See* Commission on the
　　Status of Women
King, Martin Luther, Jr., 277
Kipling, Rudyard, 134

L

La Guardia, Fiorello, 124, *128*
labor, xvii, 83. *See also* strikes; unions
　　child labor, 110
　　ER on married women in workforce,
　　　　66-69
　　ER on women and working conditions,
　　　　55-56
　　ER's address to workers at Leviton strike,
　　　　115-117, *116*
　　ER's article to women in unions during
　　　　WWII, **150-151**
　　ER's congressional testimony on
　　　　extension of minimum wage,
　　　　273-276
　　married women in workforce, **70-71**
　　"My Day" column on labor organizing,
　　　　118-120
　　"My Day" column on Taft-Hartley Act,
　　　　251-252
　　women in postwar world, 152-153
　　women in unions during WWII, **150-151**
　　women in WWII labor market, 124
　　women's participation in workforce
　　　　during Depression, 42-43, *65*
Labor Department, US, 48, 252
Ladies' Home Journal, xvi, xvii
Lape, Esther, 2-3
Lash, Joseph P., 77, *106*
Lash, Trude, *262*
League of Nations, 299
League of Women Voters (LWV), ix, 2-3
learning from experience, 288-289,
　　306-312
LeHand, Missy (Marguerite), *292*
lessons from life
　　background knowledge, **298-299**
　　"How to Take Criticism," **296-297**
　　"In Defense of Curiosity," **293-295**
　　learning from experience, **306-312**

lessons from life *(continued)*
  practical application of democratic
      principles, **312–315**
  "Seven People Who Shaped My Life,"
      300–302
  "What I Hope to Leave Behind," **289–292**
  "Where I Get My Energy," **302–306**
Leviton strike, **115–117**, *116*
Lewis, John L., 251
liberalism, xi–xii, 81–82, 246
liberty, democracy and, 256–257
Lincoln, Abraham, 159, 189
Lincoln Memorial, 166, *181, 200*
London, England, vii
loyalty tests, 246, **255–256**
Lubin, Isador, *276*
Lucy, Autherine, *210*
LWV (League of Women Voters), ix, 2–3
lynching, xii, 166–172, 189

M

magazine journalism, xvi, 42
Malik, Charles, *230*
Marianna, Florida, lynching (1934), 169
marriage
  interracial, 186, 189, 209–210
  political wives, **35–37**
  "Ten Rules for Success in Marriage,"
      26–29
Marshall, George, *224*
Marshall, Thurgood, 167, *199, 207*
Mary McLeod Bethune Human Rights
      Award, *311*
"master race," 160
McCall's, xvi, xvii
McCarthy, Joseph, 246, **264–266**
McClendon, James, *199*
McCrary, Tex, 209
Mercer, Lucy, viii, 1
military
  integration of, **114–115**
  women in, 239
minimum wage, ER's congressional
      testimony on extension of, **273–276**
Mitchell, James, *274*
"The Modern Wife's Difficult Job" (ER),
      17–21
Molotov, Vyacheslav, *219*
The Moral Basis of Democracy (ER), xvii
  civil rights, **184–185**

sacrifices necessary for democracy,
      120–121
Murray, Pauli, *175*, 204
  ER's letter on social equality to, **196–197**
  letter from ER on her rejection from the
      University of North Carolina,
      175–177, *176*
"My Day" (ER's newspaper column), xi,
      xiv, *xiv*, 42, *267*
  on aftermath of war, **160**
  on atomic bomb, **162–163**
  on *Brown v. Board of Education*,
      209–210
  on challenges of WWII, **131–132**
  on civil rights legislation, **277–278**
  on CORE and sit-ins, **277**
  on decision to enter WWII, **127–128**
  on desegregation of public schools,
      207–208
  on educational theories, 288
  on ERA, **78, 258–260**
  on FDR's death, **158–159**
  on Kennedy Commission on the Status
      of Women, **283–285**
  on labor organizing, **118–120**
  on Joseph McCarthy, **264–266**
  recurring themes in, xviii
  on resignation from DAR, 166, **177**
  on right of survival of human beings,
      136–137
  on Taft-Hartley bill, **251–252**
  on voting and freedom, **104**
  on women working outside the home,
      64–66
  on working wives, **70–71**
  on WWII conditions in Poland, **132–133**
Myer, Dillon S., *140*

N

NAACP Legal Defense and Education
      Fund, 199
National Advisory Committee on Farm
      Labor, *274*, 275
National Association for the
      Advancement of Colored People
      (NAACP), *199, 200, 202*
  ER on board of, 246
  ER's early contacts with, xi
  ER's membership in, 167
National Consumers' League, vii, 2, 273

National Council of Negro Women, 203, *311*
National Farm Labor Advisory
      Committee, 247
National Labor Relations Board (NLRB), 252
National Sharecroppers Week (poster), *185*
National Woman's Party (NWP), xvii, *55,*
      259-260
   ER's opposition to, 42
   ER's press conference on, **54**
National Women's Trade Union League,
      42, 83
National Youth Administration (NYA), xi, 85
National Youth Congress, 82
Nationality Act (1940), 145
Native Americans
   and American melting pot, 200
   and civil rights, 188-189
   in WWII, 145
NBC radio network, xv
New Caledonia, *150*
New Deal, xi-xii, xv, 81-122
   Arthurdale, **90-93**
   children and community, **107-108**
   and civil rights, 166
   Depression menus, **86-88**
   ER on bright side of the Depression,
      84-85
   ER on democracy, **120-121**
   ER on fair working conditions, **88-89**
   ER on voting and freedom, **104**
   ER's address to 1940 Democratic
      Convention, **111-113,** *113*
   ER's address to workers at Leviton
      strike, **115-117**
   ER's memo to FDR on integration of
      military, **114-115**
   first lady's dictionary, **100-102**
   homestead program, **94-97**
   "Insuring Democracy," **109-110**
   "My Day" column on labor organizing,
      118-120
   press conference on whether
      Depression is ending, **97-99**
   "The Unemployed Are Not a Strange
      Race," **103**
   during WWII, 124
New York State, x, 2-3, 11-13
New York State College of Home
      Economics of Cornell University, 86
New York State League of Women Voters,
      12

New York State Senate, vii
Newsboy's Club, 293
Nixon, Richard M., 281-282
Nixon-Kennedy debates (1960), **281-282**
NLRB (National Labor Relations Board), 252
North American Review, 14-15
NWP. see National Woman's Party
NYA (National Youth Administration), xi, 85

O

O'Day, Caroline, 3, *4,* 12
Office of Civilian Defense (OCD), xii, 124,
      128, 142
On My Own (ER), xvii
organized labor. *See* strikes; unions
"Over Our Coffee Cups" (radio series), xv

P

pacifism, xi, 124
Pan-American Coffee Bureau, xv
Parents magazine, 3
Parks, Rosa, *210*
Paul, Alice, *55*
Pavlichenko, Lyudmila, *146*
Pavlov, Alexei, 230, *230*
peace conference, WWII, **154**
Pearl Harbor, ER's radio broadcast after,
      128-130, *130*
Perkins, Frances, 3, 43, 48, 50, *50,* 76
Peterson, Esther, 282, *283, 284*
Pictorial Review, 3
"Pins and Needles" (ILGWU play), 118
"Plain Talk About Wallace" (ER), **252-254**
Poland, ER on WWII conditions in, **132-133**
polio, viii, 1
political wives, **35-37**
politics, women's place in, **51, 64, 70**
poll tax, 241, 256
Pond's Cold Cream, xiv
postwar politics, 245-285
   Christian Register article on loyalty
      tests, **255-256**
   ER on minimum wage extension,
      273-276
   ER's campaign address for Adlai
      Stevenson, **271-273**
   ER's congressional testimony on
      extension of minimum wage,
      273-276

postwar politics *(continued)*
  ER's letter to Kennedy about Nixon-Kennedy debates (1960), **281–282**
  ER's letter to Samuel Schneiderman on Israel, **260–263**
  ER's remarks to ADA, **256–257**
  "If You Ask Me" column on communism, security, and civil liberties, **268–271**
  "If You Ask Me" column on integration and segregation, **278–280**
  "My Day" column on civil rights legislation, **277–278**
  "My Day" column on CORE and sit-ins, **277**
  "My Day" column on ERA, **258–260**
  "My Day" column on Kennedy Commission on the Status of Women, **283–285**
  "My Day" column on Joseph McCarthy, **264–266**
  "My Day" column on Taft-Hartley Act, **251–252**
  "Plain Talk About Wallace," **252–254**
  "Why I Do Not Choose to Run," **247–250**
  women in postwar world, 152–153
Potofsky, Jacob, 275
poverty, 109–110, 174
prejudice, 187, 190
president, ER on woman as, **62–63, 73**
President's Commission on the Status of Women. *See* Commission on the Status of Women
press conferences, xi, *52*
  after ER's resignation from DAR, **178–179**
  ER's defense of Arthurdale, **92–93**
  ER's definition of democracy, **105**
  ER's first, **52–53,** 81
  final conference before FDR's death, **156–157**
  on married women in the labor force, **66–69**
  origins of, 41–42
  on whether Depression is ending, **97–99**
  on women in state legislatures and Congress, **70**
public school desegregation. *See* school desegregation
public speaking, xv–xvi
Public Works Administration (PWA), 85

R
radio, xiv–xv
  D-Day broadcast, **147–149**
  ER broadcast on a woman becoming president, **62–63**
  Pearl Harbor broadcast, **128–130**
  V-E Day broadcast, **161**
  V-J Day broadcast, **163**
Raleigh, North Carolina, sit-in protests, 277
Randolph, A. Philip, 114, 204, *207,* 247, *274*
Ravensbruck Women's Preventive Detention Camp, Poland, 132–133
Read, Elizabeth, 2–3
readjustment, 309–310
Red Book Magazine, xiii, 43
refugees, 124, 246, 263
religious freedom, 200–201
relocation centers. *See* Japanese American internment camps
Republican Party, 8, 16, 35
Reuther, Walter, *202,* 257
right of survival, **136–137**
right-to-work laws, 246
Robert, Jr., Mrs. Henry M. (Sarah), 178, 179, *180*
Rockefeller, Nelson, *285*
Roosevelt, Anna (daughter of ER), *14, 37, 295*
Roosevelt, (Anna) Eleanor (ER), v, *v, vi, vii, ix, x, 1, 4, 6, 10, 13, 14, 16, 20, 24, 28, 34, 37, 38, 41, 52, 53, 58, 59, 69, 77, 81, 90, 93, 100, 106, 108, 111, 114, 116, 118, 123, 128, 130, 140, 146, 147, 148, 150, 151, 152, 155, 158, 165, 195, 199, 200, 202, 207, 209, 211, 214, 216, 219, 221, 224, 226, 234, 237, 245, 254, 255, 257, 261, 262, 263, 265, 266, 270, 272, 274, 276, 280, 282, 283, 284, 287, 292, 295, 298, 302, 305, 311*
  Allenswood report card, *viii*
  birth and childhood, vi–vii
  birth of children, vii–viii
  on whether Depression is ending, vii–viii
  books by, xvi–xvii
  charitable giving, xv
  civil rights advocacy, xi
  as columnist, xi
  early journalism, x, 2
  early social reform work in New York, vii
  as educator, 3
  as first lady, 3–4

funeral of, *314*

income as speaker and writer, xv–xvi

journalism, xiii–xiv

as journalist, 3

letters to Lorena Hickok, *61*

magazine journalism, xvi

marriage to FDR, vii

and Lucy Mercer, viii

pacifism of, 124

in postwar years, xii–xiii

public speaking, xv–xvi

on radio, xiv–xv (*See also* radio)

recurring themes in writing and speech,
xviii–xix

women's rights advocacy, xvii–xviii

as writer/speaker/broadcaster, xiii–xiv

Roosevelt, Elliott (ER's father), *v*, vi

Roosevelt, Elliott (ER's son), *14*

Roosevelt, Franklin Delano (FDR), *x*, *1*, *24*,
37, *38*, *114*, *158*, *292*, *295*

campaign for New York governor
(1928), *x*, 2

character of, 300–301

and civil rights, 206

core beliefs, 314–315

death of, xii, **158–159,** 245

on death of mother, 314

early political career, vii

effect of death on ER's importance, 245

"Eleanor Clubs" investigation, 205

election of 1936, xi

and ER's activism, 249–250

ER's influence on, 82

ER's journalism, 2

ER's letter to Rose Schneiderman on
fourth term, **155**

ER's memo on integration of military,
114–115

ER's New Deal activism, xi

and ER's success, xvii

final press conference before FDR's
death, **156–157**

first White House press conference, v

marriage to ER, vii

Lucy Mercer and, viii, 1

"My Day" column on death of, **158–159**

Native Americans in WWII, 145

presidential campaign of 1932, x–xi

recurring themes in ER's writing and
speech, xviii

and Truman, 211

vice presidential campaign (1920), viii

Roosevelt, Franklin Delano, Jr., *14*

Roosevelt, Quentin, 144

Roosevelt, Sara Delano (ER's mother-in-
law), *1*, 13, *77*, 300, 313–314

Roosevelt, Theodore (ER's uncle), vi, xviii,
11, 30, 181–182, 187, 302–303

Russia. *See* Soviet Union

S

Sampson, Edith S., 204, *234*

Saturday Evening Post, xvii

Saturday Review, xvi

Schlesinger, Arthur, Jr., 257

Schneiderman, Rose, xii, 2, 43, 115, *118, 276*

ER's letter about ERA, **76–77**

ER's letter on fourth term for FDR, **155**

Schneiderman, Samuel, 260–263

school desegregation, 167, 189, **207–208,
209–210, 210**

Scott's Run, West Virginia, 94, *96*

Secret Service, 205

segregation, 196, **278–280**

Senate, US, 215, 278

"Seven People Who Shaped My Life"
(ER), **300–302**

"She, She, She" camps, *100*

Shuster, George, *119*

Simkhovitch, Mary, 291

Simmons Mattress Company, xv

Sinatra, Frank, *305*

sit-ins, **277**

Smith, Alfred E., 14–15

Smith, Hilda, 116

social equality, 167, **194–197**

social reform, vii

social revolution, 312–315

Social Security Act, 276

social services, WWII-era, 124

"Some of My Best Friends Are Negro"
(ER), **203–206**

Souvestre, Emil, 31

Souvestre, Marie, vii, xviii, 31, 293,
307–308

Soviet Union (USSR), xii

and American Youth Congress, 269

and Declaration of Human Rights, **228–
231, 232–235**

ER on UN deliberations on political
rights of women, **239–241**

Soviet Union (continued)
  ER's response to Soviet bloc criticisms of US, **235–236**
  and human rights, 223–225, 232
  "If You Ask Me" column on UN actions, **215–217**
  Look magazine piece on, **218–220**
  in UN, 213
  and US labor movement, 251–252
Spingarn Medal, *165*
State Department, US, 270
states' rights, 188
Stevenson, Adlai, *216, 257, 272*
  ER's campaign address for, **271–273**
  presidential campaigns, 246, 280
strikes, 146–147
suffrage. *See* voting rights
Supreme Court, US, 207–209
survival, right of, **136–137**
sweatshops, 273

T

Taft-Hartley Act, 246, **251–252**
Temporary Emergency Relief Administration, 86
"Ten Rules for Success in Marriage" (ER), xiii, **26–29**
Tennessee Valley Authority (TVA), 99
Tex and Jinx Show (TV program), 209
This I Remember (ER), xvii
This Is My Story (ER), xvi–xvii, 6–7
Thompson, Malvina (Tommy), xv, 59, *69,* 215
"To Undo a Mistake Is Always Harder Than Not to Create One Originally" (ER), **137–140**
Tobias, Channing, 204
"Today's Girl and Tomorrow's Job" (ER), xiii, **29–32, 34**
Todhunter School, x, 3, 33, *34,* 287, 288
"Tolerance Is an Ugly Word" (ER), **197–199**
Tomorrow is Now (ER), xvii, 289, **312–315**
Truman, Harry S, *200, 211, 255, 314*
  and civil rights, 233
  election of 1948, 246
  ER's civil rights work, 167
  ER's criticism of, 272
  ER's letter on civil rights, **231**
  ER's UN appointment, xii, 211–212, **213–214, 214–215**

Henry Wallace and, 254
TVA (Tennessee Valley Authority), 99

U

UAW (United Auto Workers), 202
UN. *see* United Nations
Un-American Activities Committee. *See* House Un-American Activities Committee
"The Unemployed Are Not a Strange Race" (ER), **103**
unemployment, **103**
unhappiness, 310
unions
  "My Day" column on Taft-Hartley Act, **251–252**
  in totalitarian states vs. in democracies, 225
  during WWII, 146–147
United Auto Workers (UAW), 202
United Jewish Appeal, 261
United Nations Commission on the Status of Women, 258–259
United Nations (UN), xix, 211–243, *216, 224, 227, 230, 237*
  ER as delegate to, xii–xiii, 211–213
  ER on making democracy mean what we say it does, **227–228**
  ER on Soviet abstention from Declaration of Human Rights, **228–231**
  ER on UN deliberations on political rights of women, **237–241**
  ER's presentation of Universal Declaration of Human Rights to General Assembly, **226–227**
  ER's presentation Universal Declaration of Human Rights to, **226–227**
  ER's reasons for accepting post, 248
  ER's reply to criticisms of Declaration of Human Rights from Soviet Bloc countries, **232–235**
  ER's response to appointment to Truman's request, **214–215**
  ER's speech on nature of freedom, **223–225**
  "If You Ask Me" column on Russia's actions in, **215–217**
  League of Nations as background knowledge for, 299

Look magazine piece on Russians, **218-220**
 in postwar world, 157
 Adlai Stevenson and, 271
 Truman's letter appointing ER to
  General Assembly, **213-214**
 Universal Declaration of Human
  Rights (*See* Universal Declaration of
  Human Rights)
Universal Declaration of Human Rights,
  xii, xix, 212-213, *222, 226, 227, 242*
 ER on importance of, **220-221**
 ER on Soviet abstention from, **228-231**
 ER's presentation to General Assembly,
  226-227
 ER's reply to criticisms from Soviet Bloc
  countries, **232-235**
 and ER's view of freedom, **223-225**
 Foreign Affairs article on Human Rights
  Commission, **220-221**
University of North Carolina, **175-177,** *176*
Urban League address, **173-175**
usefulness
 ER on women's opportunity for, **38-39**
 ER's UN appointment, 212
 as motivator, vii, x
 "What I Want Most Out of Life," 10, 13
USSR. *See* Soviet Union

V

V-E Day, 156-157, **161**
V-J Day, **163**
Val-Kill Industries, 3, 13, *20, 21, 275*
Virginia Quarterly Review, **105-107,**
  180-183
Vishinsky, Andrei, 218, *219*
voting, motivating women to take an
  interest in, 9
voting rights
 for African Americans, 240-241, 278, 279
 and civil rights, 191-192
 for women, 237-238, *240,* 240-241

W

W. Colston Leigh Lecture Bureau, xv
WAAC (Women's Army Auxiliary Corps),
  147
Wadsworth, Alice, 6-7
Wagner Labor Relations Act (1935), 83

Wald, Lillian, 291
Wallace, Henry A., 111, 246, **252-254,** *254*
war, ER's views on, **126**
War Relocation Authority, 139, 140
Watson, Edwin M., 115
"What I Hope to Leave Behind" (ER),
  289-292
"What I Want Most Out of Life" (ER),
  10-13, *14*
"What Ten Million Women Want" (ER),
  47-50
"What We Are Fighting For" (ER), **133-135**
"When Will a Woman Become President
  of the US" (ER radio talk), xv
"Where I Get My Energy" (ER), **302-306**
White, Walter, 114, 166, *170, 199, 200,* 204
 correspondence on anti-lynching
  campaign, **169-173**
 ER's early contacts with, xi
White House Conference on Children in a
  Democracy, **107-108**
"White Man's Burden," 134
"Why I Am a Democrat" (ER), **7-8**
"Why I Do Not Choose to Run" (ER),
  247-250
Why Wars Must Cease (Young, ed.), **126**
Wilkins, Roy, *199, 202*
Willow Grove Mine Number 10, *90*
Wilson, Woodrow, 159
Wirt, William A., 92
Wollcott, Marion Post, 96
Woman's Home Companion, xiii-xiv
women. *See also* women's rights
 conditions in Poland during WWII,
  132-133
 ER's press conference on women in
  workforce, **54**
 in military, 142-143, 239
 "The Modern Wife's Difficult Job," **17-21**
 in state legislatures and Congress, **70**
 "Ten Rules for Success in Marriage,"
  26-29
 "Today's Girl and Tomorrow's Job,"
  29-32, 34
 in unions during WWII, **150-151**
 "Women in the Postwar World," **152-153**
 workforce participation during
  Depression, 42-43, *65*
 during WWII, 124-125
 and WWII peace process, 142, **154**
"Women in Politics" (ER), 43, **71-76**

"Women in the Postwar World" (ER), **152–153**

"Women Must Learn to Play the Game as Men Do" (ER), xiii, **44–47**

women-only labor laws, 42–43

Women's Army Auxiliary Corps (WAAC), *147*

Women's City Club of New York, 2, 3

Women's Democratic Campaign Manual, **8, 9**

Women's Democratic News, x, xiii, 3, 4

Women's Division of New York State Democratic Party, ix, 2, 12, *13*

Women's Division of the National Democratic Committee, 50

Women's Home Companion, **51**

women's magazines, xiii

women's movement, 175, 247

women's organizations, 1–2

women's rights, 2
  equal rights amendment, xvii–xviii
  in ER's values, 290–291
  "My Day" column on ERA, **258–260**
  "My Day" column on Kennedy Commission on the Status of Women, **283–285**
  in Soviet Union, *240*
  in *This Is My Story,* **6–7**
  UN deliberations on political rights of women, **237–241**
  women in unions during WWII, **150–151**
  writings on, **41–79**

women's suffrage, 6–7, 237–238, *240,* 240–241

Women's Trade Union League, 2, 115–116

Women's Trade Union League (WTUL), *10*

workforce. *See* labor

Works Progress Administration (WPA), xi, 82, *108*

World War I, 1, 144, 145

World War II, xii, *123,* 123–163
  and American Youth Congress, 269
  D-Day radio broadcast, **147–149**
  ER on conditions in Poland, **132–133**
  ER on decision to enter war, **127–128**
  ER on women at peace conference, **154**
  ER's article to women in unions, **150–151**
  ER's civil rights work, 166
  ER's radio broadcast after Pearl Harbor, **128–130**
  ER's trip to South Pacific, *148–150*
  ER's visits to troops, 124
  final press conference before FDR's death, **156–157**
  "If You Ask Me": wartime questions, **141–147**
  letter to Rose Schneiderman on fourth term for FDR, **155**
  "My Day" column on aftermath of war, **160**
  "My Day" column on atomic bomb, **162–163**
  "My Day" column on challenges of, **131–132**
  "My Day" column on death of FDR, **158–159**
  postwar politics (*See* postwar politics)
  right of survival of human beings, **136–137**
  "To Undo a Mistake Is Always Harder Than Not to Create One Originally," **137–140**
  V-E day radio broadcast, **161**
  V-J day radio broadcast, **163**
  "What We Are Fighting For," **133–135**
  Why Wars Must Cease, **126**
  "Women in the Postwar World," **152–153**

World Youth Congress, 106

WPA. *See* Works Progress Administration

WTUL (Women's Trade Union League), *10*

Y

You Learn by Living (ER), xvii, 289, **306–312**

Z

Zionism, 261